Java 9 Data Structures and Algorithms

A step-by-step guide to data structures and algorithms

Debasish Ray Chawdhuri

BIRMINGHAM - MUMBAI

Java 9 Data Structures and Algorithms

First published: April 2017

Production reference: 1250417

Published by Packt Publishing Ltd.
Livery Place
35 Livery Street
Birmingham B3 2PB, UK.

ISBN 978-1-78588-934-9

www.packtpub.com

Credits

Author
Debasish Ray Chawdhuri

Reviewer
Miroslav Wengner

Commissioning Editor
Kunal Parikh

Acquisition Editor
Chaitanya Nair

Content Development Editor
Nikhil Borkar

Technical Editor
Madhunikita Sunil Chindarkar

Copy Editor
Muktikant Garimella

Project Coordinator
Vaidehi Sawant

Proofreader
Safis Editing

Indexer
Mariammal Chettiyar

Graphics
Abhinash Sahu

Production Coordinator
Nilesh Mohite

Cover Work
Nilesh Mohite

About the Author

Debasish Ray Chawdhuri is an established Java developer and has been in the industry for the last 8 years. He has developed several systems, right from CRUD applications to programming languages and big data processing systems. He had provided the first implementation of extensible business reporting language specification, and a product around it, for the verification of company financial data for the Government of India while he was employed at Tata Consultancy Services Ltd. In Talentica Software Pvt. Ltd., he implemented a domain-specific programming language to easily implement complex data aggregation computation that would compile to Java bytecode. Currently, he is leading a team developing a new high-performance structured data storage framework to be processed by Spark. The framework is named Hungry Hippos and will be open sourced very soon. He also blogs at `http://www.geekyarticles.com/` about Java and other computer science-related topics.

He has worked for Tata Consultancy Services Ltd., Oracle India Pvt. Ltd., and Talentica Software Pvt. Ltd.

I would like to thank my dear wife, Anasua, for her continued support and encouragement, and for putting up with all my eccentricities while I spent all my time writing this book. I would also like to thank the publishing team for suggesting the idea of this book to me and providing all the necessary support for me to finish it.

About the Reviewer

Miroslav Wengner has been a passionate JVM enthusiast ever since he joined SUN Microsystems in 2002. He truly believes in distributed system design, concurrency, and parallel computing. One of Miro's biggest hobby is the development of autonomic systems. He is one of the coauthors of and main contributors to the open source Java IoT/Robotics framework Robo4J.

Miro is currently working on the online energy trading platform for enmacc.de as a senior software developer.

I would like to thank my family and my wife, Tanja, for big support during reviewing this book.

www.PacktPub.com

eBooks, discount offers, and more

Did you know that Packt offers eBook versions of every book published, with PDF and ePub files available? You can upgrade to the eBook version at www.PacktPub.com and as a print book customer, you are entitled to a discount on the eBook copy. Get in touch with us at customercare@packtpub.com for more details.

At www.PacktPub.com, you can also read a collection of free technical articles, sign up for a range of free newsletters and receive exclusive discounts and offers on Packt books and eBooks.

https://www.packtpub.com/mapt

Get the most in-demand software skills with Mapt. Mapt gives you full access to all Packt books and video courses, as well as industry-leading tools to help you plan your personal development and advance your career.

Why subscribe?

- Fully searchable across every book published by Packt
- Copy and paste, print, and bookmark content
- On demand and accessible via a web browser

Customer Feedback

Thanks for purchasing this Packt book. At Packt, quality is at the heart of our editorial process. To help us improve, please leave us an honest review on this book's Amazon page at https://www.amazon.com/dp/1785889346.

If you'd like to join our team of regular reviewers, you can e-mail us at customerreviews@packtpub.com. We award our regular reviewers with free eBooks and videos in exchange for their valuable feedback. Help us be relentless in improving our products!

Table of Contents

Preface

Java has been one of the most popular programming languages for enterprise systems for decades now. One of the reasons for the popularity of Java is its platform independence, which lets one write and compile code on any system and run it on any other system, irrespective of the hardware and the operating system. Another reason for Java's popularity is that the language is standardized by a community of industry players. The latter enables Java to stay updated with the most recent programming ideas without being overloaded with too many useless features.

Given the popularity of Java, there are plenty of developers actively involved in Java development. When it comes to learning algorithms, it is best to use the language that one is most comfortable with. This means that it makes a lot of sense to write an algorithm book, with the implementations written in Java. This book covers the most commonly used data structures and algorithms. It is meant for people who already know Java but are not familiar with algorithms. The book should serve as the first stepping stone towards learning the subject.

What this book covers

Chapter 1, Why Bother? – Basic, introduces the point of studying algorithms and data structures with examples. In doing so, it introduces you to the concept of asymptotic complexity, big O notation, and other notations.

Chapter 2, Cogs and Pulleys – Building Blocks, introduces you to array and the different kinds of linked lists, and their advantages and disadvantages. These data structures will be used in later chapters for implementing abstract data structures.

Chapter 3, Protocols – Abstract Data Types, introduces you to the concept of abstract data types and introduces stacks, queues, and double-ended queues. It also covers different implementations using the data structures described in the previous chapter.

Chapter 4, Detour – Functional Programming, introduces you to the functional programming ideas appropriate for a Java programmer. The chapter also introduces the lambda feature of Java, available from Java 8, and helps readers get used to the functional way of implementing algorithms. This chapter also introduces you to the concept of monads.

Chapter 5, Efficient Searching – Binary Search and Sorting, introduces efficient searching using binary searches on a sorted list. It then goes on to describe basic algorithms used to obtain a sorted array so that binary searching can be done.

Chapter 6, Efficient Sorting – Quicksort and Mergesort, introduces the two most popular and efficient sorting algorithms. The chapter also provides an analysis of why this is as optimal as a comparison-based sorting algorithm can ever be.

Chapter 7, Concepts of Tree, introduces the concept of a tree. It especially introduces binary trees, and also covers different traversals of the tree: breadth-first and depth-first, and pre-order, post-order, and in-order traversal of binary tree.

Chapter 8, More About Search – Search Trees and Hash Tables, covers search using balanced binary search trees, namely AVL, and red-black trees and hash-tables.

Chapter 9, Advanced General Purpose Data Structures, introduces priority queues and their implementation with a heap and a binomial forest. At the end, the chapter introduces sorting with a priority queue.

Chapter 10, Concepts of Graph, introduces the concepts of directed and undirected graphs. Then, it discusses the representation of a graph in memory. Depth-first and breadth-first traversals are covered, the concept of a minimum-spanning tree is introduced, and cycle detection is discussed.

Chapter 11, Reactive Programming, introduces the reader to the concept of reactive programming in Java. This includes the implementation of an observable pattern-based reactive programming framework and a functional API on top of it. Examples are shown to demonstrate the performance gain and ease of use of the reactive framework, compared with a traditional imperative style.

What you need for this book

To run the examples in this book, you need a computer with any modern popular operating system, such as some version of Windows, Linux, or Macintosh. You need to install Java 9 in your computer so that `javac` can be invoked from the command prompt.

Who this book is for

This book is for Java developers who want to learn about data structures and algorithms. A basic knowledge of Java is assumed.

Conventions

In this book, you will find a number of text styles that distinguish between different kinds of information. Here are some examples of these styles and an explanation of their meaning.

Code words in text, database table names, folder names, filenames, file extensions, pathnames, dummy URLs, user input, and Twitter handles are shown as follows: "We can include other contexts through the use of the `include` directive."

A block of code is set as follows:

```
public static void printAllElements(int[] anIntArray){
    for(int i=0;i<anIntArray.length;i++){
        System.out.println(anIntArray[i]);
    }
}
```

When we wish to draw your attention to a particular part of a code block, the relevant lines or items are set in bold:

```
public static void printAllElements(int[] anIntArray){
    for(int i=0;i<anIntArray.length;i++){
        System.out.println(anIntArray[i]);
    }
}
```

Any command-line input or output is written as follows:

```
# cp /usr/src/asterisk-addons/configs/cdr_mysql.conf.sample
    /etc/asterisk/cdr_mysql.conf
```

New terms and **important words** are shown in bold. Words that you see on the screen, for example, in menus or dialog boxes, appear in the text like this: "Clicking the **Next** button moves you to the next screen."

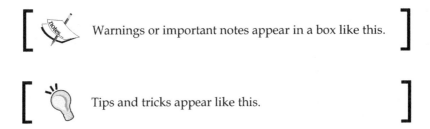

Warnings or important notes appear in a box like this.

Tips and tricks appear like this.

Reader feedback

Feedback from our readers is always welcome. Let us know what you think about this book—what you liked or disliked. Reader feedback is important for us as it helps us develop titles that you will really get the most out of.

To send us general feedback, simply e-mail feedback@packtpub.com, and mention the book's title in the subject of your message.

If there is a topic that you have expertise in and you are interested in either writing or contributing to a book, see our author guide at www.packtpub.com/authors.

Customer support

Now that you are the proud owner of a Packt book, we have a number of things to help you to get the most from your purchase.

Downloading the example code

You can download the example code files for this book from your account at http://www.packtpub.com. If you purchased this book elsewhere, you can visit http://www.packtpub.com/support and register to have the files e-mailed directly to you.

You can download the code files by following these steps:

1. Log in or register to our website using your e-mail address and password.
2. Hover the mouse pointer on the **SUPPORT** tab at the top.
3. Click on **Code Downloads & Errata**.
4. Enter the name of the book in the **Search** box.
5. Select the book for which you're looking to download the code files.
6. Choose from the drop-down menu where you purchased this book from.
7. Click on **Code Download**.

You can also download the code files by clicking on the **Code Files** button on the book's webpage at the Packt Publishing website. This page can be accessed by entering the book's name in the **Search** box. Please note that you need to be logged in to your Packt account.

Once the file is downloaded, please make sure that you unzip or extract the folder using the latest version of:

- WinRAR / 7-Zip for Windows
- Zipeg / iZip / UnRarX for Mac
- 7-Zip / PeaZip for Linux

The code bundle for the book is also hosted on GitHub at `https://github.com/PacktPublishing/Java-9-Data-Structures-and-Algorithms`. We also have other code bundles from our rich catalog of books and videos available at `https://github.com/PacktPublishing/Java9DataStructuresandAlgorithm`. Check them out!

Downloading the color images of this book

We also provide you with a PDF file that has color images of the screenshots/diagrams used in this book. The color images will help you better understand the changes in the output. You can download this file from `http://www.packtpub.com/sites/default/fles/downloads/Java9DataStructuresandAlgorithms_ColorImages.pdf`.

Errata

Although we have taken every care to ensure the accuracy of our content, mistakes do happen. If you find a mistake in one of our books—maybe a mistake in the text or the code—we would be grateful if you could report this to us. By doing so, you can save other readers from frustration and help us improve subsequent versions of this book. If you find any errata, please report them by visiting `http://www.packtpub.com/submit-errata`, selecting your book, clicking on the **Errata Submission Form** link, and entering the details of your errata. Once your errata are verified, your submission will be accepted and the errata will be uploaded to our website or added to any list of existing errata under the Errata section of that title.

To view the previously submitted errata, go to `https://www.packtpub.com/books/content/support` and enter the name of the book in the search field. The required information will appear under the **Errata** section.

Piracy

Piracy of copyrighted material on the Internet is an ongoing problem across all media. At Packt, we take the protection of our copyright and licenses very seriously. If you come across any illegal copies of our works in any form on the Internet, please provide us with the location address or website name immediately so that we can pursue a remedy.

Please contact us at `copyright@packtpub.com` with a link to the suspected pirated material.

We appreciate your help in protecting our authors and our ability to bring you valuable content.

Questions

If you have a problem with any aspect of this book, you can contact us at `questions@packtpub.com`, and we will do our best to address the problem.

Why Bother? – Basic

Since you already know Java, you have of course written a few programs, which means you have written algorithms. "Well then, what is it?" you might ask. An algorithm is a list of well-defined steps that can be followed by a processor mechanically, or without involving any sort of intelligence, which would produce a desired output in a finite amount of time. Well, that's a long sentence. In simpler words, an algorithm is just an unambiguous list of steps to get something done. It kind of sounds like we are talking about a program. Isn't a program also a list of instructions that we give the computer to follow, in order to get a desired result? Yes it is, and that means an algorithm is really just a program. Well not really, but almost. An algorithm is a program without the details of the particular programming language that we are coding it in. It is the basic idea of the program; think of it as an abstraction of a program where you don't need to bother about the program's syntactic details.

Well, since we already know about programming, and an algorithm is just a program, we are done with it, right? Not really. There is a lot to learn about programs and algorithms, that is, how to write an algorithm to achieve a particular goal. There are, of course, in general, many ways to solve a particular problem and not all ways may be equal. One way may be faster than another, and that is a very important thing about algorithms. When we study algorithms, the time it takes to execute is of utmost importance. In fact, it is the second most important thing about them, the first one being their correctness.

In this chapter, we will take a deeper look into the following ideas:

- Measuring the performance of an algorithm
- Asymptotic complexity
- Why asymptotic complexity matters
- Why an explicit study of algorithms is important

The performance of an algorithm

No one wants to wait forever to get something done. Making a program run faster surely is important, but how do we know whether a program runs fast? The first logical step would be to measure how many seconds the program takes to run. Suppose we have a program that, given three numbers, *a*, *b*, and *c*, determines the remainder when *a* raised to the power *b* is divided by *c*.

For example, say *a=2*, *b=10*, and *c = 7*, *a* raised to the power *b* = 2^{10} = *1024*, *1024 % 7 = 2*. So, given these values, the program needs to output 2. The following code snippet shows a simple and obvious way of achieving this:

```
public static long computeRemainder(long base, long power, long
divisor){
  long baseRaisedToPower = 1;
  for(long i=1;i<=power;i++){
    baseRaisedToPower *= base;
  }
  return baseRaisedToPower % divisor;
}
```

We can now estimate the time it takes by running the program a billion times and checking how long it took to run it, as shown in the following code:

```
public static void main(String [] args){
  long startTime = System.currentTimeMillis();
  for(int i=0;i<1_000_000_000;i++){
    computeRemainder(2, 10, 7);
  }
  long endTime = System.currentTimeMillis();
  System.out.println(endTime - startTime);
}
```

On my computer, it takes 4,393 milliseconds. So the time taken per call is 4,393 divided by a billion, that is, about 4.4 nanoseconds. Looks like a very reasonable time to do any computation. But what happens if the input is different? What if I pass power = 1000? Let's check that out. Now it takes about 420,000 milliseconds to run a billion times, or about 420 nanoseconds per run. Clearly, the time taken to do this computation depends on the input, and that means any reasonable way to talk about the performance of a program needs to take into account the input to the program.

Okay, so we can say that the number of nanoseconds our program takes to run is 0.42 X power, approximately.

If you run the program with the input (2, 1000, and 7), you will get an output of 0, which is not correct. The correct output is 2. So, what is going on here? The answer is that the maximum value that a long type variable can hold is one less than 2 raised to the power 63, or 9223372036854775807L. The value 2 raised to the power 1,000 is, of course, much more than this, causing the value to overflow, which brings us to our next point: how much space does a program need in order to run?

In general, the memory space required to run a program can be measured in terms of the bytes required for the program to operate. Of course, it requires the space to at least store the input and the output. It may as well need some additional space to run, which is called auxiliary space. It is quite obvious that just like time, the space required to run a program would, in general, also be dependent on the input.

In the case of time, apart from the fact that the time depends on the input, it also depends on which computer you are running it on. The program that takes 4 seconds to run on my computer may take 40 seconds on a very old computer from the nineties and may run in 2 seconds in yours. However, the actual computer you run it on only improves the time by a constant multiplier. To avoid getting into too much detail about specifying the details of the hardware the program is running on, instead of saying the program takes 0.42 X power milliseconds approximately, we can say the time taken is a constant times the power, or simply say it is proportional to the power.

Saying the computation time is proportional to the power actually makes it so non-specific to hardware, or even the language the program is written in, that we can estimate this relationship by just looking at the program and analyzing it. Of course, the running time is sort of proportional to the power because there is a loop that executes power number of times, except, of course, when the power is so small that the other one-time operations outside the loop actually start to matter.

Best case, worst case and the average case complexity

In general, the time or space required for an algorithm to process a certain input depends not only on the size of the input, but also on the actual value of the input. For example, a certain algorithm to arrange a list of values in increasing order may take much less time if the input is already sorted than when it is an arbitrary unordered list. This is why, in general, we must have a different function representing the time or space required in the different cases of input. However, the best case scenario would be where the resources required for a certain size of an input take the least amount of resources. The would also be a worst case scenario, in which the algorithm needs the maximum amount of resources for a certain size of input. An average case is an estimation of the resources taken for a given size of inputs averaged over all values of the input with that size weighted by their probability of occurrence.

Analysis of asymptotic complexity

We seem to have hit upon an idea, an abstract sense of the running time. Let's spell it out. In an abstract way, we analyze the running time of and the space required by a program by using what is known as the asymptotic complexity.

We are only interested in what happens when the input is very large because it really does not matter how long it takes for a small input to be processed; it's going to be small anyway. So, if we have $x^3 + x^2$, and if x is very large, it's almost the same as x^3. We also don't want to consider constant factors of a function, as we have pointed out earlier, because it is dependent on the particular hardware we are running the program on and the particular language we have implemented it in. An algorithm implemented in Java will perform a constant times slower than the same algorithm written in C. The formal way of tackling these abstractions in defining the complexity of an algorithm is called an asymptotic bound. Strictly speaking, an asymptotic bound is for a function and not for an algorithm. The idea is to first express the time or space required for a given algorithm to process an input as a function of the size of the input in bits and then looking for an asymptotic bound of that function.

We will consider three types of asymptotic bounds—an upper bound, a lower bound and a tight bound. We will discuss these in the following sections.

Asymptotic upper bound of a function

An upper bound, as the name suggests, puts an upper limit of a function's growth. The upper bound is another function that grows at least as fast as the original function. What is the point of talking about one function in place of another? The function we use is in general a lot more simplified than the actual function for computing running time or space required to process a certain size of input. It is a lot easier to compare simplified functions than to compare complicated functions.

For a function f, we define the notation O, called **big O**, in the following ways:

1. $f(x) = O(f(x))$.
   - For example, $x^3 = O(x^3)$.

2. If $f(x) = O(g(x))$, then $k\,f(x) = O(g(x))$ for any non-zero constant k.
   - For example, $5x^3 = O(x^3)$ and $2\,log\ x = O(log\ x)$ and $-x^3 = O(x^3)$ (taking $k = -1$).

3. If $f(x) = O(g(x))$ and $|h(x)| < |f(x)|$ for all sufficiently large x, then $f(x) + h(x) = O(g(x))$.

   ○ For example, $5x^3 - 25x^2 + 1 = O(x^3)$ because for a sufficiently large x, $|-25x^2 + 1| = 25x^2 - 1$ is much less that $|5x^3| = 5x^3$. So, $f(x) + g(x) = 5x^3 - 25x^2 + 1 = O(x^3)$ as $f(x) = 5x^3 = O(x^3)$.

   ○ We can prove by similar logic that $x^3 = O(5x^3 - 25x^2 + 1)$.

4. if $f(x) = O(g(x))$ and $|h(x)| > |g(x)|$ for all sufficiently large x, then $f(x) = O(h(x))$.

   ○ For example, $x^3 = O(x^4)$, because if x is sufficiently large, $x^4 > x^3$.

Note that whenever there is an inequality on functions, we are only interested in what happens when x is large; we don't bother about what happens for small x.

 To summarize the above definition, you can drop constant multipliers (rule 2) and ignore lower order terms (rule 3). You can also overestimate (rule 4). You can also do all combinations for those because rules can be applied any number of times.

We had to consider the absolute values of the function to cater to the case when values are negative, which never happens in running time, but we still have it for completeness.

 There is something about the sign = that is not usual. Just because $f(x) = O(g(x))$, it does not mean, $O(g(x)) = f(x)$. In fact, the last one does not even mean anything.

It is enough for all purposes to just know the preceding definition of the big O notation. You can read the following formal definition if you are interested. Otherwise you can skip the rest of this subsection.

The preceding idea can be summarized in a formal way. We say the expression $f(x) = O(g(x))$ means that positive constants M and x_0 exist, such that $|f(x)| < M|g(x)|$ whenever $x > x_0$. Remember that you just have to find one example of M and x_0 that satisfy the condition, to make the assertion $f(x) = O(g(x))$.

For example, *Figure 1* shows an example of a function $T(x) = 100x^2+2000x+200$. This function is $O(x^2)$, with some $x_0 = 11$ and $M = 300$. The graph of $300x^2$ overcomes the graph of $T(x)$ at $x=11$ and then stays above $T(x)$ up to infinity. Notice that the function $300x^2$ is lower than $T(x)$ for smaller values of x, but that does not affect our conclusion.

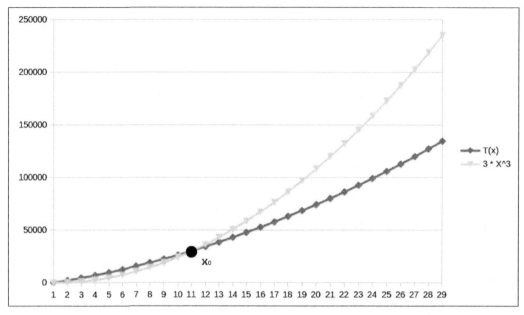

Figure 1. Asymptotic upper bound

To see that it's the same thing as the previous four points, first think of x_0 as the way to ensure that x is sufficiently large. I leave it up to you to prove the above four conditions from the formal definition.

I will, however, show some examples of using the formal definition:

- $5x^2 = O(x^2)$ because we can say, for example, $x_0 = 10$ and $M = 10$ and thus $f(x) < Mg(x)$ whenever $x > x_0$, that is, $5x^2 < 10x^2$ whenever $x > 10$.

- It is also true that $5x^2 = O(x^3)$ because we can say, for example, $x_0 = 10$ and $M = 10$ and thus $f(x) < Mg(x)$ whenever $x > x_0$, that is, $5x^2 < 10x^3$ whenever $x > 10$. This highlights a point that if $f(x) = O(g(x))$, it is also true that $f(x) = O(h(x))$ if $h(x)$ is some functions that grows at least as fast as $f(x)$.

- How about the function $f(x) = 5x^2 - 10x + 3$? We can easily see that when x is sufficiently large, $5x^2$ will far surpass the term $10x$. To prove my point, I can simply say $x>5$, $5x^2 > 10x$. Every time we increment x by one, the increment in $5x^2$ is $10x + 1$ and the increment in $10x$ is just a constant, 10. $10x+1 > 10$ for all positive x, so it is easy to see why $5x^2$ is always going to stay above $10x$ as x goes higher and higher.

In general, any polynomial of the form $a_n x^n + a_{n-1} x^{n-1} + a_{n-2} x^{n-2} + \ldots + a_0 = O(x^n)$. To show this, we will first see that $a_0 = O(1)$. This is true because we can have $x_0 = 1$ and $M = 2|a_0|$, and we will have $|a_0| < 2|a_0|$ whenever $x > 1$.

Now, let us assume it is true for some n. Thus, $a_n x^n + a_{n-1} x^{n-1} + a_{n-2} x^{n-2} + \ldots + a_0 = O(x^n)$. What it means, of course, is that some M_n and x_0 exist, such that $|a_n x^n + a_{n-1} x^{n-1} + a_{n-2} x^{n-2} + \ldots + a_0| < M_n x^n$ whenever $x>x_0$. We can safely assume that $x_0 > 2$, because if it is not so, we can simply add 2 to it to get a new x_0, which is at least 2.

Now, $|a_n x^n + a_{n-1} x^{n-1} + a_{n-2} x^{n-2} + \ldots + a_0| < M_n x^n$ implies $|a_{n+1} x^{n+1} + a_n x^n + a_{n-1} x^{n-1} + a_{n-2} x^{n-2} + \ldots + a_0| \leq |a_{n+1} x^{n+1}| + |a_{nxn} + a_{n-1} x^{n-1} + a_{n-2} x^{n-2} + \ldots + a_0| < |a_{n+1} x^{n+1}| + M_n x^n$.

This means $|a_{n+1} x^{n+1}| + M_n x^n > |a_n x^n + a_{n-1} x^{n-1} + a_{n-2} x^{n-2} + \ldots + a_0|$.

If we take $M_{n+1} = |a_{n+1}| + M_n$, we can see that $M_{n+1} x_{n+1} = |a_{n+1}| x_{n+1} + M_n x^{n+1} = |a_{n+1} x^{n+1}| + M_n x^{n+1} > |a_{n+1} x^{n+1}| + M_n x^n > |a_{n+1} x^{n+1} + a_n x^n + a_{n-1} x^{n-1} + a_{n-2} x^{n-2} + \ldots + a_0|$.

That is to say, $|a_{n+1} x^{n+1} + a_n x^{n-1} + a_{n-2} x^{n-2} + \ldots + a_0| < M_{n+1} x^{n+1}$ for all $x > x_0$, that is, $a_{n+1} x^{n+1} + a_n x^n + a_{n-1} x^{n-1} + a_{n-2} x^{n-2} + \ldots + a_0 = O(x^{n+1})$.

Now, we have it true for $n=0$, that is, $a0 = O(1)$. This means, by our last conclusion, $a_1 x + a_0 = O(x)$. This means, by the same logic, $a_2 x^2 + a_1 x + a_0 = O(x^2)$, and so on. We can easily see that this means it is true for all polynomials of positive integral degrees.

Asymptotic upper bound of an algorithm

Okay, so we figured out a way to sort of abstractly specify an upper bound on a function that has one argument. When we talk about the running time of a program, this argument has to contain information about the input. For example, in our algorithm, we can say, the execution time equals O(power). This scheme of specifying the input directly will work perfectly fine for all programs or algorithms solving the same problem because the input will be the same for all of them. However, we might want to use the same technique to measure the complexity of the problem itself: it is the complexity of the most efficient program or algorithm that can solve the problem. If we try to compare the complexity of different problems, though, we will hit a wall because different problems will have different inputs. We must specify the running time in terms of something that is common among all problems, and that something is the size of the input in bits or bytes. How many bits do we need to express the argument, power, when it's sufficiently large? Approximately log_2 *(power)*. So, in specifying the running time, our function needs to have an input that is of the size log_2 *(power)* or *lg (power)*. We have seen that the running time of our algorithm is proportional to the power, that is, constant times power, which is constant times *2 lg(power)* = *O(2x)*,where *x= lg(power)*, which is the the size of the input.

Asymptotic lower bound of a function

Sometimes, we don't want to praise an algorithm, we want to shun it; for example, when the algorithm is written by someone we don't like or when some algorithm is really poorly performing. When we want to shun it for its horrible performance, we may want to talk about how badly it performs even for the best input. An a symptotic lower bound can be defined just like how greater-than-or-equal-to can be defined in terms of less-than-or-equal-to.

A function $f(x) = \Omega(g(x))$ if and only if $g(x) = O(f(x))$. The following list shows a few examples:

- Since $x^3 = O(x^3)$, $x^3 = \Omega(x^3)$
- Since $x^3 = O(5x^3)$, $5x^3 = \Omega(x^3)$
- Since $x^3 = O(5x^3 - 25x^2 + 1)$, $5x^3 - 25x^2 + 1 = \Omega(x^3)$
- Since $x^3 = O(x^4)$, $x^4 = O(x^3)$

Again, for those of you who are interested, we say the expression $f(x) = \Omega(g(x))$ means there exist positive constants M and x_0, such that $|f(x)| > M|g(x)|$ whenever $x > x_0$, which is the same as saying $|g(x)| < (1/M)|f(x)|$ whenever $x > x_0$, that is, $g(x) = O(f(x))$.

The preceding definition was introduced by Donald Knuth, which was a stronger and more practical definition to be used in computer science. Earlier, there was a different definition of the lower bound Ω that is more complicated to understand and covers a few more edge cases. We will not talk about edge cases here.

While talking about how horrible an algorithm is, we can use an asymptotic lower bound of the best case to really make our point. However, even a criticism of the worst case of an algorithm is quite a valid argument. We can use an asymptotic lower bound of the worst case too for this purpose, when we don't want to find out an asymptotic tight bound. In general, the asymptotic lower bound can be used to show a minimum rate of growth of a function when the input is large enough in size.

Asymptotic tight bound of a function

There is another kind of bound that sort of means equality in terms of asymptotic complexity. A theta bound is specified as $f(x) = \Theta(g(x))$ if and only if $f(x) = O(g(x))$ and $f(x) = \Omega(g(x))$. Let's see some examples to understand this even better:

- Since $5x^3=O(x^3)$ and also $5x^3=\Omega(x^3)$, we have $5x^3=\Theta(x^3)$

- Since $5x^3 + 4x^2=O(x^3)$ and $5x^3 + 4x^2=\Omega(x^3)$, we have $5x^3 + 4x^2=\Theta(x^3)$

- However, even though $5x^3 + 4x^2 =O(x^4)$, since it is not $\Omega(x^4)$, it is also not $\Theta(x^4)$

- Similarly, $5x^3 + 4x^2$ is not $\Theta(x^2)$ because it is not $O(x^2)$

In short, you can ignore constant multipliers and lower order terms while determining the tight bound, but you cannot choose a function which grows either faster or slower than the given function. The best way to check whether the bound is right is to check the O and the condition separately, and say it has a theta bound only if they are the same.

Note that since the complexity of an algorithm depends on the particular input, in general, the tight bound is used when the complexity remains unchanged by the nature of the input.

In some cases, we try to find the average case complexity, especially when the upper bound really happens only in the case of an extremely pathological input. But since the average must be taken in accordance with the probability distribution of the input, it is not just dependent on the algorithm itself. The bounds themselves are just bounds for particular functions and not for algorithms. However, the total running time of an algorithm can be expressed as a grand function that changes it's formula as per the input, and that function may have different upper and lower bounds. There is no sense in talking about an asymptotic average bound because, as we discussed, the average case is not just dependent on the algorithm itself, but also on the probability distribution of the input. The average case is thus stated as a function that would be a probabilistic average running time for all inputs, and, in general, the asymptotic upper bound of that average function is reported.

Optimization of our algorithm

Before we dive into actually optimizing algorithms, we need to first correct our algorithm for large powers. We will use some tricks to do so, as described below.

Fixing the problem with large powers

Equipped with all the toolboxes of asymptotic analysis, we will start optimizing our algorithm. However, since we have already seen that our program does not work properly for even moderately large values of power, let's first fix that. There are two ways of fixing this; one is to actually give the amount of space it requires to store all the intermediate products, and the other is to do a trick to limit all the intermediate steps to be within the range of values that the `long` datatype can support. We will use binomial theorem to do this part.

As a reminder, binomial theorem says $(x+y)^n = x^n + {}^nC_1 x^{n-1}y + {}^nC_2 x^{n-2}y^2 + {}^nC_3 x^{n-3}y^3 + {}^nC_4 x^{n-4}y^4 + \ldots {}^nC_{n-1}x^1 y^{n-1} + y^n$ for positive integral values of n. The important point here is that all the coefficients are integers. Suppose, r is the remainder when we divide a by b. This makes $a = kb + r$ true for some positive integer k. This means $r = a-kb$, and $r^n = (a-kb)^n$.

If we expand this using binomial theorem, we have $r^n = a^n - {}^nC_1 a^{n-1}.kb + {}^nC_2 a^{n-2}.(kb)^2 - {}^nC_3 a^{n-3}.(kb)^3 + {}^nC_4 a^{n-4}.(kb)^4 + \ldots {}^nC_{n-1}a^1.(kb)^{n-1} \pm (kb)^n$.

Note that apart from the first term, all other terms have b as a factor. Which means that we can write $r^n = a^n + bM$ for some integer M. If we divide both sides by b now and take the remainder, we have $r^n \% b = a^n \% b$, where % is the Java operator for finding the remainder.

The idea now would be to take the remainder by the divisor every time we raise the power. This way, we will never have to store more than the range of the remainder:

```
public static long computeRemainderCorrected(long base, long
power, long divisor){
  long baseRaisedToPower = 1;
  for(long i=1;i<=power;i++){
    baseRaisedToPower *= base;
    baseRaisedToPower %= divisor;
  }
  return baseRaisedToPower;
}
```

This program obviously does not change the time complexity of the program; it just fixes the problem with large powers. The program also maintains a constant space complexity.

Improving time complexity

The current running time complexity is $O(2^x)$, where x is the size of the input as we have already computed. Can we do better than this? Let's see.

What we need to compute is *(base^{power}) % divisor*. This is, of course, the same as *(base^2)$^{power/2}$ % divisor*. If we have an even *power*, we have reduced the number of operations by half. If we can keep doing this, we can raise the *power* of *base* by 2^n in just n steps, which means our loop only has to run *lg(power)* times, and hence, the complexity is $O(lg(2^x)) = O(x)$, where x is the number of bits to store *power*. This is a substantial reduction in the number of steps to compute the value for large powers.

However, there is a catch. What happens if the *power* is not divisible by 2? Well, then we can write *(base^{power})% divisor = (base ((base$^{power-1}$))% divisor = (base ((base^2)$^{power-1}$)% divisor*, and *power-1* is, of course, even and the computation can proceed. We will write up this code in a program. The idea is to start from the most significant bit and move towards less and less significant bits. If a bit with *1* has n bits after it, it represents multiplying the result by the base and then squaring n times after this bit. We accumulate this squaring by squaring for the subsequent steps. If we find a zero, we keep squaring for the sake of accumulating squaring for the earlier bits:

```
public static long computeRemainderUsingEBS(long base, long power,
long divisor){
  long baseRaisedToPower = 1;
  long powerBitsReversed = 0;
  int numBits=0;
```

First reverse the bits of our `power` so that it is easier to access them from the least important side, which is more easily accessible. We also count the number of bits for later use:

```
while(power>0){
    powerBitsReversed <<= 1;
    powerBitsReversed += power & 1;
    power >>>= 1;
    numBits++;
}
```

Now we extract one bit at a time. Since we have already reversed the order of bit, the first one we get is the most significant one. Just to get an intuition on the order, the first bit we collect will eventually be squared the maximum number of times and hence will act like the most significant bit:

```
while (numBits-->0){
    if(powerBitsReversed%2==1){
        baseRaisedToPower *= baseRaisedToPower * base;
    }else{
        baseRaisedToPower *= baseRaisedToPower;
    }
    baseRaisedToPower %= divisor;
    powerBitsReversed>>>=1;
}
return baseRaisedToPower;
}
```

We test the performance of the algorithm; we compare the time taken for the same computation with the earlier and final algorithms with the following code:

```
public static void main(String [] args){
    System.out.println(computeRemainderUsingEBS(13, 10_000_000, 7));

    long startTime = System.currentTimeMillis();
    for(int i=0;i<1000;i++){
        computeRemainderCorrected(13, 10_000_000, 7);
    }
    long endTime = System.currentTimeMillis();
    System.out.println(endTime - startTime);

    startTime = System.currentTimeMillis();
    for(int i=0;i<1000;i++){
        computeRemainderUsingEBS(13, 10_000_000, 7);
    }
    endTime = System.currentTimeMillis();
    System.out.println(endTime - startTime);
}
```

The first algorithm takes 130,190 milliseconds to complete all 1,000 times execution on my computer and the second one takes just 2 milliseconds to do the same. This clearly shows the tremendous gain in performance for a large power like 10 million. The algorithm for squaring the term repeatedly to achieve exponentiation like we did is called... well, exponentiation by squaring. This example should be able to motivate you to study algorithms for the sheer obvious advantage it can give in improving the performance of computer programs.

Summary

In this chapter, you saw how we can think about measuring the running time of and the memory required by an algorithm in seconds and bytes, respectively. Since this depends on the particular implementation, the programming platform, and the hardware, we need a notion of talking about running time in an abstract way. Asymptotic complexity is a measure of the growth of a function when the input is very large. We can use it to abstract our discussion on running time. This is not to say that a programmer should not spend any time to make a run a program twice as fast, but that comes only after the program is already running at the minimum asymptotic complexity.

We also saw that the asymptotic complexity is not just a property of the problem at hand that we are trying to solve, but also a property of the particular way we are solving it, that is, the particular algorithm we are using. We also saw that two programs solving the same problem while running different algorithms with different asymptotic complexities can perform vastly differently for large inputs. This should be enough motivation to study algorithms explicitly.

In the following chapters, we will study the most used algorithmic tricks and concepts required in daily use. We will start from the very easy ones that are also the building blocks for the more advanced techniques. This book is, of course, by no means comprehensive; the objective is to provide enough background to make you comfortable with the basic concepts and then you can read on.

2
Cogs and Pulleys – Building Blocks

We discussed algorithms in the previous chapter, but the title of the book also includes the term "data structure." So what is a data structure? A data structure is an organization of data in memory that is generally optimized so it can be used by a particular algorithm. We have seen that an algorithm is a list of steps that leads to a desired outcome. In the case of a program, there is always some input and output. Both input and output contain data and hence must be organized in some way or another. Therefore, the input and output of an algorithm are data structures. In fact, all the intermediate states that an algorithm has to go through must also be stored in some form of a data structure. Data structures don't have any use without algorithms to manipulate them, and algorithms cannot work without data structures. It's because this is how they get input and emit output or store their intermediate states. There are a lot of ways in which data can be organized. Simpler data structures are also different types of variables. For example, `int` is a data structure that stores one 4-byte integer value. We can even have classes that store a set of specific types of values. However, we also need to think about how to store a collection of a large number of the same type of values. In this book, we will spend the rest of the time discussing a collection of values of the same type because how we store a collection determines which algorithm can work on them. Some of the most common ways of storing a collection of values have their own names; we will discuss them in this chapter. They are as follows:

- Arrays
- Linked lists
- Doubly linked lists
- Circular linked lists

These are the basic building blocks that we will use to build more complex data structures. Even if we don't use them directly, we will use their concepts.

Arrays

If you are a Java programmer, you must have worked with arrays. Arrays are the basic storage mechanisms available for a sequence of data. The best thing about arrays is that the elements of an array are collocated sequentially and can be accessed completely and randomly with single instructions.

The traversal of an array element by an element is very simple. Since any element can be accessed randomly, you just keep incrementing an index and keep accessing the element at this index. The following code shows both traversal and random access in an array:

```
public static void printAllElements(int[] anIntArray){
    for(int i=0;i<anIntArray.length;i++){
        System.out.println(anIntArray[i]);
    }
}
```

Insertion of elements in an array

All the elements in an array are stored in contiguous memory. This makes it possible to access any element in a constant amount of time. A program simply needs to compute the offset that corresponds to an index, and it reads the information directly. But this means they are also limited and have a fixed size. If you want to insert a new element into an array, you will need to create a new array with one more element and copy the entire data from the original data along with the new value. To avoid all this complexity, we will start with moving an existing element to a new position. What we are looking to do is to take an element out, shift all the elements up to the target position to make space in this position, and insert the value we extracted in the same place.

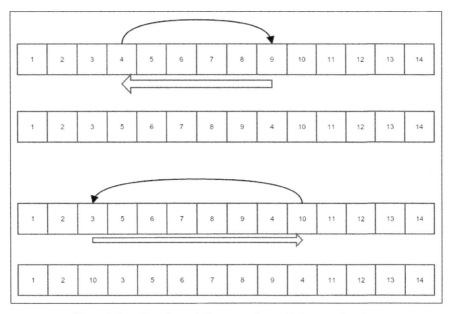

Figure 1: Insertion of an existing array element into a new location

The preceding figure explains what we mean by this operation. The thin black arrows show the movement of the element that is being reinserted, and the thick white arrow shows the shift of the elements of the array. In each case, the bottom figure shows the array after the reinsertion is done. Notice that the shifting is done either to the left or right, depending on what the start and end index are. Let's put this in code:

```
public static void insertElementAtIndex(int[] array,
int startIndex, int targetIndex){
   int value = array[startIndex];
   if(startIndex==targetIndex){
      return;
   }else if(startIndex < tarGetIndex){
      for(int i=startIndex+1;i<=targetIndex;i++){
         array[i-1]=array[i];
      }
      array[targetIndex]=value;
   }else{
      for(int i=startIndex-1;i>=targetIndex;i--){
         array[i+1]=array[i];
      }
      array[targetIndex]=value;
   }
}
```

What would be the running time complexity of the preceding algorithm? For all our cases, we will only consider the worst case. When does an algorithm perform worst? To understand this, let's see what the most frequent operation in an algorithm is. It is of course the shift that happens in the loop. The number of shifts become maximum when `startIndex` is at the beginning of the array and `targetIndex` at the end or vice versa. This is when all but one element has to be shifted one by one. The running time in this case must be some constant times the number of elements of the array plus some other constant to account for the non-repeating operations. So it is $T(n) = K(n-1)+C$ for some constants K and C, where n is the number of elements in the array and $T(n)$ is the running time of the algorithm. This can be expressed as follows:

$$T(n) = K(n-1)+C = Kn + (C-K)$$

The following steps explain the expression:

1. As per rule 1 of the definition of **big O**, $T(n) = O(Kn + (C-K))$.
2. As per rule 3, $T(n) = O(Kn)$.
3. We know $|-(C-K)| < |Kn + (C-K)|$ is true for sufficiently large n. Therefore, as per rule 3, since $T(n) = O(Kn + (C-K))$, it means $T(n) = O(Kn + (C-K) + (-(C-K)))$, that is, $T(n) = O(Kn)$.
4. And, finally, as per rule 2, $T(n) = O(n)$.

Now since the array is the major input in the algorithm, the size of the input is represented by n. So we will say, the running time of the algorithm is $O(n)$, where n is the size of the input.

Insertion of a new element and the process of appending it

Now we move on to the process of insertion of a new element. Since arrays are fixed in size, insertion requires us to create a new array and copy all the earlier elements into it. The following figure explains the idea of an insertion made in a new array:

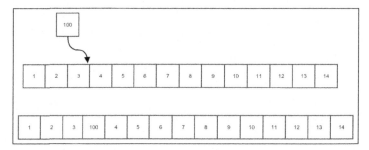

Figure 2: Insertion of a new element into an array

The following code does exactly that:

```
public static int [] insertExtraElementAtIndex(int[] array,
int index, int value){
    int [] newArray = new int[array.length+1];
```

First, you copy all the elements before the targeted position as they are in the original array:

```
for(int i=0;i<index;i++){
    newArray[i] = array[i];
}
```

Then, the new value must be put in the correct position:

```
newArray[index]=value;
```

In the end, copy the rest of the elements in the array by shifting their position by one:

```
for(int i=index+1;i<newArray.length;i++){
    newArray[i]=array[i-1];
}
return newArray;
}
```

When we have the code ready, appending it would mean just inserting it at the end, as shown in the following code:

```
public static int[] appendElement(int[] array, int value){
    return insertExtraElementAtIndex(array, array.length, value);
}
```

What is the running time complexity of the preceding algorithm? Well, no matter what we do, we must copy all the elements of the original array to the new array, and this is the operation in the loop. So the running time is $T(n) = Kn + C$ for some constants K and C, and n is the size of the array, which is the size of the input. I leave it to you to verify the steps in order to figure out this: $T(n) = O(n)$.

Linked list

Arrays are great for storing data. We have also seen that any element of an array can be read in *O(1)* time. But arrays are fixed in size. Changing the size of an array means creating a new array and copying all the elements to the original array. The simplest recourse to the resizing problem is to store each element in a different object and then hold a reference in each element to the next element. This way, the process of adding a new element will just involve creating the element and attaching it at the end of the last element of the original linked list. In another variation, the new element can be added to the beginning of the existing linked list:

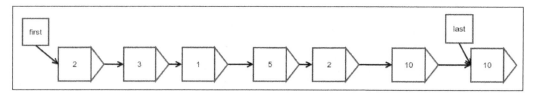

Figure 3: An example of a linked list

Figure 3 shows an example of a linked list. The arrows represent a reference. Each element is stored in a **wrapper object** that also holds a reference to the next element wrapper. There are two additional references to the first and last elements, which are required for any operation to start. The last reference is optional, but it improves the performance of appending to the end vastly, as we shall see.

To begin the discussion, let's create a linked list node in the following way:

```
public class LinkedList<E> implements Iterable<E>, Visualizable {
```

First, we create a `Node` class inside the `LinkedList` class, which will act as a wrapper for the elements and also hold the reference to the next node:

```
protected static class Node<E> {
    protected E value;
    protected Node next;

    public String toString(){
        return value.toString();
    }
}

int length = 0;
Node<E>[] lastModifiedNode;
```

Then, we must have references for the first and last elements:

```
Node<E> first;
Node<E> last;
```

Finally, we create a method called getNewNode() that creates a new empty node. We will need this if we want to use a different class for a node in any of the subclasses:

```
protected Node<E> getNewNode() {
    Node<E> node = new Node<>();
    lastModifiedNode = new Node[]{node};
    return node;
}
}
```

At this point, the unfinished class LinkedList will not be able to store any element; let's see how to do this, though. Notice that we have implemented the Iterable interface. This will allow us to loop through all the elements in an advanced for loop.

Appending at the end

Appending at the end is achieved by simply creating a link from the last element of the original linked list to the new element that is being appended and then reassigning the reference to the last element. The second step is required because the new element is the new last element. This is shown in the following figure:

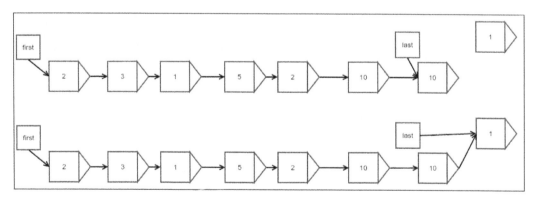

Figure 4: Appending at the end of a linked list

There is a small difference when you append an element to a linked list that is empty to start with. At this point, the first and last references are null, and this case must be handled separately. The following figure explains this case:

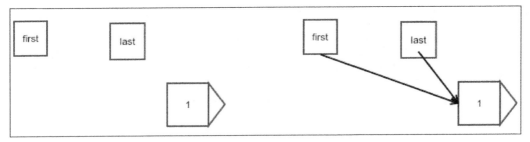

Figure 5: Appending to an empty linked list

We will achieve this by using the following simple code as is. We return the node that has just been added. This is helpful to any class that is extending this class. We will do the same in all cases, and we will see the use of this while discussing doubly linked lists:

```
public Node<E> appendLast(E value) {
    Node node = getNewNode();
    node.value = value;
```

We try to update the reference of the current last node only if the list is not empty:

```
if (last != null)
    last.next = node;
```

Then, we must update the last reference as the new element is not going to be the last element:

```
last = node;
```

Finally, if the list is empty, the new element must also be the first new element and we must update the first reference accordingly, as shown in the preceding figure:

```
if (first == null) {
    first = node;
}
length++;
return node;
}
```

Notice that we also keep track of the current length of the list. This is not essential, but if we do this, we do not have to traverse the entire list just to count how many elements are in the list.

Now, of course, there is this important question: what is the time complexity of appending to a linked list? Well, if we do it the way we have done it before — that is, by having a special reference to the last element — we don't need any loop, as we can see in the code. If the program does not have any loops, all operations would be one-time operations, hence everything is completed in constant time. You can verify that a constant function has this complexity: *O(1)*. Compare this with what was appended at the end of an array. It required the creation of a new array and also had *O(n)* complexity, where *n* was the size of the array.

Insertion at the beginning

Inserting an element at the beginning of a list is very similar to appending it at the end. The only difference is that you need to update the first reference instead of the last reference:

```
public Node<E> appendFirst(E value) {
    Node node = getNewNode();
    node.value = value;
    node.next = first;
    first = node;
    if (length == 0)
        last = node;
    length++;
    return node;
}
```

Insertion at an arbitrary position

Insertion at an arbitrary position can be achieved in the same way we perform an insertion in the first element, except that we update the reference of the previous element instead of the first reference. There is, however, a catch; we need to find the position where we need to insert the element. There is no way to find it other than to start at the beginning and walk all the way to the correct position while counting each node we step on.

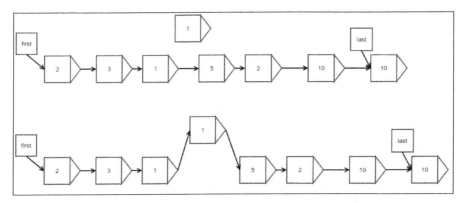

Figure 6: Insertion of an arbitrary element into a linked list

We can implement the idea as follows:

```
public Node<E> insert(int index, E value) {
    Node<E> node = getNewNode();
```

First, we take care of the special cases:

```
if (index < 0 || index > length) {
    throw new IllegalArgumentException("Invalid
        index for insertion");
} else if (index == length) {
    return appendLast(value);
} else if (index == 0) {
    return appendFirst(value);
} else {
```

As mentioned earlier, we walk all the way to the desired position while counting the nodes, or in this case, counting the index in the opposite direction:

```
Node<E> result = first;
while (index > 1) {
    index--;
    result = result.next;
}
```

Finally, we update the references:

```
        node.value = value;
        node.next = result.next;
        result.next = node;
        length++;
        return node;
    }
}
```

What is the complexity of this algorithm? There is a loop that must run as many times as the index. This algorithm seems to have a running time that is dependent on the value of the input and not just its size. In this case, we are only interested in the worst case. What is the worst case then? It is when we need to step on all the elements of the list, that is, when we have to insert the element at the end of the list, except for the last element. In this case, we must step on *n-1* elements to get there and do some constant work. The number of steps would then be $T(n) = C(n-1)+K$ for some constants C and K. So, $T(n) = O(n)$.

Looking up an arbitrary element

Finding the value of an arbitrary element has two different cases. For the first and last element, it is simple. Since we have direct references to the first and last element, we just have to traverse that reference and read the value inside it. I leave this for you to see how it could be done.

However, how do you read an arbitrary element? Since we only have forward references, we must start from the beginning and walk all the way, traversing references while counting steps until we reach the element we want.

Let's see how we can do this:

```
    public E findAtIndex(int index) {
```

We start from the first element:

```
        Node<E> result = first;
        while (index >= 0) {
            if (result == null) {
                throw new NoSuchElementException();
            } else if (index == 0) {
```

When the index is 0, we would have finally reached the desired position, so we return:

```
            return result.value;
        } else {
```

If we are not there yet, we must step onto the next element and keep counting:

```
            index--;
            result = result.next;
        }
    }
    return null;
}
```

Here too, we have a loop inside that has to run an index a number of times. The worst case is when you just need to remove one element but it is not the last one; the last one can be found directly. It is easy to see that just like you insert into an arbitrary position, this algorithm also has running time complexity of *O(n)*.

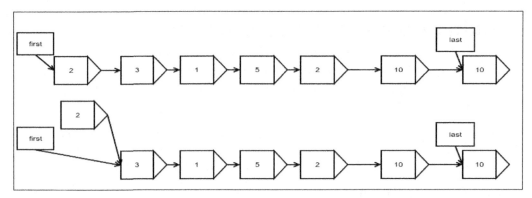

Figure 7: Removing an element in the beginning

Removing an element in the beginning means simply updating the reference to the first element with that of the next element. Note that we do not update the reference in the element that has just been removed because the element, along with the reference, would be garbage-collected anyway:

```
public Node<E> removeFirst() {
    if (length == 0) {
        throw new NoSuchElementException();
    }
```

Assign the reference to the next element:

```
Node<E> origFirst = first;
first = first.next;
length--;
```

If there are no more elements left, we must also update the last reference:

```
if (length == 0) {
    last = null;
}
return origFirst;
}
```

Removing an arbitrary element

Removing an arbitrary element is very similar to removing an element from the beginning, except that you update the reference held by the previous element instead of the special reference named first. The following figure shows this:

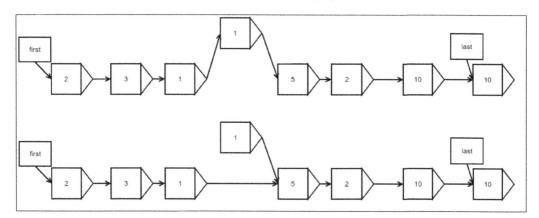

Figure 8: Removing an arbitrary element

Notice that only the link in the linked list is to be reassigned to the next element. The following code does what is shown in the preceding figure:

```
protected Node<E> removeAtIndex(int index) {
    if (index >= length || index < 0) {
        throw new NoSuchElementException();
    }
```

Of course, removing the first element is a special case:

```
if (index == 0) {
    Node<E> nodeRemoved = first;
    removeFirst();
    return nodeRemoved;
}
```

First, find out the element just before the one that needs to be removed because this element would need its reference updated:

```
Node justBeforeIt = first;
while (--index > 0) {
    justBeforeIt = justBeforeIt.next;
}
```

Update the last reference if the last element is the one that is being removed:

```
Node<E> nodeRemoved = justBeforeIt.next;
if (justBeforeIt.next == last) {
    last = justBeforeIt.next.next;
}
```

Update the reference held by the previous element:

```
    justBeforeIt.next = justBeforeIt.next.next;
    length--;
    return nodeRemoved;
}
```

It is very easy to see that the running time worst case complexity of this algorithm is $O(n)$ – which is similar to finding an arbitrary element – because this is what needs to be done before removing it. The operation of the actual removal process itself requires only a constant number of steps.

Iteration

Since we are working in Java, we prefer to implement the `Iterable` interface. It lets us loop through the list in a simplified for loop syntax. For this purpose, we first have to create an iterator that will let us fetch the elements one by one:

```
protected class ListIterator implements Iterator<E> {
    protected Node<E> nextNode = first;

    @Override
```

```
public boolean hasNext() {
    return nextNode != null;
}

@Override
public E next() {
    if (!hasNext()) {
        throw new IllegalStateException();
    }
    Node<E> nodeToReturn = nextNode;
    nextNode = nextNode.next;
    return nodeToReturn.value;
}
}
```

The code is self-explanatory. Every time it is invoked, we move to the next element and return the current element's value. Now we implement the iterator method of the Iterable interface to make our list an iterable:

```
@Override
public Iterator<E> iterator() {
    return new ListIterator();
}
```

This enables us to use the following code:

```
for(Integer x:linkedList){
    System.out.println(x);
}
```

The preceding code assumes that the variable linkedList was LinkedList<Integer>. Any list that extends this class will also get this property automatically.

Doubly linked list

Did you notice that there is no quick way to remove the element from the end of a linked list? This is because even if there is a quick way to find the last element, there is no quick way to find the element before it whose reference needs to be updated. We must walk all the way from the beginning to find the previous element. Well then, why not just have another reference to store the location of the last but one element? This is because after you remove the element, how would you update the reference otherwise? There would be no reference to the element right before that. What it looks like is that to achieve this, we have to store the reference of all the previous elements up to the beginning. The best way to do this would be to store the reference of the previous element in each of the elements or nodes along with the reference to the next element. Such a linked list is called a **doubly linked list** since the elements are linked both ways:

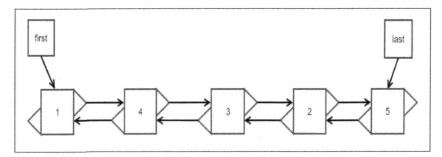

Figure 9: Doubly linked list

We will implement a doubly linked list by extending our original linked list because a lot of the operations would be similar. We can create the barebones class in the following manner:

```
public class DoublyLinkedList<E> extends LinkedList<E> {
```

We create a new `Node` class extending the original one and adding a reference for the previous node:

```
protected static class DoublyLinkedNode<E> extends Node<E> {
    protected DoublyLinkedNode<E> prev;
}
```

Of course, we need to override the `getNode()` method to use this node:

```
@Override
protected Node<E> getNewNode() {
    return new DoublyLinkedNode<E>();
}
}
```

Insertion at the beginning or at the end

Insertion at the beginning is very similar to that of a singly linked list, except that we must now update the next node's reference for its previous node. The node being inserted does not have a previous node in this case, so nothing needs to be done:

```java
public Node<E> appendFirst(E value) {
    Node<E> node = super.appendFirst(value);
    if (first.next != null)
        ((DoublyLinkedNode<E>) first.next).prev =
            (DoublyLinkedNode<E>) first;
    return node;
}
```

Pictorially, it can be visualized as shown in the following figure:

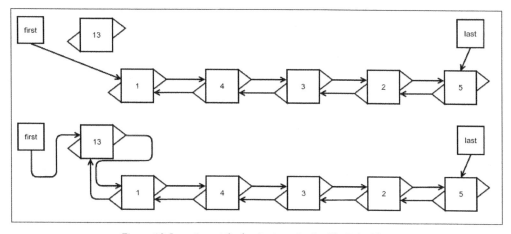

Figure 10: Insertion at the beginning of a doubly linked list

Appending at the end is very similar and is given as follows:

```java
public Node<E> appendLast(E value) {
    DoublyLinkedNode<E> origLast = (DoublyLinkedNode<E>)
                                    this.last;
    Node<E> node = super.appendLast(value);
```

If the original list were empty, the original last reference would be null:

```java
    if (origLast == null) {
        origLast = (DoublyLinkedNode<E>) first;
    }
    ((DoublyLinkedNode<E>) this.last).prev = origLast;
    return node;
}
```

The complexity of the insertion is the same as that of a singly linked list. In fact, all the operations on a doubly linked list have the same running time complexity as that of a singly linked list, except the process of removing the last element. We will thus refrain from stating it again until we discuss the removal of the last element. You should verify that the complexity stays the same as with a singly linked list in all other cases.

Insertion at an arbitrary location

As with everything else, this operation is very similar to the process of making an insertion at an arbitrary location of a singly linked list, except that you need to update the references for the previous node.

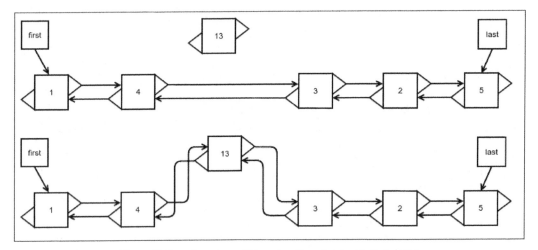

Figure 11: Insertion at an arbitrary location of a doubly linked list

The following code does this for us:

```
public Node<E> insert(int index, E value) {
    DoublyLinkedNode<E> inserted = (DoublyLinkedNode<E>)
                                    super.insert(index, value);
```

In the case of the first and last element, our overridden methods are invoked anyway. Therefore, there is no need to consider them again:

```
if(index!=0 && index!=length) {
    if (inserted.next != null) {
```

This part needs a little bit of explaining. In *Figure 11*, the node being inserted is **13**. Its previous node should be **4**, which was originally the previous node of the next node **3**:

```
inserted.prev = ((DoublyLinkedNode<E>)
                    inserted.next).prev;
```

The `prev` reference of the next node **3** must now hold the newly inserted node **13**:

```
            ((DoublyLinkedNode<E>) inserted.next).prev = inserted;
        }
    }
    return inserted;
}
```

Removing the first element

Removing the first element is almost the same as that for a singly linked list. The only additional step is to set the `prev` reference of the next node to `null`. The following code does this:

```
public Node<E> removeFirst() {
    super.removeFirst();
    if (first != null) {
        ((DoublyLinkedNode<E>) first).prev = null;
    }
    return first;
}
```

The following figure shows what happens. Also, note that finding an element does not really need an update:

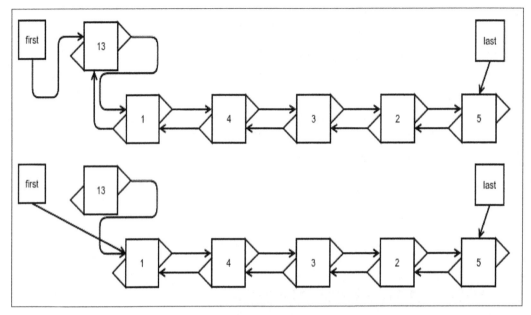

Figure 12: Removal of the first element from a doubly linked list

There can be an optimization to traverse backward from the last element to the first in case the index we are looking for is closer toward the end; however, it does not change the asymptotic complexity of the find operation. So we leave it at this stage. If interested, you would be able to easily figure out how to do this optimization.

Removing an arbitrary element

Just like other operations, removal is very similar to removal of elements in the case of a singly linked list, except that we need to update the prev reference:

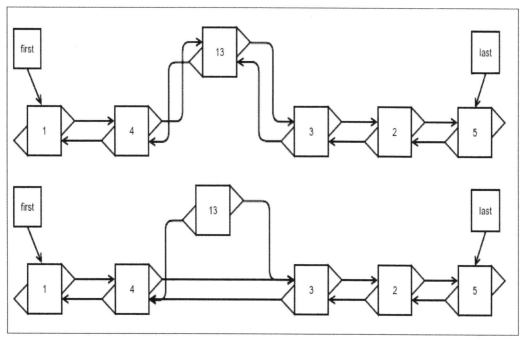

Figure 13: Removal of an arbitrary element from a doubly linked list

The following code will help us achieve this:

```
public Node<E> removeAtIndex(int index) {
    if(index<0||index>=length){
        throw new NoSuchElementException();
    }
```

This is a special case that needs extra attention. A doubly linked list really shines while removing the last element. We will discuss the removeLast() method in the next section:

```
    if(index==length-1){
        return removeLast();
    }
```

The rest of the code is fairly easy to figure out:

```
    DoublyLinkedNode<E> nodeRemoved
            = (DoublyLinkedNode<E>) super.removeAtIndex(index);
    if ((DoublyLinkedNode<E>) nodeRemoved.next != null)
        ((DoublyLinkedNode<E>) nodeRemoved.next).prev
                = nodeRemoved.prev;
    return nodeRemoved;
}
```

Removal of the last element

This is where a doubly linked list really shines. This is the reason we got started with a doubly linked list. And it's not even a lot of code. Check this out:

```
public Node<E> removeLast() {
    Node<E> origLast = last;
    if(last==null){
        throw new IllegalStateException
                    ("Removing element from an empty list");
    }
```

Just use the fact that we have access to the previous node's reference and we can update the last reference very easily:

```
    last = ((DoublyLinkedNode<E>)last).prev;
```

If the list is not empty after removal, set the next reference of the new last element to null. If the new list is empty instead, update the first element as well:

```
    if(last!=null){
        last.next = null;
    } else{
        first = null;
    }
```

Don't forget to update the length:

```
    length--;
    return origLast;
}
```

We don't need a new figure to understand the update of the references as they are really similar to the removal process of the first element. The only difference from the singly linked list is that in the case of a singly linked list, we need to walk all the way to the end of the list to find the previous element of the list. However, in the case of a doubly linked list, we can update it in one step because we always have access to the previous node's reference. This drastically reduces the running time from *O(n)* in the case of a singly linked list to *O(1)* in the case of a doubly linked list.

Circular linked list

A circular linked list is an ordinary linked list, except that the last element holds the reference to the first element as its next element. This, of course, justifies its name. It would be useful when, for example, you are holding a list of players in a list and they play in turn in a round robin fashion. The implementation is simplified if you use a circular linked list and just keep rotating as the players complete their turn:

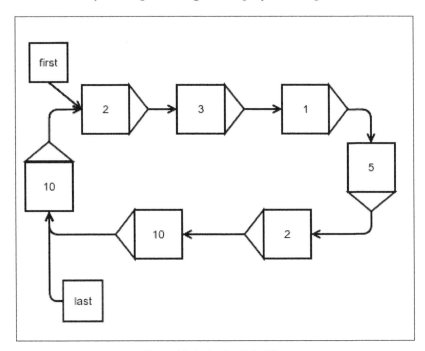

Figure 14: A circular linked list

The basic structure of a circular linked list is the same as that of a simple linked list; no more fields or methods are required:

```
public class CircularLinkedList<E> extends LinkedList<E>{
}
```

Insertion

This is the same as the insertion for a simple linked list, except that you assign the last references next to the first:

```
@Override
public Node<E> appendFirst(E value) {
    Node<E> newNode = super.appendFirst(value);
    last.next = first;
    return newNode;
}
```

From this, it is not hard to guess how it would be to append at the end:

```
@Override
public Node<E> appendLast(E value) {
    Node<E> newNode =  super.appendLast(value);
    last.next = first;
    return newNode;
}
```

Insertion at any other index, of course, remains the same as that for a simple linked list; no more changes are required. This means the complexity of the insertion stays the same as with that for a simple linked list.

Removal

Removal also only changes when you remove the first or the last element. In any case, just updating the last element's next reference solves the purpose. The only place where we need to change this is when we remove the first element. This is because the same operation we used for a simple linked list does not update the previous element's next reference, which we need to do:

```
@Override
public Node<E> removeFirst() {
    Node<E> newNode =  super.removeFirst();
    last.next = first;
    return newNode;
}
```

Nothing else needs to be done in removal.

Rotation

What we are doing here is just bringing the next element of the first element to the first position. This is exactly what the name "rotation" would imply:

```
public void rotate(){
    last = first;
    first = first.next;
}
```

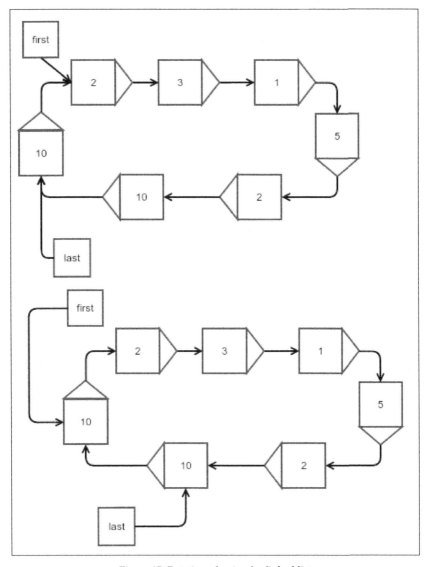

Figure 15: Rotation of a circular linked list

Doing the same with a simple linked list would require no more than assigning one more reference. You should be able to figure out how to do this with a simple linked list. But this operation looks more natural for a circular linked list, as conceptually, there is no first element.

The real power of a circular linked list is the iterator, which never ends. If the list is non-empty, the iterator will have `hasNext()`, which always returns true. This means you can simply keep calling the `next()` method on the iterator and keep processing the elements in a round robin fashion. The following code should make it clear what I mean:

```
for(int i=0;i<30;i++){
    System.out.print(" "+ linkedList.first);
    linkedList.rotate();
}
```

 Note that if you try to use the enhanced for loop with a circular linked list, you will run into an infinite loop.

Summary

We covered a few basic data structures and the algorithms for manipulating them. In addition to this, we also found out their running time complexities. To summarize this, an array provides you with the fastest random access there is with this time complexity: $O(1)$. But arrays cannot change size; the only modification they allow is to change the value of an element. A linked list allows fast append at the end and insertion at the beginning at $O(1)$ time. However, $O(1)$ removal is only available for removing the first element. This is resolved by a doubly linked list that also allows $O(1)$ removal from the end. A circular linked list holds a reference to the first element in the next reference of the last element. This makes the list a circular structure that allows one to loop indefinitely.

In the upcoming chapters, we will discuss the abstraction of data structures called abstract data types. We will use the data structures we have seen in this chapter to implement the abstract data types, which in turn will be used in later chapters.

3
Protocols – Abstract Data Types

In the last chapter, we saw a few basic data structures and some algorithms to manipulate them. However, sometimes we may want to hide the implementation details of a data structure and only want to know how they interact with other algorithms. We may want to specify a few operations that they must allow and forget about how they are achieved. This is not very different from abstraction of a part of a program in any large software application. For example, in Java, we create interfaces that only define the methods of an object that its class must implement, and then we use this interface type, being confident that they will be implemented properly. We do not want to think about how an implementation class would provide their implementation. Such interfaces of data structure are called abstract data types. To put this another way, an **abstract data type** (**ADT**) is a description of what a data structure should do for its user. It is a list of operations that any implementation must support and the complete description of what these operations are supposed to do. A few of these have very frequent usage and have names given to them. We will discuss a few of these here.

In this chapter, you will learn about the following concepts:

- The definition of some common ADTs and their operations
- How to implement these ADTs using both simple arrays and the data structures you learned in the last chapter

Stack

A **stack** is a very commonly used ADT. It is so named because it resembles a stack of plates used in a restaurant. In such a stack, a plate that has been washed and put last would stay on top. This would be the first plate to be picked up when a plate is needed. The plate that went in first would be at the bottom of the stack and would be picked last. So, the last plate to be placed in the stack is the first plate to get out, we can also call this **last in first out** (**LIFO**).

Similarly, a stack ADT has a protocol where the last value that is put in it must be returned on the first attempt to get a value out, and the value that went in first must come out last. The following figure will make it more clear:

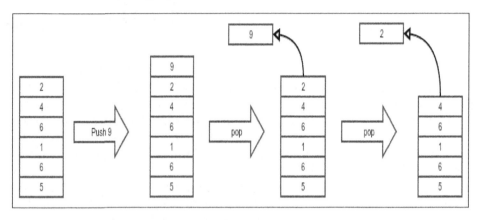

The operation of putting a new value in a stack is called push, and the operation of retrieving a value from a stack is called pop. The element that was pushed last must be popped first. The operation that allows one to see what the next pop will return is called peek. The peek operation returns the top element without modifying the stack. We expect all stack implementations to have all operations implemented in the time complexity of *O(1)*. This is also part of our stack protocol.

The stack ADT has the following operations:

- **Push**: This adds an element at the top of the stack
- **Pop**: This removes the element at the top of the stack
- **Peek**: This checks the next value to be popped

Since we know that ADTs are to data structures what interfaces are to classes, we will code an ADT as an interface. The following is our interface for a stack:

```
public interface Stack<E> {
  void push(E value);
  E pop();
  E peek();
}
```

Of course, we will not leave it at this. We will see how a stack can actually be implemented. To this end, we will see both a fixed-sized stack using an array to store it's data, and a growing stack using a linked list for storing data. We will start with the first.

Fixed-sized stack using an array

A fixed-sized stack uses a pre-allocated array to store values, that is when this stack has used up the entire array, it can no longer accept new values until the old ones are popped. This is not very different from an actual stack of plates, which most certainly has a maximum height that it can handle.

As always, we start with the basic structure of the class, as follows:

```
public class StackImplArray<E> implements Stack<E> {
```

We need an array to store the elements, and we need to remember where the top of the stack is in that array. The top always marks the index of the element that will be popped next. When there are no more elements to be popped, it is set to -1. Why -1? Because this is the natural choice as it does not require any special handling when the first element is inserted:

```
  protected E[] array;
  int top=-1;

  public StackImplArray(int size){
    array = (E[])new Object[size];
  }
}
```

The push operation in a stack can be to simply put the value in the array right next to the current top and then set the top to the new position, as illustrated in the following code:

```
@Override
public void push(E value) {
```

We first check whether the stack is already full or the current `top` is equal to the maximum index possible, like this:

```
if(top == array.length-1){
    throw new NoSpaceException("No more space in stack");
}
```

Now, we set the `top` to the new position and put the value we need to store in there as follows:

```
top++;
array[top] = value;
}
```

The exception we used is a custom exception for this purpose. The code of the exception is simple as shown in the following code:

```
public class NoSpaceException extends RuntimeException{
    public NoSpaceException(String message) {
        super(message);
    }
}
```

The `pop` operation is just the opposite. We need to first take the value of the current `top` and then update the `top` to the new position, which is one less than the current position, as shown in the following code:

```
@Override
public E pop() {
```

We first check whether the stack is already empty, in which case we return a special value, `null`. This is shown in the following code:

```
if(top==-1){
    return null;
}
```

Then we update the `top` and return the value at the current `top` as follows:

```
top--;
return array[top+1];
}
```

The `peek` operation does not change the state of the stack, and hence is even simpler:

```
@Override
public E peek() {
```

Just like the `pop` operation, we return `null` if the stack is empty:

```
if(top==-1){
    return null;
}
```

Otherwise, we return the `top` element, as follows:

```
    return array[top];
}
```

It is in fact possible to have a stack without an upper limit backed up by an array. What we really need to do is that whenever we run out of space, we can resize the array. Array actually cannot be resized, so the operation would be to create a new array with a higher size (maybe twice as much as the original size), and copy all the old elements into this array. Since this involves copying all the *n* elements to the new array one by one, the complexity of this operation is *O(n)*.

Variable-sized stack using a linked list

The problem with an array-based implementation is that since arrays are fixed in size, the stacks cannot grow beyond a fixed-size. To resolve this, we have to do what we did to fix the same problem for an array, that is, use a linked list instead. We start such an implementation with the following bare bone class. The linked list will store the values. Instead of assigning a new linked list to it, we do so using an overridable method `getNewLinkedList()`. This will be useful in the class that extends from this one:

```
public class StackImplLinkedList<E> implements Stack<E> {
    protected LinkedList<E> list = getNewLinkedList();

    protected LinkedList<E> getNewLinkedList(){
        return new LinkedList<>();
    }
}
```

To see which end of the linked list must be used as the top of the stack, we need to remember that our stack protocol expects the operations to be *O(1)*, so we must choose an end that allows both insertion and removal in *O(1)* time. That end is of course the front of the list as we saw in the last chapter. This makes the following code for the push operation self-explanatory:

```
@Override
public void push(E value) {
  list.appendFirst(value);
}
```

Note that this time, we did not check whether the stack is full because this implementation of the stack is never full, it grows as it needs and the underlying linked list takes care of that.

The pop operation, however, does need to check whether the stack is empty and return null at that point. The following code for the pop operation is also quite self-explanatory:

```
@Override
public E pop() {
  if(list.getLength()==0){
    return null;
  }
  E value = list.getFirst();
  list.removeFirst();
  return value;
}
```

The peek operation is, of course, the same, except it does not remove the top element:

```
@Override
public E peek() {
  if(list.getLength()==0){
    return null;
  }
  return list.getFirst();
}
```

This concludes our linked list-based implementation of a stack. In the next section, we will check out another ADT called a **queue**.

Queue

What is the opposite of a stack? This may be a weird question. However, a stack follows LIFO, last in first out. The opposite of that is **first-in-first-out** (**FIFO**). So, in some sense, a FIFO ADT can be considered as the opposite of a stack. This is not very different from a queue of people waiting for a bus or at a doctor's clinic. The first person to show up gets the first chance to get onto the bus or to get to see the doctor. The second person gets the second chance. No wonder, such an abstract data type is called a queue. Appending to the end of a queue is called **enqueuing** and removing from it is called **dequeuing**. The contract is, of course, that the first value that is enqueued would be the first to be dequeued. The following figure illustrates this operation:

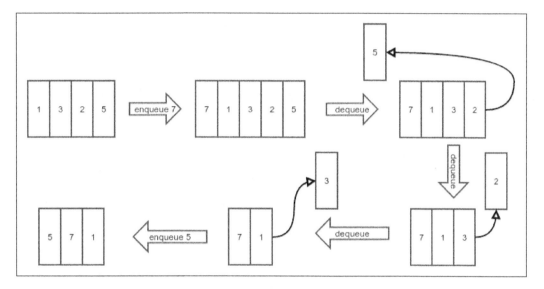

The queue ADT has the following operations:

- **Enqueue**: This adds an element at the back of the queue
- **Dequeue**: This removes an element from the front of the queue
- **Peek**: This checks the element that would be dequeued next

The queue will be represented by the following interface:

```
public interface Queue<E> {
  void enqueue(E value);
  E dequeue();
  E peek();
}
```

Fixed-sized queue using an array

Just like the stack, we have an array-based implementation of a queue. However, since a queue receives new values and removes old values from opposite sides, the body of the queue moves as it does. The following figure will illustrate this point:

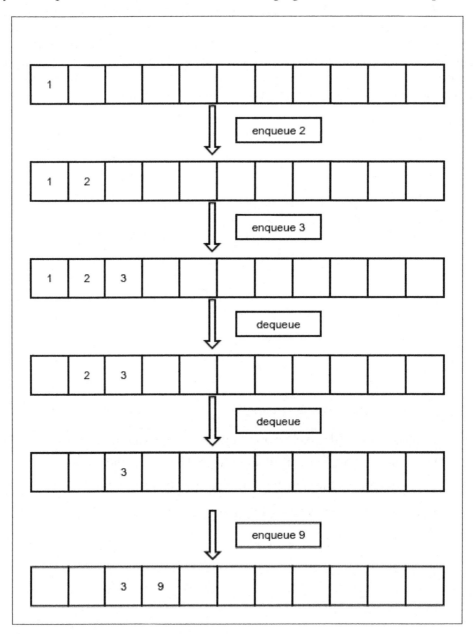

This means that after a sequence of a few such operations, the end of the queue will reach the end of the array, and there will be space left at the beginning of the array. At this point, we don't want to stop receiving new values as there is space left, so we roll over to the beginning of the array. That is to say, we continue adding the new values at the beginning of the array.

To do all these manipulations, we must have separate variables storing the indexes of the beginning and the end of the queue. Also, since due to roll over, sometimes the end is smaller than the beginning, we store the length separately to avoid confusion. We start with the bare bone implementation of the class just as before. The start represents the index of the element that would be dequeued next and the end represents the position of the next value that would be enqueued. This is illustrated in the following code:

```
public class QueueImplArray<E>  implements Queue<E>{
  protected E[] array;
  protected int start=0;
  protected int end=0;
  protected int length=0;
  public QueueImplArray(int size){
    array = (E[]) new Object[size];
  }
}
```

The enqueue operation does not change the start position. The new value is put at the end position of the array and the end is incremented by one. The end, of course, needs to be rolled over in case it goes beyond the maximum index of the array, as shown in the following code:

```
@Override
public void enqueue(E value) {
  if(length>=array.length){
    throw new NoSpaceException("No more space to add an element");
  }
  array[end] = value;
```

The modulo operator will make sure that the index goes to the beginning of the array when it hits the end of the array, as follows:

```
  end = (end+1) % array.length;
  length++;
}
```

The `dequeue` operation does not change the end position. We read from the start index and then increment the start index with rollover, as follows:

```
@Override
public E dequeue() {
  if(length<=0){
    return null;
  }
  E value = array[start];
  start = (start+1) % array.length;
  length--;
  return value;
}
```

The `peek` operation lets us see the element that would be dequeued next, without removing it. It is, of course, simpler. We just return the next element to be dequeued. This is shown in the following code:

```
@Override
public E peek() {
  if(length<=0){
    return null;
  }
  return array[start];
}
```

A queue backed up by an array can be resized in a similar manner as described for the case of a stack, and this too will be *O(n)*, since we must copy all the old elements to the newly allocated array one by one.

Variable-sized queue using a linked list

Just like a stack, we want to implement a queue using a linked list. We need to remember that all operations must be *O(1)* in running time. If we enqueue by appending new elements at the beginning of the linked list, we will need to remove elements from the end of the list during dequeuing. This will not work as removal of an element from the end of a linked list is *O(n)*. But appending at the end of a linked list is *O(1)* and so is removing from the beginning of the list. Hence, the end of the queue, where new elements are enqueued, would be the end of the list. And the start of the queue, where the elements are dequeued from, would be the beginning of the linked list.

Given this, the implementation of a queue using a linked list is straightforward. Again, we create an instance of the list only using a `getNewLinkedList()` method, which can be overridden by a subclass to use a different linked list, as follows:

```
public class QueueImplLinkedList<E> implements Queue<E>{
   protected LinkedList<E> list = getNewLinkedList();

   protected LinkedList<E> getNewLinkedList(){
      return new LinkedList<>();
   }
}
```

The `enqueue` operation simply appends at the end of the list as follows:

```
@Override
public void enqueue(E value) {
   list.appendLast(value);
}
```

The `dequeue` operation first checks if the list is empty so it can return `null`, and then it simply removes the first element from the list. It must also return the element that it just removed:

```
@Override
public E dequeue() {
   if(list.getLength()==0){
      return null;
   }
   E value = list.getFirst();
   list.removeFirst();
   return value;
}
```

Just like the `dequeue` operation, the `peek` operation first needs to check whether the list is empty, in which case it has to return a `null` value, otherwise it simply returns the element at the beginning of the list that would be dequeued on the next `dequeue` operation, as shown in the following code:

```
@Override
public E peek() {
   if(list.getLength()==0){
      return null;
   }
   return list.getFirst();
}
}
```

Double ended queue

A double ended queue is a combination of a stack and a queue. The idea is that you are allowed to insert and remove elements at both ends of the queue. If you remove elements from the side you have inserted, it will behave like a stack. On the other hand, if you insert and remove on opposite ends, it will behave like a queue. You can mix these operations and use them in any order you like. The following figure shows a few operations to clarify this idea:

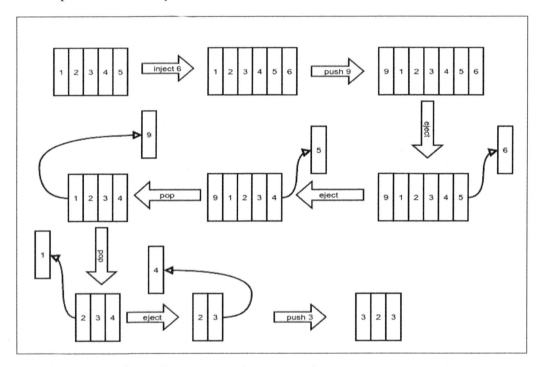

A double ended queue has the following operations all with a complexity of *O(n)*:

- **Push**: This inserts an element at the beginning
- **Pop**: This removes an element from the beginning
- **Inject**: This inserts an element at the end
- **Eject**: This removes an element from the end
- **Peek**: This checks the first element
- **PeekLast**: This checks the last element

A double ended queue will be represented by the following interface:

```
public interface DoubleEndedQueue<E> extends Stack<E> {
  void inject(E value);
  E eject();
  E peekLast();
}
```

Note that since a double ended queue has push and pop operations just like a stack and it preserves the same meaning, we create this interface extending the Stack interface.

Fixed-length double ended queue using an array

Since we have created the double ended queue as an extension of a stack, one would expect its implementation to extend a stack implementation as well. However, remember that a double ended queue is both a stack and a queue. The array-based implementation for a queue was more complex than that for a stack due to rollover of the indexes. We don't want to reprogram those, so we choose to extend a queue implementation instead of a stack implementation, as shown in the following code:

```
public class DoubleEndedQueueImplArray<E> extends
QueueImplArray<E> implements DoubleEndedQueue<E> {
```

We initialize the queue to the fixed length, as follows:

```
public DoubleEndedQueueImplArray(int size) {
  super(size);
}
```

This is appended at the end of the double ended queue, which is the same as the enqueue operation of a queue:

```
@Override
public void inject(E value) {
  enqueue(value);
}
```

The eject operation is the removal of an element from the end of the double ended queue. We don't have an equivalent operation in a simple queue. So, we must code for it as follows:

```
@Override
public E eject() {
  if (length <= 0) {
    return null;
  }
```

The end has to decrement by one with a provision for rollover. But if the end is already at zero, it will become negative, which will not work well with the modulo operator, because it will return a negative value. To always keep it positive, we add the length of the array to it. Note that it does not change the remainder when divided by the length of the array. This is shown in the following code:

```
end = (end + array.length - 1) % array.length;
E value = array[end];
length--;
return value;
}
```

The peekLast operation simply needs to return the element that would have been returned by the eject operation without modifying anything, as shown in the following code:

```
@Override
public E peekLast() {
  if (length <= 0) {
    return null;
  }
  return array[(end + array.length - 1) % array.length];
}
```

The push operation is the insertion of an element at the beginning of the double ended queue. There is no equivalent operation in a simple queue. Hence, we need to code for it as follows:

```
@Override
public void push(E value) {
  if (length >= array.length) {
    throw new NoSpaceException("No more space to add an
                               element");
  }
```

This operation is very similar to updating the end index eject operation, as shown in the following code:

```
start = (start + array.length - 1) % array.length;
array[start] = value;
length++;
}
```

The `pop` operation is the removal of the element at the beginning of the queue, which is the same as the `dequeue` operation of an ordinary queue. This is illustrated in the following code:

```
@Override
public E pop() {
  return dequeue();
}
}
```

Note that we don't write any code for the peek operation, which should return the element at the beginning of the double ended queue, as it is the same as the peek operation for a simple queue.

The array-based implementation is, of course, fixed in size and cannot hold more elements than it's fixed size. Next, we develop a linked list-based implementation.

Variable-sized double ended queue using a linked list

We had earlier used a simple linked list to implement both a queue and a stack. However, remember again that all operations must be *O(1)*. Now, we must both add and remove elements at both ends of the underlying linked list. We know that removal from the end of a singly linked list is *O(n)* and we cannot use it. So, we must use a doubly linked list instead.

This time we do not have to worry about rollovers and so we will extend the linked list implementation of a stack, which is the natural choice. We will replace its singly linked list with a doubly linked list by overriding the `getLinkedList()` method, as follows:

```
public class DoubleEndedQueueImplLinkedList<E> extends
StackImplLinkedList<E> implements DoubleEndedQueue<E> {

  @Override
  protected LinkedList<E> getNewLinkedList() {
    return new DoublyLinkedList<E>();
  }
}
```

The `inject` operation inserts a new element at the end of the list as shown in the following code:

```
@Override
public void inject(E value) {
  list.appendLast(value);
}
```

The `eject` operation must remove and return the last element of the list. This is illustrated in the following code:

```
@Override
public E eject() {
  if(list.getLength()==0){
    return null;
  }
  E value = list.getLast();
  list.removeLast();
  return value;
}
```

Finally, the `peekLast()` method will just return the last element of the doubly linked list as follows:

```
@Override
public E peekLast() {
  if(list.getLength()==0){
    return null;
  }
  return list.getLast();
}
}
```

We only had to implement the `inject()`, `eject()`, and `peekLast()` methods as the other methods are already implemented by the stack we extend.

Summary

In this chapter, we saw that an abstract data type or ADT is an abstraction of a data structure. It is a contract that an underlying data structure is supposed to adhere to. The contract involves different operations on the data structure and their specific behavior. We then saw a few simple ADTs as examples. These ADTs are, however, extremely useful as we will see in the course of this book when we encounter other algorithms. Abstraction allows different implementations of the structures. We will also see more ADTs in the course of this book and their implementations.

In the next chapter, we will take a detour into a new area of algorithms called **functional programming**. Remember that an algorithm is a sequence of steps that may be followed to achieve a desired processing; it turns out that there is another way of looking at it, which we will explore in the next chapter.

4
Detour – Functional Programming

In the beginning of this book, we saw that an algorithm is a sequence of steps to achieve a result. This way of solving a problem by following a sequence of instructions is called imperative programming. Each statement in the program can be thought of as an imperative sentence asking the computer to do something. However, this is not the only way of looking at it. Functional programming sees an algorithm as a composition of components rather than as a sequence of steps. A problem to solve is seen as a composition of smaller-sized problems. Instead of using a loop, we combine smaller versions of the same problem. Functional programming uses recursion as a basic component. A recursion is nothing but solving the same problem for a smaller size and then composing the result with something else to get the solution for the given size of the problem. This has a far-reaching implication in how easy it is to read and understand a program. This makes it very important to study.

There are really two worlds in the programming paradigm. The imperative style of programming is favored by C-like languages, such as C, C++, and Java. On the purely functional side, there are languages such as Lisp, Haskell, and Scheme. Apart from these, some languages try to have the best of both worlds, such as Python or Scala. This is easier said than done; trying to mix both ideas in a language means you have features to support both, but to use them effectively is truly an art.

So, if Java is imperative in nature, why are we talking about functional programming in this book? Well, as I pointed out, sometimes, it is better to mix both concepts and get the best of both worlds. Recently, the Java community has taken note of this fact and has introduced a feature lambda from Java version 8 to provide some level of functional programming support. So, our intention is not to program completely in functional style, as that is not the preferred programming style of Java, but we will do it just enough to make our programs more beautiful and to aid our understanding of algorithms.

This chapter will introduce this rather foreign concept to you and provide some basic tools that are commonly used in functional programming. You will learn the following concepts:

- Recursive algorithms and the immutability of variables
- Monads
- Aggregations on monads
- Java's support for functional programming, that is, lambda.

Recursive algorithms

As I have already pointed out, recursive algorithms are a different way of thinking about solving a problem. For example, say our problem is to write a program that, given a positive integer n, returns the sum of numbers from zero to n. The known imperative way of writing it is simple:

```
public int sum_upto(int n){
  int sum=0;
  for(int i=0;i<=n;i++){
    sum+=i;
  }
  return sum;
}
```

The following would be the functional version of the problem:

```
public int sum_upto_functional(int n){
  return n==0?0:n+sum_upto_functional(n-1);
}
```

That's it–just a one-liner! This is probably nothing new to Java programmers, as they do understand recursive functions. However, an imperative programmer would use recursion only when nothing else worked. But this is a different way of thinking. How do we justify that it is equivalent to solving the problem for a smaller input and then composing it with something else? Well, we are certainly first computing the same function for an input that is smaller by one and then just adding *n* to it. There is one more thing to note here: in the imperative version, we are updating the variable called sum for each value of the loop variable i. However, in the functional version, we are not updating any variable. What do we achieve by that? When a variable is updated multiple times in a program, it is hard to understand or debug it because you need to keep track of the latest value. When this does not happen, it is far easier to understand what is happening. In fact, it makes it simpler in such a way that we can even prove the correctness of the program completely formally, which is rather hard to do for imperative programs where variables change values.

Let's check out another example. This one is about choosing r objects from n objects, where the order does not matter. Let's have a set A of a finite amount of objects. Let the number of objects in this set be n. How many subsets B of this set A have exactly r elements? Of course, the maximum number of elements any subset of A can have is n; hence $r \leq n$. We will call this function `choose`. So, we write this as `choose(n,r)`. Now, the only subset that has an equal number of elements as A is A itself. So, `choose(n,n)` equals 1.

How do we break this problem into subproblems of a similar nature but with smaller input? To find out how many subsets B have r elements, we first think of the set A as a combination of a subset C with `n-1` elements and one particular element a. So, we can say $A = C \cup \{a\}$. Now, we consider two disjoint cases: the element a is a member of the subset B and when it is not a member of the subset B. When a is not a member of the subset B, B is also a subset of C. The number of such subsets B with exactly r elements is `choose(n-1,r)`, since C has `n-1` elements. On the other hand, when a is a member of the set B, then B can be thought of as a union of two sets – a set D that has all the elements of B except a, and the other is just $\{a\}$. So, $B = D \cup \{a\}$. Now, you can see that D is a subset of C that we defined. How many such subsets D are there of C? There are `choose(n-1,r-1)` subsets, since C has `n-1` elements and D has `r-1` elements. So, the number of such subsets B is `choose(n-1,r-1)`. This means that the total number of sets B with or without a as an element is `choose(n-1,r)` + `choose(n-1,r-1)`. If we put this in recursive calls, the r and n will get reduced until r equals zero or n equals r. We have already considered the case when n equals r, that is, `choose(n,n)`. When r equals zero, it means B is the null set. Since there is only one null set, `choose(n,0)` equals 1. Now, we put this in code:

```java
public long choose(long n, long r){
  if(n<r){
    return 0;
  }else if(r==0){
    return 1;
  }else if(n==r){
    return 1;
  }else{
    return choose(n-1,r) + choose(n-1,r-1);
  }
}
```

That was a little complex, but note that not only did we compute the value of the `choose` function, we also sort of proved that it will work. The `choose` function is the binomial coefficient function for integral exponents.

The aforementioned implementation is not efficient. To see why, just consider what each recursive call of the choose function will evaluate to when they both fall in the final else case: choose(n-1,r) = choose(n-2,r) + choose(n-2,r-1) and choose(n-1,r-1) = choose(n-2,r-1) + choose(n-2,r-2). Now note that choose(n-2,r-1) is being evaluated in both cases, which then would have its own recursive calls. This actually significantly increases the asymptotic complexity. We'll defer the analysis of this complexity to the end of this chapter.

Lambda expressions in Java

Before moving on, we need to learn about a feature in Java called **Lambda**. Many of you may already know about it. However, since the feature was only introduced in version 8, it is better to get familiar with it if you aren't already. It lets you pass a block of code, called a lambda expression, as an argument to another function. To talk about lambda, we must first see what a functional interface is.

Functional interface

A functional interface is an interface that has only one unimplemented method, that is to say, a class that implements it needs to implement exactly one method. The functional interface may have more than one method declared or inherited, but as long as we can implement it by implementing exactly one method, it is a functional interface. The following example shows one such interface:

```
@FunctionalInterface
public interface SampleFunctionalInterface {
  int modify(int x);
}
```

Note that we also marked it as a functional interface with an annotation, but it is not necessary. Marking it ensures that Java will show a compile-time error if the interface does not have exactly one method that needs to be implemented. The following example shows another valid functional interface:

```
public interface AnotherFunctionalInterface{
  public void doSomething(int x);
  public String toString();
}
```

There are two methods in it. However, since the toString() method is already implemented in the object class, you need to implement only one method.

Similarly, an interface with more than one method can be a functional interface if all but one has a default implementation. For example, look at the following interface.

```
@FunctionalInterface
public interface FunctionalInterfaceWithDefaultMethod {
    int modify(int x);
    default int modifyTwice(int x){return modify(modify(x));}
}
```

Even though this interface has two methods, only one needs to be implemented by any implementation. This makes it a functional interface.

Implementing a functional interface with lambda

So, what happens if we have a functional interface? We can provide an inline implementation of it using a cool syntax called lambda, as follows:

```
SampleFunctionalInterface sfi = (x)->x+1;
int y = sfi.modify(1);
```

Take note of the parentheses and the arrow sign. The parentheses contain all the parameters. The types of parameters are not specified because they are already specified in the interface method. There can be zero or more parameters.

There are two kinds of lambda syntax–one that has an expression as the body and one that has one or more steps as the body. These lambdas look a bit different from each other. A lambda that is implemented as a one liner looks like the one we just saw. This is called an **expression** syntax. The expression syntax can be used if the lambda expression is a one liner. For multi-line code, we use the block syntax as shown below:

```
Thread t = new Thread(()->{for(int i=0;i<500;i++)
System.out.println(i);});
```

One can use block syntax for functions that return a value as well, especially when using multiple lines of code. In that case, one just needs to use a return statement to return a value.

Since in a functional program all variables must not ever be reassigned, we should declare them final to avoid accidentally modifying them. However, since typing `final` for every variable clutters the code a bit, we avoid doing so. In a purely functional language, the variables are immutable by default. Even in a semifunctional language, such as Scala, it is so if it generally encourages the functional style. However, since Java mostly prefers an imperative style, the `final` keyword is necessary, causing a little clutter.

Now that we know about lambda, we can start learning about functional data structures.

Functional data structures and monads

Functional data structures are data structures that follow the principle of immutability and inductive (or recursive) definition. Immutability means that any modification of the data structure would result in a new data structure, and any old reference to the original version would still have access to the original version. Inductive definition means that the definition of the structure is defined as a composition of smaller versions of the same data structure. Take, for example, our linked list. When we add an element to or remove an element from the beginning of the list, it will modify the linked list. That means any reference to the linked list will now hold a reference to the modified linked list. This doesn't conform to the principle of immutability. A functional linked list would make sure that the older references still held reference to an unmodified version. We will discuss how to do it in the next section.

Functional linked lists

To make a linked list that is immutable, we consider a linked list to be made of two parts:

- A head containing the first element of the list
- A tail containing another linked list containing the rest of the elements

Note that we have now defined the linked list recursively, being true to our functional design. This recursion says that a linked list is:

- Either an empty list
- Or a set of two objects, as follows:
    ◦ A head containing one element of its element type
    ◦ A tail containing another linked list of the same type

This version of the definition is the same as the previous simplified one, except that we have now specified how we represent where the list terminates. The list terminates where there are no more elements, that is, when the tail is an empty list. Let's put all these in code.

First, we define a version according to the simplified definition:

```
public class LinkedList<E> {
  private E head;
  private LinkedList<E> tail;

  private LinkedList(){

}

  private LinkedList(E head, LinkedList<E> tail){
    this.head = head;
    this.tail = tail;
  }


  public E head(){
    return head;
  }
  public LinkedList<E> tail(){
    return tail;
  }
```

This is the core of immutability for our linked list. Note that every time we add a new value to our linked list, we create a new linked list so that the old references still hold references to the unmodified list:

```
  public LinkedList<E> add(E value){
    return new LinkedList<E>(value,this);
  }
}
```

The code is self-explanatory, now that we already know how we think about our linked list. But note that we have made the constructors private. We don't want people to create inconsistent versions of our linked lists, such as a null `tail` or something. We insist that everyone creates our linked list by first creating an empty linked list and then adding elements to it. So, we add the following `EmptyList` class and `add()` method:

```
public static final class EmptyList<E> extends LinkedList<E>{
  @Override
  public E head() {
```

```
            throw new NoValueException("head() invoked on empty list");
    }

    @Override
    public LinkedList<E> tail() {
        throw new NoValueException("tail() invoked on empty list");
    }
}

public static <E> LinkedList<E> emptyList(){
    return new EmptyList<>();
}
```

Now we can use the linked list as follows:

```
LinkedList<Integer> linkedList = LinkedList.<Integer>emptyList()
.add(5).add(3).add(0);
while(!(linkedList instanceof LinkedList.EmptyList)){
    System.out.println(linkedList.head());
    linkedList = linkedList.tail();
}
```

But wait, did we just modify the linkedList variable in the while loop? Yes, but that does not comply with the principle of immutability. To solve this, let's see what we would mostly want to do with a list. In general, we would want to perform the following operations:

- Do something for each element of the list. For example, print all the elements to the console.

- Get a new list where each element is transformed using a function that is provided.

- Compute a function of all the elements in the list. This is an aggregation of the elements. For example, find the sum of all the elements.

- Create a new list containing only selected elements of the list. This is called **filtering**.

We will deal with them one by one. At the end of the next section, you will be prepared to learn about monads as well.

The forEach method for a linked list

The `forEach()` method on a linked list would do something for each element of the list. This something would be passed as a lambda. For this purpose, we will first create a functional interface that consumes one parameter but does not return anything:

```
@FunctionalInterface
public interface OneArgumentStatement<E> {
  void doSomething(E argument);
}
```

With this interface available, we will define the `forEach()` method for a list, as follows:

```
public class LinkedList<E> {
...

  public static class EmptyList<E> extends LinkedList<E>{
    ...

    @Override
    public void forEach(OneArgumentStatement<E> processor) {}
  }

  ...

  public void forEach(OneArgumentStatement<E> processor){
    processor.doSomething(head());
    tail().forEach(processor);
  }
}
```

The ellipsis represent more code that we have already discussed and need not be repeated. The `forEach()` method simply processes the head and then recursively calls itself on the tail. Note again that, true to our philosophy of recursion, we have implemented the `forEach()` method using recursion. Of course, this will not work on an empty list because the head and tail are null. The empty list represents when the method needs to stop calling itself. We achieve this by overriding the `forEach()` method in the `EmptyList` class to not do anything.

Now we can print all the elements using the following code:

```
linkedList.forEach((x) -> {System.out.println(x);});
```

We pass a lambda that, given any element x, calls `System.out.println` on x. But, if you see, this lambda just works as a delegation to the `System.out.println` method that already has the required form of the lambda. Java allows you to use a method as a lambda with the following syntax. The `::` operator is used to tell the compiler that you are not looking for a field with that name; instead you are looking for a method with that name:

```
linkedList.forEach(System.out::println);
```

Note that this time we did not even modify the list while printing the elements, unlike last time, when we did it using a loop.

Map for a linked list

Now we move on to the next thing we want to do with a list, which is to create a new list where all the elements are transformed according to a lambda that is provided. What I mean is that we want to do the following:

```
LinkedList<Integer> tranformedList = linkedList.map((x)->x*2);
```

We need to implement the `map()` method in a way that `transformedList` holds all the elements of `linkedList` multiplied by 2, in the same order. The following is the implementation of the `map()` method:

```
public class LinkedList<E> {
...
    public static class EmptyList<E> extends LinkedList<E>{
        ...

        @Override
        public <R> LinkedList<R> map(OneArgumentExpression<E,
        R> transformer) {

        return LinkedList.emptyList();
        }
    }
...

    public <R> LinkedList<R> map(OneArgumentExpression<E,R> transformer){
        return new LinkedList<>(transformer.compute(head()),
        tail.map(transformer));
    }
}
```

As usual, the method is defined recursively. The transformed list is just the head transformed followed by the tail transformed. We have also overridden the method in the EmptyList class to return an empty list because an empty list transformed is just another empty list of a possibly different type. With this implementation in place, we can do the following:

```
LinkedList<Integer> tranformedList = linkedList.map((x)->x*2);
tranformedList.forEach(System.out::println);
```

This should print a list with all the values multiplied by 2. You can even change the type of the elements by transformation, such as the following:

```
LinkedList<String> tranformedListString
  = linkedList.map((x)->"x*2
  = "+(x*2));
tranformedListString.forEach(System.out::println);
```

The tranformedListString list is a list of strings, and printing each element on the next line shows the strings obtained.

Now we move on to the next thing we want to do with a list, which is to compute some function that uses all the values in the list. This is called an **aggregation** operation. But before looking at a general case, we will concentrate on a specific one, called a **fold** operation.

Fold operation on a list

A fold operation on a list is an aggregation operation that can be done element by element. For example, if we want to compute the sum of all the elements of a list, we can do it by taking each element of the list and adding it to a moving sum, so when we are done with processing all the elements, we will have the sum of all elements.

There are two operations that suit this purpose: foldLeft and foldRight. The foldLeft operation aggregates the head first and moves on to the tail. The foldRight method aggregates the tail first and then moves on to the head. Let's start with foldLeft. But before doing anything, we need a functional interface that represents an expression of two parameters:

```
@FunctionalInterface
public interface TwoArgumentExpression<A,B,R> {
  R compute(A lhs, B rhs);
}
```

With this interface available, we define the `foldLeft` method in the following way:

```
public class LinkedList<E> {

  ...

  ...


  public static class EmptyList<E> extends LinkedList<E>{


    ...


    @Override
    public <R> R foldLeft(R initialValue, TwoArgumentExpression<R,
    E, R> computer) {
      return initialValue;
    }
  }


  ...

  public <R> R foldLeft(R initialValue,
  TwoArgumentExpression<R,E,R> computer){
    R newInitialValue = computer.compute(initialValue, head());
    return tail().foldLeft(newInitialValue, computer);
  }
}
```

We compute a new value from `initialValue` and the head using the lambda passed, and then we use this updated value to compute `foldLeft` on the tail. The empty list overrides this method to just return the `initialValue` itself because it just marks the end of the list. Now we can compute the sum of all elements as follows:

```
int sum = linkedList.foldLeft(0, (a,b)->a+b);
System.out.println(sum);
```

We have passed 0 as the initial value and the lambda that sums up the values passed. This looks complicated until you get used to this idea, but once you get used to it, it is very simple. Let's see what is happening step by step; the list from head to `tail` is {0,3,5}:

1. In the first invocation, we pass the initial value 0. The computed `newInitialValue` is 0+0 = 0. Now, we pass this `newInitialValue` to the tail to `foldLeft`, which is {3,5}.

2. The {3,5} has a head 3 and `tail` {5}. 3 is added to the `initialValue` 0 to give a `newInitialValue` 0+3=3. Now, this new value 3 is passed to the tail {5} to `foldLeft`.

3. The {5} has a head 5 and tail and empty list. 5 is added to the initialValue 3 to get 8. Now this 8 is passed as initialValue to the tail, which is an empty list.

4. The empty list, of course, just returns the initial value for a foldLeft operation. So it returns 8, and we get the sum.

Instead of computing one value, we can even compute a list as a result. The following code reverses a list:

```
LinkedList<Integer> reversedList =
linkedList.foldLeft(LinkedList.emptyList(),(l,b)->l.add(b) );
reversedList.forEach(System.out::println);
```

We have simply passed an empty list as an initial operation, and then our operation simply adds a new element to the list. In the case of foldLeft, the head will be added before the tail, causing it to be placed more in the tail side in the newly constructed list.

What if we want to process the right-most end (or away from the head) first and move to the left? This operation is called foldRight. This can be implemented in a very similar manner, as follows:

```
public class LinkedList<E> {
   ...

   public static class EmptyList<E> extends LinkedList<E>{
      ...

      @Override
      public <R> R foldRight(TwoArgumentExpression<E, R,
      R> computer, R initialValue) {
        return initialValue;
      }
   }

   ...

   public <R> R foldRight(TwoArgumentExpression<E,R,R> computer,
   R initialValue){
      R computedValue = tail().foldRight(computer, initialValue);
      return computer.compute(head(), computedValue);
   }
}
```

We have switched the order of the arguments to make it intuitive that the initialValue is being combined from the right end of the list. The difference from foldLeft is that we compute the value on the tail first, calling a foldRight on it. Then we return the result of the computed value from the tail being combined with the head to get the result. In the case of computing a sum, it does not make any difference which fold you invoke because sum is commutative, that is, a+b always equals b+a. We can call the foldRight operation for the computation of sum in the following way, which will give the same sum:

```
int sum2 = linkedList.foldRight((a,b)->a+b, 0);
System.out.println(sum2);
```

However, if we use an operator that is not commutative, we will get a different result. For example, if we try reversing the list with the foldRight method, it will give the same list instead of being reversed:

```
LinkedList<Integer> sameList = linkedList.foldRight((b,l)-
>l.add(b), LinkedList.emptyList());
sameList.forEach(System.out::println);
```

The final thing we wanted to do with a list was filtering. You will learn it in the next subsection.

Filter operation for a linked list

Filter is an operation that takes a lambda as a condition and creates a new list that has only those elements that satisfy the condition. To demonstrate this, we will create a utility method that creates a list of a range of elements.

First, we create a helper method that appends a range of numbers to the head of an existing list. This method can call itself recursively:

```
private static LinkedList<Integer> ofRange(int start, int end,
LinkedList<Integer> tailList){
  if(start>=end){
    return tailList;
  }else{
    return ofRange(start+1, end, tailList).add(start);
  }
}
```

Then we use the helper method to generate a list of a range of numbers:

```
public static LinkedList<Integer> ofRange(int start, int end){
   return ofRange(start,end, LinkedList.emptyList());
}
```

This will let us create a list of a range of integers. The range includes the start and excludes the end. For example, the following code will create a list of numbers from 1 to 99 and then print the list:

```
LinkedList<Integer> rangeList = LinkedList.ofRange(1,100);
rangeList.forEach(System.out::println);
```

We now want to create a list of all even numbers, say. For that, we create a `filter` method in the `LinkedList` class:

```
public class LinkedList<E> {

  ...

    public static class EmptyList<E> extends LinkedList<E>{

      ...

      @Override
      public LinkedList<E> filter(OneArgumentExpression<E,
      Boolean> selector) {
        return this;
      }
    }

  ...

    public LinkedList<E> filter(OneArgumentExpression<E,
    Boolean> selector){
      if(selector.compute(head())){
        return new LinkedList<E>(head(), tail().filter(selector));
      }else{
        return tail().filter(selector);
      }
    }
}
```

The `filter()` method checks whether the the condition is met. If yes, then it includes the `head` and calls the `filter()` method on the `tail`. If not, then it just calls the `filter()` method on the `tail`. The `EmptyList` of course needs to override this method to just return itself because all we need is an empty list. Now, we can do the following:

```
LinkedList<Integer> evenList =
LinkedList.ofRange(1,100).filter((a)->a%2==0);
evenList.forEach(System.out::println);
```

This will print all the even numbers between 1 and 99. Let's go through some more examples in order to get used to all this stuff. How do we add all numbers from 1 to 100? The following code will do that:

```
int sumOfRange = LinkedList.ofRange(1,101).foldLeft(0, (a,b)-
>a+b);
System.out.println(sumOfRange);
```

Note that we have used the range of `(1,101)` because the end number is not included in the generated linked list.

How do we compute the factorial of a number using this? We define a `factorial` method as follows:

```
public static BigInteger factorial(int x){
   return LinkedList.ofRange(1,x+1)
   .map((a)->BigInteger.valueOf(a))
   .foldLeft(BigInteger.valueOf(1),(a,b)->a.multiply(b));
}
```

We have used Java's `BigInteger` class because factorials grow too fast and an `int` or a `long` cannot hold much. This code demonstrates how we converted the list of integers to a list of `BigIntegers` using the `map` method before multiplying them with the `foldLeft` method. We can now compute the `factorial` of `100` with the following code:

```
System.out.println(factorial(100));
```

This example also demonstrates the idea that we can combine the methods we developed to solve more complicated problems. Once you get used to this, reading a functional program and understanding what it does is a lot simpler than doing the same for their imperative versions. We have even used one-character variable names. Actually, we could use meaningful names, and in some cases, we should. But here the program is so simple and the variables used are so close to where they are defined that it's not even necessary to name them descriptively.

Let's say we want to repeat a string. Given an integer, n, and a string, we want the resultant string to be a repetition of the original string n number of times. For example, given an integer 5 and a string Hello, we want the output to be HelloHello HelloHello Hello. We can do this with the following function:

```
public static String repeatString(final String seed, int count){
    return LinkedList.ofRange(1,count+1)
    .map((a)->seed)
    .foldLeft("",(a,b)->a+b);
}
```

What we are doing here is first creating a list of length count and then replacing all its elements with the seed. This gives us a new list with all the elements equal to the seed. This can be folded to get the desired repeated string. This is easy to understand because it is very much like the sum method, except we are adding strings instead of integers, which causes repetition of the string. But we don't even need to do this. We can do this even without creating a new list with all the elements replaced. The following will do it:

```
public static String repeatString2(final String seed, int count){
    return LinkedList.ofRange(1,count+1)
    .foldLeft("",(a,b)->a+seed);
}
```

Here, we just ignore the integer in the list and add the seed instead. In the first iteration, a would be set to the initial value, which is an empty string. Every time, we just ignore the content and instead add the seed to this string. Note that in this case, variable a is of the String type and variable b is of the Integer type.

So, we can do a lot of things using a linked list, using its special methods with lambda parameters. This is the power of functional programming. What we are doing with lambda, though, is that we are passing the implementation of interfaces as pluggable code. This is not a new concept in an object-oriented language. However, without the lambda syntax, it would take a lot of code to define an anonymous class to do the equivalent, which would clutter the code a lot, thus undermining the simplicity. What has changed though is the immutability, leading to chaining of methods and other concepts. We are not thinking about state while analyzing the programs; we are simply thinking of it as a chain of transformations. The variables are more like variables in algebra, where the value of x stays the same throughout a formula.

Append on a linked list

We have completed all the things that were in the list of the things we wanted to do. There may be a few more. One important thing, for example, is append. This operation sticks one list to another. This can be done using the foldRight method that we have already defined:

```
public LinkedList<E> append(LinkedList<E> rhs){
  return this.foldRight((x,l)->l.add(x),rhs);
}
```

Now, we perform the following:

```
LinkedList<Integer> linkedList =

LinkedList.<Integer>emptyList().add(5).add(3).add(0);
LinkedList<Integer> linkedList2 =

LinkedList.<Integer>emptyList().add(6).add(8).add(9);
linkedList.append(linkedList2).forEach(System.out::print);
```

This will output 035986, which is the first list stuck in front of the second list.

To understand how it works, first remember what a foldRight operation does. It starts with an initial value–in this case, the **right hand side** (**RHS**). Then it takes one element at a time from the tail end of the list and operates on that with the initial list using the provided operation. In our case, the operation simply adds an element to the head of the initial list. So, in the end, we get the entire list appended to the beginning of the RHS.

There is one more thing that we want to do with a list, but we have not talked about it until now. This concept requires an understanding of the earlier concepts. This is called a flatMap operation, and we will explore it in the next subsection.

The flatMap method on a linked list

The flatMap operation is just like the map operation, except we expect the operation passed to return a list itself instead of a value. The job of the flatMap operation is to flatten the lists thus obtained and append them one after another. Take for example the following code:

```
LinkedList<Integer> funnyList
=LinkedList.ofRange(1,10)
.flatMap((x)->LinkedList.ofRange(0,x));
```

The operation passed returns a range of numbers starting from 0 to x-1. Since we started the flatMap on a list of numbers from 1 to 9, x will get values from 1 to 9. Our operation will then return a list containing 0,x-1 for each value of x. The job of the flatMap operation is to then flatten all these lists and stick them one after another. Take a look at the following line of code, where we print funnyList:

```
funnyList.forEach(System.out::print);
```

It will print 001012012301234012345012345601234567012345678 on the output.

So, how do we implement the flatMap operation? Let's have a look:

```
public class LinkedList<E> {

  public static class EmptyList<E> extends LinkedList<E>{

    ...

    @Override
    public <R> LinkedList<R> flatMap(OneArgumentExpression<E,
    LinkedList<R>> transformer) {
      return LinkedList.emptyList();
    }
  }

  ...

  public <R> LinkedList<R> flatMap(OneArgumentExpression<E,
  LinkedList<R>> transformer){
    return transformer.compute(head())
    append(tail().flatMap(transformer));
  }
}
```

So what is happening here? First, we compute the list obtained by the head and the result of the flatMap operation on the tail. Then we append the result of the operation on the head of the list in front of the list obtained by flatMap on the tail. In case of an empty list, the flatMap operation just returns an empty list because there is nothing for the transformation to be called on.

The concept of a monad

In the previous section, we saw quite a few operations for a linked list. A few of them, namely map and flatMap, are a common theme in many objects in functional programming. They have a meaning outside of the list. The map and flatMap methods, and a method to construct a monad from a value are what make such a wrapper object a monad. A monad is a common design pattern that is followed in functional programming. It is a sort of container, something that stores objects of some other class. It can contain one object directly as we will see; it can contain multiple objects as we have seen in the case of a linked list, it can contain objects that are only going to be available in the future after calling some function, and so on. There is a formal definition of monad, and different languages name its methods differently. We will only consider the way Java defines the methods. A monad must have two methods, called map() and flatMap(). The map() method accepts a lambda that works as a transformation for all the contents of the monad. The flatMap method also takes a method, but instead of returning the transformed value, it returns another monad. The flatMap() method then extracts the output from the monad and creates a transformed monad. We have already seen an example of a monad in the form of a linked list. But the general theme does not become clear until you have seen a few examples instead of just one. In the next section, we will see another kind of monad: an option monad.

Option monad

An option monad is a monad containing a single value. The whole point of this is to avoid handling null pointers in our code, which sort of masks the actual logic. The point of an option monad is to be able to hold a null value in a way that null checks are not required in every step. In some way, an option monad can be thought of as a list of zero or one objects. If it contains just zero objects, then it represents a null value. If it contains one object, then it works as the wrapper of that object. The map and flatMap methods then behave exactly like they would behave in the case of a one-argument list. The class that represents an empty option is called None. First, we create an abstract class for an option monad. Then, we create two inner classes called Some and None to represent an Option containing a value and one without a value, respectively. This is a more general pattern for developing a monad and can cater to the fact that the non-empty Option has to store a value. We could do this with a list as well. Let's first see our abstract class:

```
public abstract class Option<E> {
  public abstract E get();
  public abstract <R> Option<R> map(OneArgumentExpression<E,R>
  transformer);
  public abstract <R> Option<R> flatMap(OneArgumentExpression<E,
  Option<R>> transformer);
```

```
public abstract void forEach(OneArgumentStatement<E> statement);

    ...

}
```

A static method `optionOf` returns the appropriate instance of the `Option` class:

```
public static <X> Option<X>  optionOf(X value){
  if(value == null){
    return new None<>();
  }else{
    return new Some<>(value);
  }
}
```

We now define the inner class, called `None`:

```
public static class None<E> extends Option<E>{

  @Override
  public <R> Option<R> flatMap(OneArgumentExpression<E,
  Option<R>> transformer) {
    return new None<>();
  }

  @Override
  public E get() {
    throw new NoValueException("get() invoked on None");
  }

  @Override
  public <R> Option<R> map(OneArgumentExpression<E, R> transformer) {
    return new None<>();
  }

  @Override
  public void forEach(OneArgumentStatement<E> statement) {
  }
}
```

We create another class, `Some`, to represent a non-empty list. We store the value as a single object in the class `Some`, and there is no recursive tail:

```
public static class Some<E> extends Option<E>{
  E value;
  public Some(E value){
```

```
      this.value = value;
   }
   public E get(){
      return value;
   }
   ...
}
```

The `map` and `flatMap` methods are pretty intuitive. The `map` method accepts a transformer and returns a new `Option` where the value is transformed. The `flatMap` method does the same, except it expects the transformer to wrap the returned value inside another `Option`. This is useful when the transformer can sometimes return a null value, in which case the `map` method will return an inconsistent `Option`. Instead, the transformer should wrap it in an `Option`, for which we need to use a `flatMap` operation. Have a look at the following code:

```
public static class Some<E> extends Option<E>{

   ...

   public <R> Option<R> map(OneArgumentExpression<E,R> transformer){
      return Option.optionOf(transformer.compute(value));
   }
   public <R> Option<R> flatMap(OneArgumentExpression<E,
   Option<R>> transformer){
      return transformer.compute(value);
   }
   public void forEach(OneArgumentStatement<E> statement){
      statement.doSomething(value);
   }
}
```

To understand the usage of an `Option` monad, we will first create a **JavaBean**. A JavaBean is an object exclusively intended to store data. It is the equivalent of a structure in C. However, since encapsulation is a defining principle of Java, the members of the JavaBean are not accessed directly. They are instead accessed through special methods called getters and setters. However, our functional style dictates that the beans be immutable, so there won't be any setter methods. The following set of classes gives a few examples of JavaBeans:

```
public class Country {
   private String name;
   private String countryCode;

   public Country(String countryCode, String name) {
      this.countryCode = countryCode;
```

```
      this.name = name;
    }

    public String getCountryCode() {
      return countryCode;
    }

    public String getName() {
      return name;
    }
}
public class City {
    private String name;
    private Country country;

    public City(Country country, String name) {
      this.country = country;
      this.name = name;
    }

    public Country getCountry() {
      return country;
    }

    public String getName() {
      return name;
    }

}
public class Address {
    private String street;
    private City city;

    public Address(City city, String street) {
      this.city = city;
      this.street = street;
    }

    public City getCity() {
      return city;
    }

    public String getStreet() {
      return street;
```

```
    }
  }
  public class Person {
    private String name;
    private Address address;

    public Person(Address address, String name) {
      this.address = address;
      this.name = name;
    }

    public Address getAddress() {
      return address;
    }

    public String getName() {
      return name;
    }
  }
```

There is not much to understand in these four classes. They are there to store a person's data. In Java, it is not very uncommon to hit a case where you will hit a very similar kind of object.

Now, let's say, given a variable person of type Person, we want to print the name of the country he/she lives in. If the case is that any of the state variables can be null, the correct way to do it with all null checks would look like the following:

```
if(person!=null
  && person.getAddress()!=null
  &&
person.getAddress().getCity()!=null
  &&
person.getAddress().getCity().getCountry()!=null){
    System.out.println(person.getAddress().getCity().getCountry());
}
```

This code would work, but let's face it–it's a whole bunch of null checks. We can get a hold of the address simply by using our Options class, as follows:

```
String countryName = Option.optionOf(person)
.map(Person::getAddress)
.map(Address::getCity)
.map(City::getCountry)
.map(Country::getName).get();
```

Note that if we just print this address, there is a chance that we will print null. But it would not result in a null-pointer exception. If we don't want to print null, we need a `forEach` method just like the one in our linked list:

```
public class Option<E> {
  public static class None<E> extends Option<E>{

    ...

    @Override
    public void forEach(OneArgumentStatement<E> statement) {
    }
  }

  ...

  public void forEach(OneArgumentStatement<E> statement){
    statement.doSomething(value);
  }
}
```

The `forEach` method just calls the lambda passed on the value it contains, and the `None` class overrides it to do nothing. Now, we can do the following:

```
Option.optionOf(person)
.map(Person::getAddress)
.map(Address::getCity)
.map(City::getCountry)
.map(Country::getName)
.forEach(System.out::println);
```

This code will now not print anything in case of a null name in `country`.

Now, what happens if the `Person` class itself is functionally aware and returns `Options` to avoid returning null values? This is where we need a `flatMap`. Let's make a new version of all the classes that were a part of the `Person` class. For brevity, I will only show the modifications in the `Person` class and show how it works. You can then check the modifications on the other classes. Here's the code:

```
public class Person {
  private String name;
  private Address address;

  public Person(Address address, String name) {
    this.address = address;
    this.name = name;
```

```
  }

  public Option<Address> getAddress() {
    return Option.optionOf(address);
  }

  public Option<String> getName() {
    return Option.optionOf(name);
  }
}
```

Now, the code will be modified to use `flatMap` instead of `map`:

```
Option.optionOf(person)
.flatMap(Person::getAddress)
.flatMap(Address::getCity)
.flatMap(City::getCountry)
.flatMap(Country::getName)
.forEach(System.out::println);
```

The code now fully uses the `Option` monad.

Try monad

Another monad we can discuss is the `Try` monad. The point of this monad is to make exception handing a lot more compact and avoid hiding the details of the actual program logic. The semantics of the `map` and `flatMap` methods are self-evident. Again, we create two subclasses, one for success and one for failure. The `Success` class holds the value that was computed, and the `Failure` class holds the exception that was thrown. As usual, `Try` is an abstract class here, containing one static method to return the appropriate subclass:

```
public abstract class Try<E> {
  public abstract <R> Try<R> map(
OneArgumentExpressionWithException<E, R> expression);

  public abstract <R> Try<R> flatMap(
OneArgumentExpression<E, Try<R>> expression);

  public abstract E get();

  public abstract void forEach(
OneArgumentStatement<E> statement);

  public abstract Try<E> processException(
```

```
OneArgumentStatement<Exception> statement);

  ...

  public static <E> Try<E> of(
NoArgumentExpressionWithException<E> expression) {
    try {
      return new Success<>(expression.evaluate());
    } catch (Exception ex) {
      return new Failure<>(ex);
    }
  }
  ...
}
```

We need a new `NoArgumentExpressionWithException` class and a
`OneArgumentExpressionWithException` class that allows exceptions in its body.
They are as follows:

```
@FunctionalInterface
public interface NoArgumentExpressionWithException<R> {
  R evaluate() throws Exception;
}


@FunctionalInterface
public interface OneArgumentExpressionWithException<A,R> {
  R compute(A a) throws Exception;
}
```

The `Success` class stores the value of the expression passed to the `of()` method.
Note that the `of()` method already executes the expression to extract the value.

```
protected static class Success<E> extends Try<E> {
  protected E value;

  public Success(E value) {
    this.value = value;
  }
```

The fact is that this is a class that represents the success of the earlier expression;
the `flatMap` has to only handle exceptions in the following expression, which the
following `Try` passed to it handles itself, so we can just return that `Try` instance itself:

```
@Override
public <R> Try<R> flatMap(
  OneArgumentExpression<E, Try<R>> expression) {
    return expression.compute(value);
}
```

The map() method, however, has to execute the expression passed. If there is an exception, it returns a Failure; otherwise it returns a Success:

```
@Override
public <R> Try<R> map(
  OneArgumentExpressionWithException<E, R> expression) {
  try {
    return new Success<>(
      expression.compute(value));
  } catch (Exception ex) {
    return new Failure<>(ex);
  }
}
```

The get() method returns the value as expected:

```
@Override
public E get() {
  return value;
}
```

The forEach() method lets you run another piece of code on the value without returning anything:

```
@Override
public void forEach(
  OneArgumentStatement<E> statement) {
    statement.doSomething(value);
}
```

This method does not do anything. The same method on the Failure class runs some code on the exception:

```
@Override
public Try<E> processException(
  OneArgumentStatement<Exception> statement) {
    return this;
  }
}
```

Now, let's look at the Failure class:

```
protected static class Failure<E> extends Try<E> {
  protected Exception exception;

  public Failure(Exception exception) {
    this.exception = exception;
  }
```

Here, in both the `flatMap()` and `map()` methods, we just change the type of `Failure`, but return one with the same exception:

```
@Override
public <R> Try<R> flatMap(
    OneArgumentExpression<E, Try<R>> expression) {
        return new Failure<>(exception);
}


@Override
public <R> Try<R> map(
    OneArgumentExpressionWithException<E, R> expression) {
        return new Failure<>(exception);
}
```

There is no value to be returned in the case of a `Failure`:

```
@Override
public E get() {
    throw new NoValueException("get method invoked on Failure");
}
```

We don't do anything in the `forEach()` method because there is no value to be worked on, as follows:

```
@Override
public void forEach(
    OneArgumentStatement<E> statement) {
        ...
}
```

The following method runs some code on the exception contained in the `Failure` instance:

```
@Override
public Try<E> processException(
    OneArgumentStatement<Exception> statement) {
        statement.doSomething(exception);
        return this;
}
}
```

With this implementation of the `Try` monad, we can now go ahead and write some code that involves handing exceptions. The following code will print the first line of the file demo if it exists. Otherwise, it will print the exception. It will print any other exception as well:

```
Try.of(() -> new FileInputStream("demo"))
.map((in)->new InputStreamReader(in))
.map((in)->new BufferedReader(in))
.map((in)->in.readLine())
.processException(System.err::println)
.forEach(System.out::println);
```

Note how it removes the clutter in handling exceptions. You should, at this stage, be able to see what is going on. Each `map()` method, as usual, transforms a value obtained earlier, only, in this case, the code in the `map()` method may throw an exception and that would be gracefully contained. The first two `map()` methods create a `BufferedReader` in from a `FileInputStream`, while the final `map()` method reads a line from the `Reader`.

With this example, I am concluding the monad section. The monadic design pattern is ubiquitous in functional programming and it's important to understand this concept. We will see a few more monads and some related ideas in the next chapter.

Analysis of the complexity of a recursive algorithm

Throughout the chapter, I have conveniently skipped over the complexity analysis of the algorithms I have discussed. This was to ensure that you grasp the concepts of functional programming before being distracted by something else. Now is the time to get back to it.

Analyzing the complexity of a recursive algorithm involves first creating an equation. This is naturally the case because the function is defined in terms of itself for a smaller input, and the complexity is also expressed as a function of itself being calculated for a smaller input.

For example, let's say we are trying to find the complexity of the `foldLeft` operation. The `foldLeft` operation is actually two operations, the first one being a fixed operation on the current initial value and the head of the list, and then a `foldLeft` operation on the tail. Suppose $T(n)$ represents the time taken to run a `foldLeft` operation on a list of length n. Now, let's assume that the fixed operation takes a time A. Then, the definition of the `foldLeft` operation suggests that $T(n) = A + T(n-1)$. Now, we would try to find a function that solves this equation. In this case, it is very simple:

$T(n) = A + T(n-1)$

$=> T(n) - T(n-1) = A$

This means *T(n)* is an arithmetic progression and thus can be represented as $T(n) = An + C$, where *C* is the initial starting point, or *T(0)*.

This means $T(n) = O(n)$. We have already seen how the `foldLeft` operation works in linear time. Of course, we have assumed that the the operation involved is constant with time. A more complex operation will result in a different complexity.

You are advised to try to compute the complexity of the other algorithms, which are not very different from this one. However, I will provide a few more of these.

Earlier in this chapter, we implemented the `choose` function as follows:

```
choose(n,r) = choose(n-1,r) + choose(n-1, r-1)
```

If we assume that the time taken is given by the function `T(n,r)`, then `T(n,r)` = `T(n-1,r) + T(n-1,r-1) + C`, where `C` is a constant. Now we can do the following:

```
T(n,r) = T(n-1,r) + T(n-1,r-1) + C

=>T(n,r) -  T(n-1,r) = T(n-1,r-
1) + C
```

Similarly, `T(n-1,r) - T(n-2,r) = T(n-2,r-1) + C`, by simply having `n-1` in place of *n*. By stacking such values, we have the following:

```
T(n,r)   -   T(n-1,r) = T(n-1,r-1) + C
T(n-1,r) -   T(n-2,r) = T(n-2,r-1) + C
T(n-2,r) -   T(n-3,r) = T(n-3,r-1) + C
...
T(r+1,r) -   T(r,r) = T(r,r-1) + C
```

The preceding equation considers *n-r* such steps in total. If we sum both sides of the stack, we have the following:

$$T(n,r) - T(r,r) = \left(\sum_{i=r}^{n-1} T(i,r-1) \right) + (n-r)C$$

Of course, *T(r,r)* is constant time. Let's call it *B*. Hence, we have the following:

$$T(n,r) = \left(\sum_{i=r}^{n-1} T(i,r-1) \right) + (n-r)C + B$$

Note that we can apply the same formula to *T(i,r-1)* too. This will give us the following:

$$T(n,r) = \left(\sum_{i=r}^{n-1} \left(\sum_{j=r-1}^{i-1} T(j,r-2) \right) + (n-r)C + B \right) + (n-r)C + B$$

This gives the the following after simplification:

$$T(n,r) = \left(\sum_{i=r}^{n-1} \left(\sum_{j=r-1}^{i-1} T(j,r-2) \right) \right) + \left\{ (n-r)^2 + (n-r) \right\} C + \left\{ (n-r)+1 \right\} B$$

We can continue this way and we will eventually get an expression with multiple nested summations, as follows:

$$T(n,r) = \left(\sum_{i=r}^{n-1} \sum_{j=r-1}^{i-1} \cdots \sum_{t=1}^{s-1} T(t,0) \right)$$

$$+ \left\{ A_r (n-r)^r + A_{(r-1)} (n-r)^{(r-1)} + \ldots + A_2 (n-r)^2 + A_1 (n-r) \right\} C$$

$$+ \left\{ D_{(r-1)} (n-r)^{(r-1)} + D_{(r-2)} (n-r)^{(r-2)} + \ldots + D_1 (n-r) + 1 \right\} B$$

Here A's and D's are also constants. When we are talking about asymptotic complexity, we need to assume that a variable is sufficiently large. In this case, there are two variables, with the condition that *r* is always less than or equal to *n*. So, first we consider the case where *r* is fixed and *n* is being increased and being made sufficiently large. In this case, there would be a total of *r* summations nested in one another. *T(t,0)* is a constant time. The summation has *r* depth, each having a maximum of *(n-r)* elements, so it is *O((n-r)r)*. The other terms are *O((n-r)r)*. Hence we can say the following:

```
T(n,r) = O((n-r)r) = O(nr)
```

The size of the input is of course not *n*; it is *log n = u (say)*. Then, we have the complexity of computation of *T(n,r) = O(2sr)*.

Another interesting case would be when we increase both *r* and *n* while also increasing the difference between them. To do that, we may want a particular ratio between the two, we assume *r/n= k* , *k<1* always. Then we can see the asymptotic growth of the function *T(n, kn)*. But computing this requires calculus and is outside the scope of this book.

This shows that even though the analysis of algorithms in functional form can be easier, the analysis of the time complexity can be fairly difficult. It is easy to understand why it is more difficult to compute the complexity of a functional algorithm. At the end of the day, computing complexity involves counting the number of steps required to do the computation. In the imperative style, steps of computation are direct, so it is easy to count them. On the other hand, a recursive style is a higher level of abstraction, and hence, counting the number of steps is harder. In the succeeding chapters, we will see more of these analyses.

Performance of functional programming

If we think about it, the whole point of functional programming is to have immutability and recursive definitions (or inductive definitions) of programs so that they can be analyzed easily. In general, adding additional constraints on your program would make it simpler to analyze but would reduce what you can do with it. Functional programming, of course, adds additional constraints on imperative programming in the form of immutability, that is, you are no longer allowed to reassign a variable. This is done so that the analysis of the program, that is, understanding how the program works, is now simpler. It is also simpler to prove theorems about the programs. However, we also lose some of the things that we could do without such restrictions. It turns out that any program can be rewritten in a functional style in a way to produce the same results. However, no guarantees are made about their performance or complexity in general. So, a functional version of a program can be a lot less efficient than its imperative counterpart. And indeed, in real life, we face many such scenarios. So, it is really a tradeoff between performance and simplicity. The general direction should then be that when working with a large input size, it is better to do away with restrictions in order to be able to optimize more. On the other hand, when the input sizes are small, it makes sense to stick to a functional style because the performance is probably not affected much by it.

There are some cases, though, where the functional version has the same running time complexity as the imperative version. In such a case, a functional version might be preferred because of its simplicity. It should be noted that since Java does not provide any explicit way of garbage collection and really, it happens by chance or outside the control of the programmer, a functional programming style will fill up the heap very quickly because of being immutable and thus being thrown away right after being created. So, it will not be advisable to use them where performance is really a problem.

This would seem really contrary to the fact that many large data processing systems, such as Spark, use a functional programming style. However, these systems only have a specialized language that gives an appearance of a functional programming style; they get translated to an almost non-functional form before they are even executed. To elaborate a little more, a map method in a monad may not evaluate anything at all; instead, it may just create a new object that contains this operator. A general program can then analyze these structures and construct an imperative program that does the same work. This provides a simple interface to the person using the framework as well as keeping the resource usage under control. In the next chapter, we will explore some of these ideas.

Summary

In this chapter, we learned a new way of looking at algorithms. The functional style of writing a program can simplify the analysis of its correctness, that is, you can easily understand why the program produces correct output. We saw a few patterns in functional programming, especially monads. We also saw how Java provides support for the functional style of programming through the syntax called lambda, which has existed from version 9 of Java. Finally, we saw how to use lambda effectively for functional programming.

Functional programs are, in general, easier to verify for correctness, but it is harder to compute their complexity. They generally perform either at the same speed as or slower than their imperative counterparts. It is a trade-off between development effort and computational efficiency. For smaller inputs, it is thus desirable to have a functional style of programming, whereas for processing large inputs, imperative style may be preferred.

Efficient Searching – Binary Search and Sorting

What is searching? Searching is trying to locate a given value in a collection of values. For example, you are given an array of integers, and your problem is to check whether the integer 5 is in that array. This is a search problem. In addition to just deciding whether the element 5 is in the array, we may be interested in its location as well when it is found. This is also a search problem.

Another interesting take on it would be to imagine a dictionary, that is, an array of values and associated values. For example, you have an array of names of students and their marks, as shown in the following table:

Name	Marks
Tom	63
Harry	70
Merry	65
Aisha	85
Abdullah	72
...	...

The list continues. Suppose, our system lets the student view his/her own marks. They would type their name and the system would show their marks. For simplicity, let's assume that there are no duplicate names. Now, we have to search for the name provided and return the corresponding values. This is, thus, another search problem. As we will see, search problems are quite ubiquitous in programming.

In this chapter, you will learn the following:

- Search algorithms
- Efficient searching in a sorted list
- Some sorting algorithms

Search algorithms

Suppose you are given an array of values and you are required to check whether a particular value is in that array, what is the most natural way to find that element? Well, it seems that the natural way is to go through each element one by one and check whether they match the given value. If any one does, we have found that element and we can return the index; if not, we can return -1 at the end of processing all the elements to report that such an element could not be found. This is what we would call a **linear search**. The following demonstrates a linear search algorithm in an array:

```
public static <E, F extends E> int linearSearch(E[] values,
valueToLookup) {
    for (int i = 0; i < values.length; i++) {
        if (values[i].equals(valueToLookup)) {
            return i;
        }
    }
    return -1;
}
```

The function `linearSearch` takes an array of values and a value to search in it, and returns the index if the value is found. If not, it returns a special value, -1. The program simply goes through each element and checks whether the current element matches with the value to lookup; if it does, then it just returns the current index, otherwise it keeps looking. At the end of the array, it returns the special value, -1. Now the following piece of code should return -1 in the first case and the value 5 in the second case:

```
Integer[] integers = new Integer[]{232,54,1,213,654,23,
                                    6,72,21};
System.out.println(ArraySearcher.linearSearch(integers,5));
System.out.println(ArraySearcher.linearSearch(integers,23));
```

Now, if we want to solve the student-marks problem described in the introduction of this chapter, we just need to have the marks of the students stored in a different array in the same order, as follows:

```
static String[] students = new String[]{"Tom","Harry",
                            "Merry","Aisha", "Abdullah"};
static int[] marks = new int[]{63,70, 65, 85, 72};
```

Now we can write a function to search for a name:

```
public static Integer marksForName(String name){
    int index = linearSearch(students, name);
    if(index>=0){
        return marks[index];
    }else{
        return null;
    }
}
```

First, we look for the name of the students in the list of students. If the name is found, the corresponding index would be assigned to the variable index and the value would be greater than or equal to zero. In such a case, we return the marks stored in the same index as of the marks array. If it is not found, we return null. To lookup the marks for Merry, for example, we call as shown here:

```
System.out.println(marksForName("Merry"));
```

We correctly obtain her marks, that are, 65.

What is the complexity of linear search? We have a `for` loop that moves through each element of an array of length n (say); in the worst case, we would go through all the elements, so the worst case complexity is $\theta(n)$. Even on an average, we would be visiting half the elements before we hit the correct element, so the average case complexity is $\theta(n/2) = \theta(n)$.

Binary search

Is a linear search the best we can do? Well, it turns out that if we are looking at an arbitrary array, this is what we have to do. After all, in an arbitrary array, there is no way to know whether an element is there without potentially looking at all of them. More specifically, we cannot say for sure that some element does not exist, without verifying all the elements. The reason is that the value of one element does not say anything about the values of the other elements.

But, what information can one element have about other elements in an array? One way to make elements have information about the other elements is to have a sorted array instead of just an arbitrary array. What is a sorted array? A sorted array is an array that has all the elements arranged in order of their values. When an array is sorted, every element contains the information that everything on the left is smaller than that particular element, and everything on the right is bigger (or the other way round if the order of the elements is opposite, but we will consider the arrays that are sorted in an increasing order from left to right). This information can, amazingly, make this search a lot faster. Here is what we do:

- Check the middle element of the array. If it matches the element we are searching for, we are done.
- If the middle element is smaller than the value we are searching for, search on the subarray on the right of the current array. This is because everything on the left is even smaller.
- If the middle element is bigger than the value we are searching for, search only in the left sub-array.

To avoid creating copies of the array while creating a sub-array, we just pass on the whole array, but we remember the start and end positions we are looking at. The start is included in the range and end is excluded. So, only elements on the right of the start position and the left of the end position are included in the subarray being searched. The following figure gives a visual understanding of binary search:

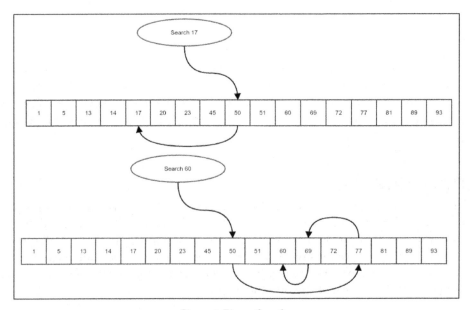

Figure 1: Binary Search.

An arrow representing moving one element to another during the search.

But, before implementing this algorithm, we need to understand the concept of `Comparable`. `Comparable` is an interface in the Java standard library that looks like this:

```
package java.lang;
public interface Comparable<T> {
    public int compareTo(T o);
}
```

Any class implementing this interface has to compare a different object with itself. It is required that the type parameter, *T*, must be instantiated with the same class that implements it, like this:

```
public class Integer implements Comparable<Integer>{
    public int compareTo(Integer o){
        ...
    }
}
```

The `compareTo` method intends to compare an object of the same type. If the current object (the one that the `this` reference refers to) is smaller than the object passed, `compareTo` must return a negative value. If the object passed is smaller, the method must return a positive value. Otherwise, if they are equal, it must return 0. The following conditions are required to be fulfilled by the `compareTo` method:

- If `a.compareTo(b) == 0`, then `a.equals(b)` must be `true`
- If `a.compareTo(b) < 0` and `b.compareTo(c) < 0`, then `a.compareTo(c) <0`
- If `a.compareTo(b) <0`, then `b.compareTo(a) > 0`
- If `b.equals(c)` is true and `a.compareTo(b) <0`, then `a.compareTo(c) <0`
- If `b.equals(c)` is true and `a.compareTo(b) >0`, then `a.compareTo(c) >0`

Basically, the conditions are the same for a total order where equality is represented by the equals method. It basically generalizes the concept of the `<` and `<=` operators, which are there for numbers. Of course, the `compareTo` method for the `Wrapper` objects are implemented exactly as the `<` and `<=` operators are on the primitives inside them.

Now, we write the search function to do the search, as per the preceding steps:

```
private static <E extends Comparable<E>,
  F extends E> int binarySearch( E[] sortedValues,
  F valueToSearch, int start, int end) {
    if(start>=end){
        return -1;
    }
}
```

```
        int midIndex = (end+start)/2;
        int comparison = sortedValues[midIndex].compareTo(
                    valueToSearch);
        if(comparison==0){
            return midIndex;
        }else if(comparison>0){
            return binarySearch(sortedValues, valueToSearch,
                            start, midIndex);
        }else{
            return binarySearch(sortedValues, valueToSearch,
                            midIndex+1, end);
        }
    }
```

Note that in this case, we have mandated that the objects in the array must be comparable so that we can know if an object is greater than or less than another object. It does not matter exactly how this relationship is determined; the array must be sorted using the same comparison – that the comparison between two consecutive elements will make sure the element on the left is smaller than the one on the right, as provided by Comparable.

The first if condition checks whether the array passed is empty, if so, obviously the element to be searched is not found and we return -1 to represent this. Then, we find the midIndex and recursively search for the element in either the left or the right subarray. Once we have this function, we create another wrapper function to run the search without having to mention the start and the end positions:

```
        public static <E extends Comparable<E>, F extends E>
        int binarySearch(
                E[] sortedValues, F valueToSearch) {
            return binarySearch(sortedValues, valueToSearch, 0,
                            sortedValues.length);
        }
```

Complexity of the binary search algorithm

In every step, we are partitioning the total array into two parts, barring the one element that we are comparing. In the worst case, that is, the case where the element searched is not present in the array, we will have to get down all the way to the point where we are dealing with an empty array, in which case we return -1 and stop recursing. We must have had an array of only one element in the previous step. For our analysis, we will consider this step as the last step. So, let's have a sorted array of n elements and $T(.)$ is the time required for searching in the array. So, we have the following:

```
    T(n) = T((n-1)/2) + C, where C is a constant.
```

In general, the two search branches in every step would be of different sizes, one potentially being of size one less than that of the other part. But we will ignore these small differences, which hardly matter for a large *n*. Hence, we will work with the following equation:

```
T(n) = T(n/2) + C
```

Now, let's assume that *n* is an integral power of 2 so that *n = 2m* for some integer *m*. So, we have this:

```
T(2m) = T(2m-1) + C
```

Now we take another function *S(.)*, such that *S(m) = T(2m)* for all *m*. Then, we have:

```
S(m) = S(m-1) + C
```

This is the formula for an arithmetic progression. And hence, we have this:

```
S(m) = mC + D, where D is also a constant.
=> T(2m) = mC + D
=> T(n) = C lg(n) + D
```

So, we have the asymptotic complexity of *T(n)*:

```
T(n) = O(lg(n))
```

The function, *T(n)*, grows only as fast as the logarithm of the size of the array passed, which is really slow. This makes binary search an extremely efficient algorithm.

To sort of field test the algorithms, we run both linear and binary search algorithms on an array of a hundred million elements with the following code:

```
int arraySize = 100000000;
Long array[] = new Long[arraySize];
array[0] = (long)(Math.random()*100);
for(int i=1;i<array.length;i++){
    array[i] = array[i-1] + (long)(Math.random()*100);
}

//let us look for an element using linear and binary search
long start = System.currentTimeMillis();
linearSearch(array, 31232L);
long linEnd = System.currentTimeMillis();
binarySearch(array, 31232L);
long binEnd = System.currentTimeMillis();

System.out.println("linear search time :=" + (linEnd -start));
System.out.println("binary search time :=" +
                (binEnd -linEnd));
```

On my computer, the linear search took 282 milliseconds and binary search took 0 milliseconds. Also, note that the value we are looking for is expected to be quite near to the beginning of the array; in case of values near the middle, a binary search would have an even higher advantage.

Sorting

Okay, so we are convinced that if we have a sorted array, it takes a lot less time to find an element in it. But how do we get a sorted array? An arbitrary array is unlikely to be sorted. The algorithm of getting a sorted array out of an arbitrary array while keeping all the elements same, that is, by only rearranging the elements of an input array, is called sorting. There are a lot of algorithms for sorting. But in this chapter, we will start with a few simple ones that are not efficient. In the next chapter, we will explore efficient sorting algorithms.

Selection sort

This is the most natural algorithm for sorting. We choose each position of the array and find the element in the array that belongs in that position. The functional definition of selection sort is as follows:

- Find the minimum element in an array
- Swap this element with the first element of the array
- Sort the rest of the array after the first element recursively

Finding the minimum element has the functional structure as follows:

- Consider the array as a composition of the first element and the rest of the array.
- Find the index of the minimum element in the rest of the array.
- Compare this element with the first element. If this element is smaller than the first element, then it is the minimum element in the entire array. Otherwise, the first element is the minimum element.

Instead of making copies of the array, we represent subarrays by simply storing the starting index we want to consider, and then we work on the index recursively.

First, we write a function to find the index of the minimum element in a given array, starting from a position:

```
public static <E extends Comparable<E>> int findMin(E[] array,
int start){
```

Then, we check whether the start position is the last position in the array, in which case we just simply return the start position as there are no more elements:

```
if(start==array.length-1){
    return start;
}
```

We find the index of the minimum element in the array to the right of the current start position and compare that element with the current start element. We return whichever has the minimum element, as demonstrated in the following:

```
int restMinIndex = findMin(array, start+1);
E restMin = array[restMinIndex];
if(restMin.compareTo(array[start])<0){
    return restMinIndex;
}else {
    return start;
}
}
```

The `swap` function swaps or interchanges two elements in the array at the given positions. This function is pretty straightforward:

```
public static <E> void swap(E[] array, int i, int j){
    if(i==j)
        return;
    E temp = array[i];
    array[i]=array[j];
    array[j] = temp;
}
```

With the `findMin` and `swap` functions in our repository, we can finally put down the `selectionSort` algorithm. We start off by passing the position zero as the value of the start parameter:

```
public static <E extends Comparable<E>> void selectionSort(
E[] array, int start){
```

Firstly, there is no sorting to be done if the array is empty:

```
if(start>=array.length){
    return;
}
```

Now, we just find the index of the minimum element and swap the current position with the index of the minimum position. This will put the minimum element in the current position:

```
int minElement = findMin(array, start);
swap(array,start, minElement);
```

Then, we recursively sort the rest of the array:

```
    selectionSort(array, start+1);
}
```

Now, we can write a wrapper function to just do `selectionSort` without having to pass a start index:

```
public static <E extends Comparable<E>> void selectionSort(
E[] array) {
    selectionSort(array, 0);
}
```

We can test our code by creating an arbitrary array and then sorting it using our algorithm:

```
Integer[] array = new Integer[]{10, 5, 2, 3, 78, 53, 3};
selectionSort(array);
System.out.println(Arrays.toString(array));
```

And the output would be as follows:

```
[2, 3, 3, 5, 10, 53, 78]
```

Note how all the elements are repositioned in ascending order, which means that the array is sorted.

> The form of selection sort shown is not functional in a strict sense because we are modifying the contents of an array. A truly functional sort of an array will make a copy of the array on every modification. However, this is very expensive. On the other hand, thinking of the algorithm in terms of smaller versions of the same problem, like we have done, does make the algorithm simpler to understand. I tried to hit a sweet spot where I have the simplicity of the recursive algorithm, but don't have to keep creating copies of the array.

Complexity of the selection sort algorithm

To compute the complexity of the selection sort algorithm, first we have to compute the complexity of the `findMin` and `swap` functions. Let's start with the `findMin` function. As with any recursive function, we start with assuming that with an array of length *n* (in this case, the effective length of the array, starting from the start position), it takes us *T(n)* time to compute the `findMin` function. While recursively calling itself, it passes on an effective array of length *n-1*. So, we have the following equation:

```
T(n) = T(n-1) + A where A is a constants
=> T(n) - T(n-1) = A, so it is an arithmetic progression
=> T(n) = An + B where B is a constant
=> T(n) = θ(n)
```

Now, let's move on to the `swap` function. It has no recursion and no loops, so the complexity is constant or *θ(1)*.

Finally, we are ready to compute the complexity of the function `selectionSort`. Say, for an effective length *n* of an array, the time taken is *T(n)*. It calls itself with effective length *n-1*, it also calls `findMin` and `swap` functions, which are *θ(n)* and *θ(1)*, respectively. So, we have this:

```
T(n) = T(n-1) + θ(n) + θ(1)
```

Note that some expressions that are *θ (n)* have been written as *θ (n)* itself. It should be read as, *"Some function of n that has the asymptotic complexity, θ (n)."* It turns out, for computing complexity of *T(n)*, we don't have to actually know the actual expression, we can simply put *Cn* and *D* for functions that are *θ (n)* and *θ (1)*, respectively, where *C* and *D* are constants. So, we form the following equation:

```
T(n) = T(n-1) + Cn + D
=> T(n) - T(n-1) = Cn + D
```

Similarly, *T(n-1) - T(n-2) = C(n-1) + D* and so on. If we stack these equations, we get the following:

```
T(n)   - T(n-1) = Cn + D
 T(n-1) - T(n-2) = C(n-1) + D
 T(n-2) - T(n-3) = C(n-2) + D
 T(n-3) - T(n-4) = C(n-3) + D
 ...
 T(1) - T(0) = C(1) + D
```

Adding both sides, we get this:

$$T(n) - T(0) = \sum_{i=1}^{n} Ci + nD$$

$$\Rightarrow T(n) - T(0) = C \cdot \frac{n(n+1)}{2} + nD$$

$$\Rightarrow T(n) = C \cdot \frac{n(n+1)}{2} + nD + T(0)$$

$$\Rightarrow T(n) = \theta(n^2)$$

So, the selection sort has a complexity of $\theta(n2)$, where n is the size of the array being sorted. Now, we will see the next sorting algorithm, which is the insertion sort.

Insertion sort

In selection sort, we first selected a position and then found the element that should sit there. In the insertion sort, we do the opposite; we first select an element and then insert the element into position where it should sit. So, for every element, we first find out where it should be and then we insert the element in the right place. So, we first see how to insert an element into a sorted array. The idea is that we are given an array of sorted elements and we are supposed to insert another element in the correct position, so that the resulting array remains sorted. We will consider a simpler problem. We are given an array that is sorted except for the last element. Our job is to insert the last element in the correct position. The recursive way to achieve this insertion is as follows:

* If the element to be inserted is bigger than the end element of the sorted array, it belongs in the end and the insertion is complete.

* Otherwise, we swap the last element with the element to be inserted and recursively insert this element in the rest of the smaller array in front of it.

We do it with the following function. The function takes an array and a position that represents this last position:

```
public static <E extends Comparable<E>> void insertElementSorted(
E[] array, int valueIndex) {

    if (valueIndex > 0 && array[valueIndex].compareTo(
        array[valueIndex - 1]) < 0) {
        swap(array, valueIndex, valueIndex - 1);
```

```
        insertElementSorted(array, valueIndex - 1);
    }

}
```

If the last position or the `valueIndex` is `0`, there is nothing to be done, as the element is already in the correct position, that is, `0`. There is no array to the left of `valueIndex` in this case. If not, we compare the last element to the previous element. Since the array on the left is presumed to be sorted, the previous element is the largest element in the sorted part of the array. If the last element is bigger than even this one, there is nothing more to be done. If not, we swap the last element with the previous one and run the insertion recursively on the array with one less element. The last element has moved to the previous position and it must now be compared with the element before that, and so on.

With the insertion function available for sorted arrays, we are now ready to write the algorithm for an insertion sort. In every step of the insertion sort, we consider a boundary in the array. Everything on the left of the boundary has already been sorted. Our job in the current step is to insert the element at the boundary index into the left sorted array, which we achieve using the `insertElementSorted` function. We implement this sort with the following simple strategy. In any step, we do the following:

- We first sort the left-hand side of the boundary so that our assumption about it being sorted is achieved
- Then we invoke the `insertElementSorted` function to insert the current boundary element in the sorted array

Of course, when `boundary` is zero, it means that there is no array to be sorted and we simply return:

```
public static <E extends Comparable<E>> void insertionSort(
E[] array, int boundary) {
    if(boundary==0){
        return;
    }
    insertionSort(array, boundary-1);
    insertElementSorted(array, boundary);
}
```

Complexity of insertion sort

To compute the complexity of insertion sort, we must first compute it for the
`insertElementSorted` function. Let the time taken for an array of effective length
(that is, from *zero to boundary-1*), *n* be *T(n)*. From there, we recursively call it with
n-1. So, we have the following:

```
T(n)  = T(n-1) + C where C is a constant
=> T(n)  = θ(n)
```

Let's now assume that the time taken for sorting an array of *n* elements is *S(n)*.
Apart from the base case, it calls itself with one less argument and then calls the
`insertElementSorted` function with an array of effective length *n-1*. Thus, we
have this:

```
S(n)  = S(n-1) + T(n)  + D where D is a constant.
```

Again, when *n* is large, *T(n)* = θ(*n*); hence, it can be approximated by *An* where *A* is a
constant. So, we have this:

```
S(n)   = S(n-1) + An + D
=> S(n)  - S(n-1) = An + D,
```

Since this is true for all *n*, we have:

```
S(n)  - S(n-1)  = An + D
S(n-1)  - S(n-2)  = A(n-1)  + D
S(n-2)  - S(n-3)  = A(n-2)  + D
...
S(1)  - S(0)  = A + D
```

Summing both sides, we get the following:

$$S(n) - S(0) = \sum_{i-1}^{n} Ai + nD$$

$$\Rightarrow S(n) - S(0) = A\frac{n(n+1)}{2} + nD$$

$$\Rightarrow S(n) = A\frac{n(n+1)}{2} + nD + S(0)$$

$$\Rightarrow S(n) = \theta(n^2)$$

Thus, insertion sort has the same asymptotic complexity as selection sort.

Bubble sort

Another interesting sorting algorithm is a bubble sort. Unlike the previous algorithms, this one works at a very local level. The strategy is as follows:

- Scan through the array, searching pairs of consecutive elements that are ordered wrongly. Then find *a j*, such that *array[j+1] < array[j]*.

- Whenever such a pair is found, swap them and continue searching until the end of the array and then back from the beginning again.

- Stop when a scan through the entire array does not even find a single pair.

The code that does this is as follows:

```java
public static <E extends Comparable<E>> void bubbleSort(
E[] array) {
    boolean sorted = false;
    while (!sorted) {
        sorted = true;
        for (int i = 0; i < array.length - 1; i++) {
            if (array[i].compareTo(array[i + 1]) > 0) {
                swap(array, i, i + 1);
                sorted = false;
            }
        }
    }
}
```

The flag, `sorted`, keeps track of whether any inverted pairs were found during a scan. Each iteration of the `while` loop is a scan through the entire array, the scan being done inside the `for` loop. In the `for` loop, we are, of course, checking each pair of elements, and if an inverted pair is found, we swap them. We stop when `sorted` is `true`, that is, when we have not found a single inverted pair in the entire array.

To see that this algorithm will indeed sort the array, we have to check two things:

- When there are no inverted pairs, the array is sorted. This justifies our stopping condition.

> This is, of course, true because when there are no inverted pairs, we have that for all *j< array.length-1*, we have *array[j+1]>=array[j]*. This is the definition of an array being in an increasing order, that is, the array being sorted.

- Irrespective of the input, the program will eventually reach the preceding condition after a finite number of steps. That is to say that we need the program to finish in a finite number of steps. To see this, we need to understand the concept of **inversions**. We will explore them in the next section.

Inversions

Inversion in an array is a pair of elements that are wrongly ordered. The pair may be close together or very far apart in the array. For example, take the following array:

```
Integer[] array = new Integer[]{10, 5, 2, 3, 78, 53, 3};
```

How many inversions does the array have? Let us count:

```
10>5, 10>2, 10>3, 10<78,  10<53, 10>3
        5>2,    5>3,      5<78,   5<53,   5>3
            ,   2<3,     2<78,    2<53,   2<3
                  ,             3<78,     3<53,    3=3
                              , 78>53,  78>3
                                         53>3
```

In this listing, every element is compared with the elements following it. There is an inversion when there is a greater-than sign, highlighted by bold characters. Counting the bold ones, we see there are 10 inversions.

For any input array, there is a number of inversions. In a sorted array, the number of inversions would be zero. Now, think about what happens to the number of inversions when a swap is made. A swap interchanges a pair of consecutive elements, thus breaking one inversion (the swap happens only when there is an inversion between consecutive elements). To see this more clearly, consider the following case of a swap between *j* and *j+1* indexes:

```
…........., j, j+1, ….....
```

Let's take the jth element first. Let it have x number of inversions with the left part of the array. Since these elements are on the left, all inversions of this type are with elements greater than the jth element. When the jth element moves to the $(j+1)^{th}$ position, they still remain to the left, and the only element added to the left of the jth element is the element it is swapped with. Hence, no changes to the number of inversion happens to the jth element, other than the one due to the $(j+1)^{th}$ element. The same logic can be applied to the inversions with it in the right part of the array, and also to both sides of the array for the $(j+1)^{th}$ element. Because of the swap, one inversion is broken between j^{th} and $(j+1)^{th}$ elements. Hence, the number of inversions reduce by exactly one in each inversion. This means the number of swaps in bubble sort would be exactly equal to the number of inversions in the input array, which is finite. And since each scan through the array requires a swap in the previous scan, the total number of scans is at most one more that the number of swaps; this is finite too. This makes sure that the algorithm always finishes.

Complexity of the bubble sort algorithm

To understand the complexity of a bubble sort, we have to count the number of steps. Is the number of steps equal to the number of swaps? The answer is, not really. In case of asymptotic analysis, we must always count the step that happens a maximum number of times. In this case, that step is comparison. How many comparisons are there per scan of the array? *n-1* of course. So, now the analysis of complexity is reduced to the number of scans we need to sort the array.

Let's see what happens to the maximum element after the first scan. Let's say the maximum element is at the index *j*. So, it will be compared with the element at *j+1*. For simplicity, let's assume that all elements are different. Now, since it is the maximum element, the element at the *j+1* position will be less than it, and hence it will be swapped. Now the maximum element is at the position, *j+1*, and is being compared with the element at position, *j+2*, and the same thing happens. It will continue until the maximum element is at the end of the array. If the elements are not unique, the same will happen to the rightmost maximum element. In the next cycle, the maximum element will already be at the end of the array, and we will hit the second maximum (or another maximum element) somewhere in the array. Now, since one maximum element is at the end of the array, we can think of the rest of the array apart from the last element. In this array, the current maximum is the maximum and it will reach the end of the current part of the array at the end of the current scan.

This shows that at the end of each scan, at least one element reaches the correct final position without altering the correct positions of the ones that got there before the scan, which means that at the end of n scans, all of the elements would be in the correct position and the array would be sorted. That is to say that after at most n scans, the bubble sort would be complete. In each of those scans, there are $O(n)$ operations. So, the worst case complexity of bubble sort is $O(n2)$.

This is not the end of this analysis; we still have to show that there is a case that takes that many steps, and only then can we have a theta bound on the worst case. We take the case where all the elements are sorted in the opposite order, that is, they are in a decreasing order and are all distinct. In such a case, every element has an inversion with all the others. This means that each one of the n elements have an inversion with $n-1$ other elements, that is, $n(n-1)$ inversions in total. But since each inversion would be counted twice, once from each of the elements that are members of the inversion, it is actually $n(n-1)/2$. Now, note that the maximum number of swaps that can be done in one scan is $n-1$, which will happen if every comparison results in a swap because there are $n-1$ comparisons per scan. So, we will need at least $(n(n-1)/2)/(n-1) = n/2$ scans to complete all the swaps, each requiring $n-1$ comparisons. So, the complexity is at least $n(n-1)/2 = \Omega(n2)$. Of course then, the worst case is at least this much complex because the worst case is, by definition, the most complex case.

So, the worst case is both $O(n2)$ and $\Omega(n2)$, that is to say that it is $\theta(n2)$.

A problem with recursive calls

A problem with recursive calls is that they are expensive; a method invocation entails considerable overhead on the processor. It is, in general, better to avoid invoking methods if you want to improve performance to the last bit. On top of that, there is a limit to the depth of function calls that you can go to, before the program breaks. This is because a program has a stack to enable method invocation semantics, that actually gets a new element containing all variables and the position of the current instruction to the stack. This stack does not grow indefinitely, but instead is fixed in size; usually, it can hold a few thousand values, which means that if your method invocation is deeper than that, it will break and the program will exit with an error. This means that our insertion sort will break for an array containing more than a few thousand entries. On the other hand, it is generally easier to explain an algorithm in a functional form. To balance between these two aspects, we need to be able to convert to and from the recursive and non-recursive versions of the same algorithm. We will do this step by step from the simplest form to the more complicated form.

Tail recursive functions

A recursive function is called a tail recursive function if all the recursive calls to itself in the function are the last operations. I say it like there are multiple calls and all of them must be the last operations. How is that possible? I mean there can be different calls from different conditional branches of the code inside the function. However, whenever the function calls itself that must be the last operation in that conditional branch of the function. For example, take our binary search algorithm again:

```java
private static <E extends Comparable<E>, F extends E>
int binarySearch(
    E[] sortedValues, F valueToSearch, int start, int end) {
    if(start>=end){
        return -1;
    }
    int midIndex = (end+start)/2;
    int comparison = sortedValues[midIndex]
                        .compareTo(valueToSearch);
    if(comparison==0){
        return midIndex;
    }else if(comparison>0){
        return binarySearch(sortedValues, valueToSearch,
                            start, midIndex);
    }else{
        return binarySearch(sortedValues, valueToSearch,
                            midIndex+1, end);
    }
}
```

Note that the function calls itself in two different conditional branches. However, in each branch, the recursive call is the last operation. There is nothing to be done after the call to itself. This is a tail recursive function.

Tail recursive functions can be turned into a loop absolutely mechanically. In fact, all functional language compilers do this automatically during compiler optimization. The Java compiler, however, does not do this because Java generally prefers loops over recursion in the code, at least until very recently. But we can do this conversion by ourselves.

The idea is that since there are no more operations after the recursive call, the program does not have to remember the values of the variables of the calling function. So, they can simply be overwritten by the values of the same variables of the called function instead, and we just have to process the code of the function again. So, the following is the mechanical procedure to achieve this:

Wrap the entire content in an infinite `while` loop.

Replace all recursive calls by updating the values of the parameters to the values that are passed in the recursive calls.

The following shows this update in the binary search algorithm:

```
private static <E extends Comparable<E>, F extends E>
int binarySearchNonRecursive(
    E[] sortedValues, F valueToSearch, int start, int end) {
    while(true) {
        if (start >= end) {
            return -1;
        }
        int midIndex = (end + start) / 2;
        int comparison = sortedValues[midIndex]
                            .compareTo(valueToSearch);
        if (comparison == 0) {
            return midIndex;
        } else if (comparison > 0) {
            end = midIndex;
        } else {
            start = midIndex + 1;
        }
    }
}
```

Note that we updated only those arguments that changed, which is only one update per branch in this case. This will produce the exact same result as the earlier function, but now it would not cause a stack overflow. This conversion is not really required in case of a binary search though, because you need only *lg n* steps to search an array of length *n*. So, if your allowed depth of invocation is *1000*, then you can search in an array of maximum size of *21000* elements. This number is way more than the total number of atoms in the entire universe, and hence we will never be able to store an array of that enormous size. But the example shows the principle of converting a tail recursion into a loop.

Another example is the `insertElementSorted` function, used in our insertion sort algorithm:

```
public static <E extends Comparable<E>> void
    insertElementSorted(
    E[] array, int valueIndex) {

    if (valueIndex > 0 && array[valueIndex]
            .compareTo(array[valueIndex - 1]) < 0) {
        swap(array, valueIndex, valueIndex - 1);
        insertElementSorted(array, valueIndex - 1);
```

```
        }

    }
```

Note that there is no operation pending after the recursive call to itself. But we need to be a little more careful here. Note that the invocation only happens inside a code branch. The else case is implicit here, which is else { return; }. We need to make it explicit in our code first, as shown below:

```
public static <E extends Comparable<E>> void insertElementSorted(
E[] array, int valueIndex) {

    if (valueIndex > 0 && array[valueIndex].compareTo(
        array[valueIndex - 1]) < 0) {
        swap(array, valueIndex, valueIndex - 1);
        insertElementSorted(array, valueIndex - 1);
    } else{
     return;
    }
}
```

Now we can use our old technique to make it non-recursive, that is, to wrap it in an infinite loop and replace recursive calls with argument updates:

```
public static <E extends Comparable<E>> void
insertElementSortedNonRecursive(
    E[] array, int valueIndex) {
    while(true) {
        if (valueIndex > 0 && array[valueIndex].compareTo(
            array[valueIndex - 1]) < 0) {
            swap(array, valueIndex, valueIndex - 1);
            valueIndex =  valueIndex - 1;
        }else{
            return;
        }
    }

}
```

This gives the exact same result as the previous recursive version of the function. So, the corrected steps would be as follows:

1. First, make all implicit branches explicit and all implicit returns explicit.

2. Wrap the entire content in an infinite while loop.

3. Replace all recursive calls by updating the values of the parameters to the values that are passed in the recursive calls.

Non-tail single recursive functions

By single recursion, I mean that the function invokes itself at most once per conditional branch of the function. They may be tail-recursive, but they are not always so. Consider the example of the recursion of our insertion sort algorithm:

```
public static <E extends Comparable<E>> void insertionSort(
    E[] array, int boundary) {
    if(boundary==0){
        return;
    }
    insertionSort(array, boundary-1);
    insertElementSorted(array, boundary);
}
```

Note that the function calls itself only once, so it is a single recursion. But since we have a call to `insertElementSorted` after the recursive call to itself, it is not a tail recursive function, which means that we cannot use the earlier method. Before doing this though, let's consider a simpler example. Take the factorial function:

```
public static BigInteger factorialRecursive(int x){
    if(x==0){
        return BigInteger.ONE;
    }else{
        return factorialRecursive(x-1).multiply(
            BigInteger.valueOf(x));
    }
}
```

First, note that the function is singly recursive, because there is at most one recursive call per branch of the code. Also, note that it is not tail recursive because you have to do a multiplication after the recursive call.

To convert this into a loop, we must first figure out the actual order of the numbers being multiplied. The function calls itself until it hits 0, at which point, it returns 1. So, the multiplication actually starts from 1 and then accumulates the higher values.

Since it accumulates the values on its way up, we need an accumulator (that is a variable storing one value) to collect this value in a loop version. The steps are as follows:

1. First, make all implicit branches explicit and all implicit returns explicit.

2. Create an accumulator of the same type as the return type of the function. This is to store intermediate return values. The starting value of the accumulator is the value returned in the base case of the recursion.

3. Find the starting value of the recursion variable, that is, the one that is getting smaller in each recursive invocation. The starting value is the value that causes the next recursive call to fall in the base case.

4. The exit value of the recursion variable is the same as the one passed to the function originally.

5. Create a loop and make the recursion variable your loop variable. Vary it from the start value to the end value calculated earlier in a way to represent how the value changes from higher depth to lower depth of recursion. The higher depth value comes before the lower depth value.

6. Remove the recursive call.

What is the initial value of the accumulator prod? It is the same as the value that is returned in the exit branch of the recursion, that is, 1. What is the highest value being multiplied? It is x. So we can now convert it to the following loop:

```
public static BigInteger factorialRecursiveNonRecursive(int x){
    BigInteger prod = BigInteger.ONE;
    for(int i=1;i<=x;i++){
        prod = prod.multiply(BigInteger.valueOf(x));
    }
    return prod;
}
```

Now let's consider the `insertionSort` algorithm. What is the accumulator? It is the same thing that would be the final output, that is, an array of sorted elements. What is the starting value? It is the same that is returned in the recursive version in the exit branch. This is an array of length zero. What is the final value? The array of sorted elements of the length provided to sort. Again, just like our recursive version, we represent these partial arrays with, simply, a boundary value. So, the code is as follows:

```
public static <E extends Comparable<E>> void
  insertionSortNonRecursive(
    E[] array) {
    for(int boundary = 0;boundary<array.length;boundary++) {
        insertElementSortedNonRecursive(array, boundary);
    }
}
```

Note that in this case, the function `return` type is `void`. But what we are really returning is the sorted array; we just resorted to modifying the same array to avoid creating duplicate arrays.

The most general case is the multiple recursion, that is, the function calls itself multiple times in the same conditional branch of the function. This case cannot be done without a stack. In case of a recursive call, we use the method-invocation stack. Otherwise, we can even use an external stack. Since we do not have such an example in this chapter, we defer its explanation to the next chapter, where we will have an example.

Summary

In this chapter, we saw how to do an efficient search in an ordered array. This search is called a binary search. You also learned some methods of obtaining an ordered array out of an unordered one. This process is called sorting. We saw three basic algorithms of sorting. Although they are not particularly efficient, they are simple to understand the concept. You also learned how to convert a recursive algorithm to a non-recursive one that uses a loop. In the next chapter, we will see efficient sorting algorithms.

6
Efficient Sorting – quicksort and mergesort

In the last chapter, we explored a few simple sorting algorithms. The problem with those is that they are not efficient enough. In this chapter, we will cover two efficient sorting algorithms and we will also see how they are efficient.

In this chapter, you will learn the following topics:

- quicksort
- mergesort
- Optimality of efficiency in sorting algorithms

quicksort

We want to develop an algorithm that sorts an array of elements efficiently. Our strategy will be simple; we will somehow try to divide the array into two halves in such a way that sorting each half will complete the sorting. If we can achieve this, we can recursively call the sorting algorithm this way. We already know that the number of levels of recursive call will be of the order of $lg\ n$ where $lg\ m$ is the logarithm of m with the base 2. So, if we can manage to cut the array in a time in the order of n, we will still have a complexity of $O(n\ lg\ n)$ This is much better than $O(n^2)$, which we saw in the previous chapter. But how do we cut the array that way? Let's try to cut the following array as follows:

```
10, 5, 2, 3, 78, 53, 3,1,1,24,1,35,35,2,67,4,33,30
```

If we trivially cut this array, each part will contain all sorts of values. Sorting these individual parts would then not cause the entire array to be sorted. Instead, we have to cut the array in such a way that all the elements in the left part are less than all the elements in the right part. If we can achieve this, sorting the parts will achieve sorting the whole. But, of course, we need to make some swaps for us to be able to cut the array in such a way. So, we use the following trick:

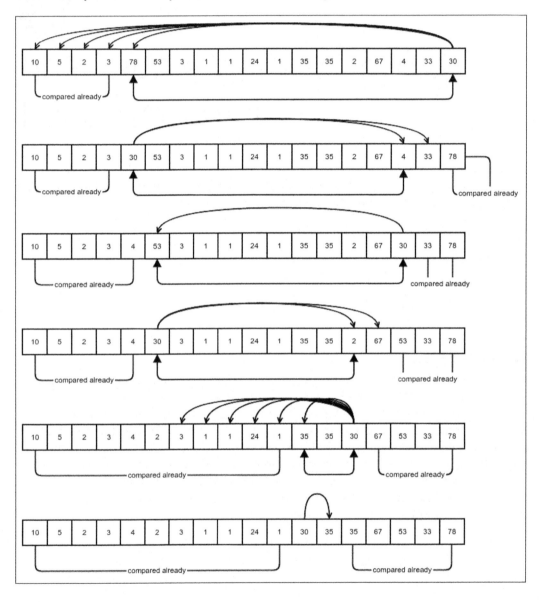

This is an example of pivot positioning in quicksort. The one headed arrows represent comparison and double headed arrows represent swap.

We first choose the last element and call it *pivot*. Our aim is to make all the elements that are less than the pivot to be on its left and all the elements that are greater than the pivot to be on its right. Note that this means that the pivot is already at the correct position of the array. The preceding figure shows how to do it with an example. In the figure, our pivot is **30**. We start comparing with the first element and move on. The moment we find an inversion, we swap the pivot with that element and keep comparing in the opposite direction. We continue this way, swapping every time there is an inversion and reversing the direction of comparison each time. We stop when all the elements have been compared. Note that after this process, all the elements less than the pivot are on its left, and all the elements greater than the pivot are on its right. Why does this work? Let's take a closer look.

Suppose we start comparing from the left. After the first swap, the pivot is at the position of the element that was found to be greater than it. All the elements that were on the left of it have already been compared with the pivot and found to be less than it. The previous figure shows the parts that have already been compared. Now it starts comparing from its earlier position in the opposite direction. After the second swap, it sits in the position of the element that it has been swapped with. All the elements on the right have already been compared with it and found to be greater than it. We keep going in the same way, always ensuring that the parts that have already been compared follow the rule that the part on the left of the pivot contains only elements that are less than or equal to it and the part on the right of the pivot contains only elements that are greater than or equal to it. So, when we are done with the comparisons, we still hold this condition, thus achieving the result. Once we know that all the elements on the left of the pivot are less than or equal to all the elements that are on its right, we can sort these parts separately and the entire array will be sorted as a result. Of course, we sort these parts recursively in the same way.

However, before we dive into the code, I would like to introduce a different interface for comparison. It is called `java.util.Comparator` and allows us to specify any comparison logic while sorting, thus providing more flexibility. Here is how it looks:

```
@FunctionalInterface
public interface Comparator<T> {
    int compare(T o1, T o2);
}
```

This is, of course, a very simplified version of the actual interface but has got all that we care about. As you can see, this is a functional interface and thus can be implemented using a lambda. It should return the same value that is conceptually similar to the value returned by o1.compareTo(o2), but a different sorting can use a different comparison lambda. The compare method has to follow the same rules that are there for the compareTo method in the java.util.Comparable interface we studied in the previous chapter.

Now let's jump into the code for quicksort. We know we don't have to sort any more when the array to be processed is empty, which would be our base case. Otherwise, We create two indexes i and j, one storing the current end of the left part and the other storing the current beginning of the right part that has already been compared with the pivot at any given point of time, while the pivot is being placed in its correct position. Both the index variables store the indexes that are to be compared next. At any given point of time, one of these variables holds the position of the pivot and the other stores the current value being compared with it. The variable that currently stores the position of the pivot is flagged by the Boolean variable, movingI. If it is true, it means that we are currently moving i and hence, j is pointing to the pivot. We update the position variables and keep comparing, in a loop, until both indexes point to the pivot, when the comparison suggests that there is an inversion, we swap and reverse the direction of movement. We reverse the direction of movement because the pivot has moved to the position indexed by the opposite variable, marked by movingI switching its value. Otherwise, we just keep updating the appropriate position variable.

When movingI is false, it means that i is storing the position of the pivot. And finally, when the pivot is at the correct position and all the elements on its left are less than or equal to all the elements on its right, we recursively call **quicksort** on each part:

```
public static <E> void quicksort(E[] array, int start, int end,
Comparator<E> comparator) {

    if (end - start <= 0) {
        return;
    }

    int i = start;
    int j = end - 1;
    boolean movingI = true;

    while (i < j) {
```

```
        if (comparator.compare(array[i], array[j]) > 0) {
            swap(array, i, j);
            movingI = !movingI;
        } else {
            if (movingI) {
                i++;
            } else {
                j--;
            }
        }
    }

    quicksort(array, start, i, comparator);
    quicksort(array, i + 1, end, comparator);
}
```

We can wrap this method to avoid having to pass the start and end parameters:

```
public static <E> void quicksort(E[] array, Comparator<E> comparator){
    quicksort(array, 0, array.length, comparator);
}
```

We can use this method to sort an array. Let's see how to sort an integer array:

```
Integer[] array =
new Integer[]{10, 5, 2, 3, 78, 53, 3, 1, 1, 24, 1, 35,
35, 2, 67, 4, 33, 30};

quicksort(array, (a, b) -> a - b);
System.out.println(Arrays.toString(array));
```

The following would be the output:

```
[1, 1, 1, 2, 2, 3, 3, 4, 5, 10, 24, 30, 33, 35, 35, 53, 67, 78]
```

Note how we passed the simple comparator using a lambda. If we pass a lambda (a,b)->b-a instead, we will get the array reversed. In fact, this flexibility lets us sort arrays containing complex objects according to any comparison we like. For example, it is easy to sort an array of Person objects by age using the lambda, (p1, p2)->p1.getAge() - p2.getAge().

Complexity of quicksort

Like always, we will try to figure out the worst case of quicksort. To begin with, we notice that after the pivot has been positioned correctly, it is not positioned in the middle of the array. In fact, its final position depends on what value it has with respect to the other elements of the array. Since it is always positioned as per its rank, its rank determines the final position. We also notice that the worst case for quicksort would be when the pivot does not cut the array at all, that is, when all the other elements are either to its left or to its right. This will happen when the pivot is the largest or the smallest element. This will happen when the highest or the lowest element is at the end of the array. So, for example, if the array is already sorted, the highest element would be at the end of the array in every step, and we will choose this element as our pivot. This gives us the counter intuitive conclusion that an array that is already sorted would be the worst case for the quicksort algorithm. An array that is sorted in the opposite direction is also one of the worst cases.

So, what is the complexity if the worst case happens? Since it is the worst case where every step is made out of two recursive calls, one of which is with an empty array and thus needing a constant time to process, and another having an array with one less element. Also, in each step, the pivot is compared with every other element, thus taking time proportional to *(n-1)* for an *n*-element step. So, we have the recursive equation for the time $T(n)$ as follows:

```
T(n) = T(n-1) + a(n-1) + b where a and b are some constants.
=> T(n) - T(n-1) = a(n-1) + b
```

Since this is valid for all values of n, we have:

```
T(n)   - T(n-1) = a(n-1) + b
T(n-1) - T(n-2) = a(n-2) + b
T(n-2) - T(n-3) = a(n-3) + b
...
T(2)   - T(1)   = a(1) + b
```

Summing both sides, we have the following:

```
T(n) - T(1) = a (1+2+3+...+(n-1)) + (n-1)b
=> T(n) - T(1) = an(n-1)/2 + (n-1)b
=> T(n) = an(n-1)/2 + (n-1)b + T(1)
=> T(n) = O(n²)
```

This is not very good. It is still $O(n^2)$. Is it really an efficient algorithm? Well, to answer that, we need to consider the average case. The average case is the probabilistically weighted average of the complexities for all possible inputs. This is quite complicated. So, we will use something that we can call a typical case, which is sort of the complexity of the usual case. So, what would happen in a typical randomly unsorted array, that is, where the input array is arranged quite randomly? The rank of the pivot will be equally likely to be any value from 1 to n, where n is the length of the array. So, it will sort of split the array near the middle in general. So, what is the complexity if we do manage to cut the array in halves? Let's find out:

```
T(n) = 2T((n-1)/2) + a(n-1) + b
```

This is a little difficult to solve, so we take `n/2` instead of `(n-1)/2`, which can only increase the estimate of complexity. So, we have the following:

```
T(n) = 2T(n/2) + a(n-1) + b
```

Let m = lg n and S(m) = T(n), and hence, n = 2m. So, we have this:

```
S(m) = 2S(m-1) + a 2ᵐ + (b-a)
```

Since this is valid for all `m`, we can apply the same formula for `S(m-1)` as well. So, we have the following:

```
S(m) = 2(2S(m-2) + a 2ᵐ⁻¹ + (b-a)) + a 2ᵐ + (b-a)
=> S(m) = 4 S(m-2) + a (2ᵐ + 2ᵐ) + (b-a)(2+1)
```

Proceeding similarly, we have this:

```
S(m) = 8 S(m-3) + a (2ᵐ + 2ᵐ  + 2ᵐ) + (b-a)(4+2+1)
...
S(m) = 2ᵐ S(0) + a (2ᵐ + 2ᵐ  + 2ᵐ + 2ᵐ) + (b-a)(2ᵐ⁻¹+ 2ᵐ⁻²+ ... + 2+1)
=>S(m) = 2ᵐ S(0) + a m . 2ᵐ+ (b-a) (2ᵐ - 1)
=> T(n) = nT(1) + a . (lg n) . n + (b-a) (n-1)
=> T(n) =  θ(n lg n)
```

This is pretty good. In fact, this is way better than the quadratic complexity we saw in the previous chapter. In fact, *n lg n* grows so slow that *n lg n* = *O(na)* for any a greater than *1*. That is to say that the function *n1.000000001* grows faster than *n lg n*. So, we have found an algorithm that performs quite well in most cases. Remember that the worst case for quicksort is still *O(n2)*. We will try to address this problem in the next subsection.

Random pivot selection in quicksort

The problem with quicksort is that it performs really badly if the array is already sorted or sorted in the reverse direction. This is because we would be always choosing the pivot to be the smallest or the largest element of the array. If we can avoid that, we can avoid the worst case time as well. Ideally, we want to select the pivot that is the median of all the elements of the array, that is, the middle element when the array is sorted. But it is not possible to compute the median efficiently enough. One trick is to choose an element randomly among all the elements and use it as a pivot. So, in each step, we randomly choose an element and swap it with the end element. After this, we can perform the quicksort as we did earlier. So, we update the quicksort method as follows:

```
public static <E> void quicksort(E[] array, int start, int end,
Comparator<E> comparator) {
    if (end - start <= 0) {
        return;
    }
    int pivotIndex = (int)((end-start)*Math.random()) + start;
    swap(array, pivotIndex, end-1);
    //let's find the pivot.
    int i = start;
    int j = end - 1;
    boolean movingI = true;
    while (i < j) {
        if (comparator.compare(array[i], array[j]) > 0) {
            swap(array, i, j);
            movingI = !movingI;
        } else {
            if (movingI) {
                i++;
            } else {
                j--;
            }
        }
    }
    quicksort(array, start, i, comparator);
    quicksort(array, i + 1, end, comparator);
}
```

Even now we can be very unlucky and pick the end element every time, but it is very unlikely to happen. In this case, we will almost always get an $n\ lg\ n$ complexity, as desired.

mergesort

In the previous section, we tried to divide the array in such a way that when we sort each part, the entire array is sorted. We faced the problem that when we try to do that, the two parts are not equal in size causing the algorithm to sometimes take a quadratic amount of time. What if, instead of trying to divide the array in a way that sorting the parts would sort the whole, we just divide the array into two equal halves? Of course then, sorting the parts will not sort the entire array. However, if we have two array parts sorted on their own, can we merge them together to produce a sorted array as a whole? If we can do this efficiently enough, we would have an algorithm guaranteed to be efficient. As it turns out, it is possible. But we need to think about where the merged array will be stored. Since the values are being copied from the source array, the result needs to be stored in a separate place. So, we will need another storage of equal size for mergesort.

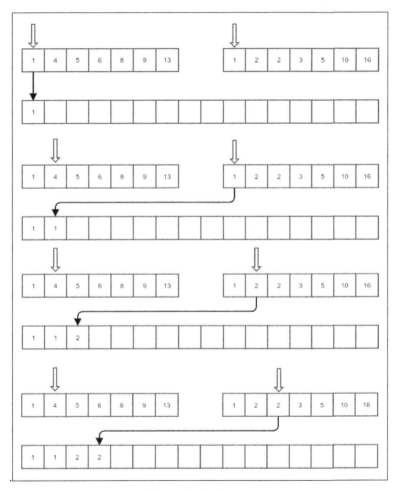

Merge of sorted arrays

The preceding figure shows a part of the merging operation. We keep the current position of each of the arrays. In each step, we compare the values in the current positions in both the input sorted arrays.

We copy whichever of them is smaller to the target location and increment the corresponding current position. We keep doing this until we finish one of the arrays, after which the elements of the other array can just be copied over. The following shows the code for the merge operation. One thing to note is that, since the merge will be used for a mergesort, it presumes both the input arrays to be the same array with different indexes and the target arrays to have the same size. The source has three indexes: start, mid, and end. It is assumed that the source parts are residing side by side in the source array. The variable start points to the start of the first part. The integer mid stores the index of the start of the second part and also acts as the end of the first part, as the parts are contiguous. Finally, the end variable stores the end of the second array:

```
private static <E> void merge(E[] array, int start, int mid,
    int end, E[] targetArray, Comparator<E> comparator) {
    int i = start;
    int j = mid;
    int k = start;
    while (k < end) {
```

The first two cases are for the time when one of the source arrays has been exhausted:

```
if (i == mid) {
    targetArray[k] = array[j];
    j++;
} else if (j == end) {
    targetArray[k] = array[i];
    i++;
}
```

If none of the arrays are exhausted, copy from the correct array:

```
else if (comparator.compare(array[i], array[j]) > 0) {
    targetArray[k] = array[j];
    j++;
} else {
    targetArray[k] = array[i];
    i++;
}
```

Finally, the target location must also be incremented:

```
            k++;
        }
    }
```

With this `merge` function available to us, we can now proceed to do the mergesort. It involves the following steps:

1. Divide the array into two equal parts.

2. Mergesort the parts.

3. Merge the sorted parts into a full sorted array.

Of course, we do not need to do anything for an array with zero or one element. So, that will be our exit case:

```
public static <E> void mergeSort(E[] sourceArray, int start,
    int end, E[] tempArray, Comparator<E> comparator) {
```

Just return to the calling function for an array of zero or one element. This is our base case:

```
        if (start >= end - 1) {
            return;
        }
```

For any array of size bigger than 1, divide the array into two halves–start to mid and mid to end. Then merge-sort them separately, and then merge the two sorted subarrays to a combined sorted array in `tempArray`, which is an auxiliary space that we are using:

```
        int mid = (start + end) / 2;
        mergeSort(sourceArray, start, mid, tempArray, comparator);
        mergeSort(sourceArray, mid, end, tempArray, comparator);
        merge(sourceArray, start, mid, end, tempArray, comparator);
```

Finally, copy the contents of `tempArray` to `sourceArray` so that the source is now sorted:

```
System.arraycopy(tempArray, start, sourceArray, start,
    end - start);
}
```

The complexity of mergesort

Let's start from the complexity of the merge operation. The merge operation is not recursive. In every step, it increments either i or j. When both these variables reach the end of the respective arrays, the merge ends. The comparison happens at most once per any of these increments. This means that there are at most as many comparisons as there are elements in both the sub-arrays combined. The copying of the contents of `tempArray` to `sourceArray` also, of course, takes operations proportional to the number of elements in `tempArray`, which is the same as the number of elements in the `sourceArray`. So, the number of operations in each step is proportional to *n*, apart from the recursive call. The recursive call works on both parts of the array, which are themselves half the size of the entire array. Thus, if *T(n)* is the time taken, we have the following:

```
T(n) = 2T(n/2) + an + b
```

Here, a and b are constants.

This is the same equation as the one obtained for the typical case of the quicksort algorithm, and we know that the solution gives us $T(n) = \theta(n\ lg\ n)$. This is the estimate for the both the average case and the worst case because, in both cases, the array will always be divided into two equal halves irrespective of the contents of the array. In fact, the worst case is when all the copying also requires a comparison, which is the case we considered.

In the best case, one of the arrays will have all its elements copied before even the first element of the second array is copied, thus requiring only half as many comparisons. But this case gives the same complexity of $T(n) = \theta(n\ lg\ n)$. So, irrespective of the actual contents of the array we started with, mergesort will always have the same asymptotic complexity.

Avoiding the copying of tempArray

In our rather simplistic example, we first merged the subarrays into tempArray, and then we copied it back to sourceArray. Can the copying be avoided? Can we use tempArray itself as the result of the merge? It turns out that we can. In this case, both sourceArray and tempArray would be used rather symmetrically, the only difference being that sourceArray holds the original input array. Otherwise, they are two pre-allocated arrays of the same size. However, the code will get a little more complicated.

Let us first consider what would happen if we do not copy the contents of tempArray to sourceArray and try to use tempArray itself as the content of the sorted array. Then, in each step, sourceArray and tempArray would need to be swapped, that is, tempArray would become sourceArray and vice versa. Since in each step, tempArray and sourceArray are getting swapped, the actual array that holds the result depends on whether the number of steps required to sort the array is odd or even.

Now, if the array we started with had a number of elements equal to an exact integral power of 2, the source array could always be divided into two sub-arrays of the exact same size. This means, the number of steps required to sort each of these sub-arrays would be exactly the same. This means that the actual array that holds the sorted result would be the same after sorting either sub-array. However, in reality, the number of elements in the array is not an exact power of 2 most of the time, and hence, one sub-array is a little bigger than the other. This results in a different number of steps being required to sort either sub-array, causing them to potentially store the resultant sorted array in different arrays. We have to consider these cases as well. So, when the result of sorting either sub-array is stored in the same array, we store the output of the merge in the other array. If not, we always store the output of the merge in the array that holds the result of sorting the second part of the array.

First, we change the merge function to handle two different arrays holding the contents of two different inputs:

```
private static <E> void merge(E[] arrayL, E[] arrayR,
int start, int mid, int end, E[] targetArray,
Comparator<E> comparator) {
    int i = start;
    int j = mid;
    int k = start;
    while (k < end) {
        if (i == mid) {
            targetArray[k] = arrayR[j];
```

```
                j++;
            } else if (j == end) {
                targetArray[k] = arrayL[i];
                i++;
            } else if (comparator.compare(arrayL[i], arrayR[j]) > 0) {
                targetArray[k] = arrayR[j];
                j++;
            } else {
                targetArray[k] = arrayL[i];
                i++;
            }
            k++;
        }
    }
```

With this `merge` function available, we write our efficient mergesort in the following way. Note that we need some way to inform the calling function about which pre-allocated array contains the result, so we return that array:

```
public static <E> E[] mergeSortNoCopy(E[] sourceArray, int start,
int end, E[] tempArray, Comparator<E> comparator) {
    if (start >= end - 1) {
        return sourceArray;
    }
```

First, split and merge-sort the sub-arrays as usual:

```
    int mid = (start + end) / 2;
    E[] sortedPart1 =
    mergeSortNoCopy(sourceArray, start, mid, tempArray,
                comparator);
    E[] sortedPart2 =
    mergeSortNoCopy(sourceArray, mid, end, tempArray,
                comparator);
```

If both the sorted sub-arrays are stored in the same pre-allocated array, use the other pre-allocated array to store the result of the merge:

```
    if (sortedPart2 == sortedPart1) {
        if (sortedPart1 == sourceArray) {
            merge(sortedPart1, sortedPart2, start, mid, end,
                tempArray, comparator);
```

```
            return tempArray;
        } else {
            merge(sortedPart1, sortedPart2, start, mid, end,
            sourceArray, comparator);
            return sourceArray;
        }
    } else {
```

In this case, we store the result in `sortedPart2` because it has the first portion empty:

```
        merge(sortedPart1, sortedPart2, start, mid, end,
            sortedPart2, comparator);
        return sortedPart2;
    }
}
```

Now we can use this mergesort as follows:

```
Integer[] anotherArray = new Integer[array.length];
array = mergeSortNoCopy(array, 0, array.length, anotherArray,
(a, b)->a-b);
System.out.println(Arrays.toString(array));
```

Here is the output:

```
[1, 1, 1, 2, 2, 3, 3, 4, 5, 10, 24, 30, 33, 35, 35, 53, 67, 78]
```

Note that this time, we had to ensure that we use the output returned by the method as, in some cases, `anotherArray` may contain the final sorted values. The efficient no-copy version of the mergesort does not have any asymptotic performance improvement, but it improves the time by a constant. This is something worth doing.

Complexity of any comparison-based sorting

Now that we have seen two algorithms for sorting that are more efficient than the ones described in the previous chapter, how do we know that they are as efficient as a sorting can be? Can we make algorithms that are even faster? We will see in this section that we have reached our asymptotic limit of efficiency, that is, a comparison-based sorting will have a minimum time complexity of $\theta(m\ lg\ m)$, where m is the number of elements.

Suppose we start with an array of *m* elements. For the time being, let's assume they are all distinct. After all, if such an array is a possible input, we need to consider this case as well. The number of different arrangements possible with these elements is *m!*. One of these arrangements is the correct sorted one. Any algorithm that will sort this array using comparison will have to be able to distinguish this particular arrangement from all others using only comparison between pairs of elements. Any comparison divides the arrangements into two sets–one that causes an inversion as per the comparison between those two exact values and one that does not. This is to say that given any two values *a* and *b* from the arrays, a comparison that returns *a<b* will divide the set of arrangements into two partitions; the first set will contain all the arrangements where *b* comes before *a*, and the second set will contain all the arrangements where *a* comes before *b*. The sorted arrangement is, of course, a member of the second set. Any algorithm that sorts based on comparisons will have to do enough of them to pin down on the single correct arrangement, that is, the sorted arrangement. Basically, it will first perform a comparison, choose the correct subset, then perform another comparison and choose the correct subset of the subset, and so on, until it reaches a set of arrangements containing just one arrangement. This particular arrangement is the sorted version of the array. What is the minimum number of comparisons that are required to find one particular arrangement out of *m!* arrangements? This is the same as asking how many times you have to halve a set of *m!* elements to reach a set of only one element. It is, of course, *lg (m!)*. This is a rough estimation; in fact, the number of comparisons required would be a bit more than this because the two subsets that each comparison creates may not be equal in size. But we know that the number of comparisons required is *lg (m!)* at the minimum.

Now, how much is *lg m!*? Well, it is *(ln (m!)) (lg e)*, where *ln (x)* is the natural logarithm of *x*. We will find a simpler asymptotic complexity for the function *ln(m!)*. It requires a little bit of calculus.

Let's look at the following figure:

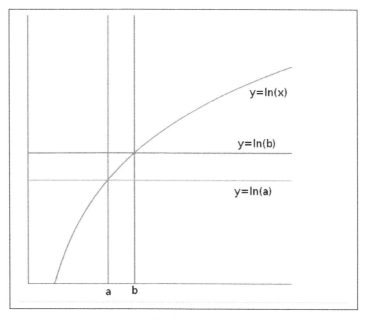

Area under the curve y = ln x.

The diagram shows some plots. We know that the integral measures the area under the curve of a function. Now, the area under the curve *y=ln b* between *a* and *b* is *(b-a) ln b*, and the area under the curve *y=ln a* is *(b-a) ln a*. The area under the curve *y=lg x* in the same interval is as follows:

$$\int_a^b \ln x \, dx$$

From the graph in the preceding figure, the following is clear:

$$(b-a)\ln(a) < \int_a^b \ln x \, dx < (b-a)\ln b$$

In particular, having *b=a+1*, we get the following:

$$\ln(a) < \int_{a}^{a+1} \ln x \, dx < \ln(a+1)$$

So, we set *a = 1* and move up to *a = m-1*, to get the following set of inequalities:

$$\ln(1) < \int_{1}^{2} \ln x \, dx < \ln(2)$$

$$\ln(2) < \int_{2}^{3} \ln x \, dx < \ln(3)$$

$$\ln(3) < \int_{3}^{4} \ln x \, dx < \ln(4)$$

$$\ln(4) < \int_{4}^{5} \ln x \, dx < \ln(5)$$

$$\dots$$

$$\ln(m-1) < \int_{m-1}^{m} \ln x \, dx < \ln(m)$$

Adding respective sides, we get the following:

$$\ln((m-1)!) < \int_{1}^{m} \ln x \, dx < \ln(m!)$$

Now, of course we know the following:

$$\int_{1}^{m} \ln x \, dx = \left[x \ln x - x\right]_{1}^{m} = m \ln m - (m-1)$$

So, we have the following inequalities:

$$\ln((m-1)!) < m \ln m - (m-1) < \ln(m!)$$

In the left inequality, if we put m instead of *m-1*, we will have the following:

$$\ln\left(m!\right) < \left(m+1\right)\ln\left(m+1\right) - m$$

This, combined with the right inequality, gives the following relations:

$$m\ln m - \left(m-1\right) < \ln\left(m!\right) < \left(m+1\right)\ln\left(m+1\right) - m$$

This gives a pretty good upper bound and lower bound on the value of *ln(m!)*. Both the upper bound and lower bound are $\theta(m\ ln\ m)$. So, we can conclude that *ln(m!)* = $\theta(m\ ln\ m)$. This means that *lg(m!)* = *(ln (m!))(lg e)* is also $\theta(m\ ln\ m) = \theta(m\ lg\ m)$ because *lg(m)* = *(ln m)(lg e)*.

So, the minimum time complexity of a comparison-based sorting algorithm would have to be at least $\theta(m\ lg\ m)$ just because of the minimum number of comparisons that would be needed to do this. Therefore, mergesort and the typical case of quicksort are asymptotically optimal.

The stability of a sorting algorithm

The stability of a sorting algorithm is the property that the elements that compare to be equal preserve their original order after sorting. For example, if we have an array of objects containing the ID number and the age of some people and we want to sort them in increasing order of age, a stable sorting algorithm will preserve the original order of the people with the same age. This can be helpful if we are trying to sort multiple times. For example, if we want the IDs to be in increasing order for people with the same age, we can first sort the array by ID and then sort it again by age. If the sorting algorithm is stable, it will ensure that the final sorted array is in increasing order of age, and for the same age, it is in increasing order of ID. Of course, this effect can also be achieved by having a more complex comparison with a single sorting operation. Quicksort is not stable, but mergesort is. It is easy to see why mergesort is stable. During merging, we preserve the order, that is, values from the left half precede values from the right half when they compare as equal.

Summary

In this chapter, we explored two efficient sorting algorithms. The basic principle, in both cases, was to divide the array and to sort the parts separately. If we ensure that sorting the parts will cause the entire array to be sorted by readjusting the elements, it is quicksort. If we just divide the array into two equal parts first and–after sorting each part–merge the results to cause the entire array to be sorted, it is a mergesort. This way of dividing the input into smaller parts, solving the problem for the smaller parts and then combining the results to find the solution for the entire problem is a common pattern in solving computational problems, and it is called the divide and conquer pattern.

We have also seen an asymptotic lower bound for any sorting algorithm that works using comparisons. Both quicksort and mergesort achieve this lower bound and hence, are asymptotically optimal. In the next chapter, we will move to a different kind of data structures called trees.

7
Concepts of Tree

We have already seen data structures such as linked list and array. They represent data stored in a linear fashion. In this chapter, we will discuss a new kind of data structure, called a tree. A tree is a generalization of a linked list. While a linked list node has one reference to the next node, a tree node has references to possibly more than one next node. These next nodes are called children of the node, and the node holding the references to the children is called a parent node. In this chapter, we will explore the following topics:

- Concept of a tree as a data structure
- Concept of a tree as an ADT
- Binary trees
- Different kinds of tree traversals
- Tree search algorithms

So, let's jump into it right away.

A tree data structure

A tree data structure looks very much like a real tree, the kind you can see in a garden or by the roadside. If we look at a tree, we will see that it has a root that makes the stem outside of the ground. The stem splits into branches, and at the end of the branches, we find leaves. In our tree data structure, we start from the root. The root is the node that does not have any parent. The children can be thought of as being attached to the stem by lines just like the branches of a real tree. At the end, we find some nodes that have no children and hence are called leaves. The following figure shows an example of a tree:

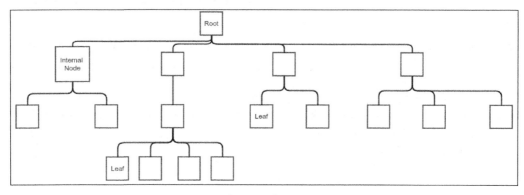

An example tree

Note that the tree is drawn upside down. The root is at the top and the leaves are below. This is just a convention that most people prefer. Think of this as the reflection of a tree on water.

A tree can be represented in many ways, but we will get started with the idea of generalization of a **linked** list. In the case of a linked list, a node stores a single reference that points to the next node. In a tree, a node needs to store the references to all its children. Multiple children could be stored in an array, but since we have access to our own class LinkedList, we will use that. We will use our non-functional version of the linked list because our first tree will be non-functional and will allow modification.

We start with the following class:

```
public class Tree<E> {
    public static class Node<E>{
        private E value;
        private LinkedList<Node<E>> children;
        private Tree<E> hostTree;
        private Node<E> parent;
```

```
public LinkedList<Node<E>> getChildren() {
    return children;
}

public E getValue() {
    return value;
}

private Node(LinkedList<Node<E>> children, Tree<E> hostTree,
E value, Node<E> parent) {
    this.children = children;
    this.hostTree = hostTree;
    this.value = value;
    this.parent = parent;
}
}

...
}
```

We have defined our Node class as an inner class. Apart from remembering the value it stores inside and the list of children, it also stores the parent and the tree that it is a member of. Once we create an instance of a tree, we must be able to store a node in it. The node that does not have a parent is called the root of the tree. So, we add an addRoot method to add a root to the tree. The tree, itself, only has to store the reference of the root node as all the other nodes can be reached from this node by traversing the references:

```
private Node<E> root;
```

```
public void addRoot(E value){
    if(root == null){
        root = new Node<>(new LinkedList<>(), this, value, null );
    }else{
        throw new IllegalStateException(
            "Trying to add new node to a non empty tree");
    }
}
```

Note that we test whether the tree already has a root node, in which case, we throw an exception.

Okay, now that we have a way of adding a root node, we need to have a method for adding nodes as we like. The method takes a parent node and a value in order to add a new node. This method will return the newly added node so that we keep adding more nodes as its children:

```
public Node<E> addNode(Node<E> parent, E value){
    if(parent==null){
        throw new NullPointerException("Cannot add child
        to null parent");
    }else if(parent.hostTree != this){
        throw new IllegalArgumentException(
            "Parent node not a part of this tree");
    }else{
        Node<E> newNode = new Node<>(new LinkedList<>(),
                                    this, value, parent);
        parent.getChildren().appendLast(newNode);
        return newNode;
    }
}
```

In the preceding code, we first check whether the parent is null or whether the parent is the node of a different tree instance. In either case, an exception must be thrown. Otherwise, we just add a new node as the child of the parent node passed as an argument.

But wait a second! How would we ever be able to pass a parent node if we do not have a reference to the root node in the calling code? So, we add a method, getRoot, to access the root node of the Tree:

```
public Node<E> getRoot() {
    return root;
}
```

Okay, now let's create a Tree instance:

```
public static void main(String [] args){
    Tree<Integer> tree = new Tree<>();
    tree.addRoot(1);
    Node<Integer> node1 = tree.getRoot();
    Node<Integer> node2 = tree.addNode(node1, 5);
    Node<Integer> node3 = tree.addNode(node1, 1);
    Node<Integer> node4 = tree.addNode(node2, 2);
    Node<Integer> node5 = tree.addNode(node2, 5);
    Node<Integer> node6 = tree.addNode(node2, 9);
```

```
Node<Integer> node7 = tree.addNode(node3, 6);
Node<Integer> node8 = tree.addNode(node3, 2);
Node<Integer> node9 = tree.addNode(node5, 5);
Node<Integer> node10 = tree.addNode(node6, 9);
Node<Integer> node11 = tree.addNode(node6, 6);
}
```

The code is self-explanatory. We just create a tree by adding the nodes one by one. But how do we see what the tree looks like? For that, we will have to learn about the traversal of a tree. The preceding code will create the tree shown in the following figure:

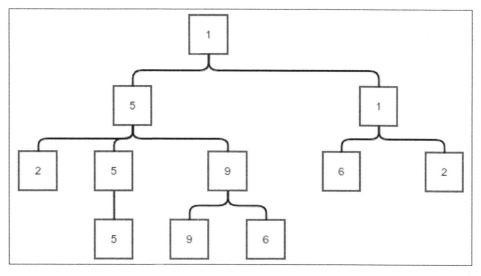

Example tree

The traversal of a tree

Tree traversal is an algorithm to visit or to process all nodes of a tree exactly once. This obviously involves recursively looking into the children of the nodes. The order in which the children are processed depends on the particular algorithm we use. The simplest algorithm for traversing a tree is the depth-first traversal.

The depth-first traversal

In the depth-first traversal, we process every child of a node recursively and wait for it to finish with all its descendants before proceeding to the next child. To understand the depth-first search, we have to understand what a subtree is. A subtree is a node with all its descendants up to the leaves. The following figure shows some examples of subtrees.

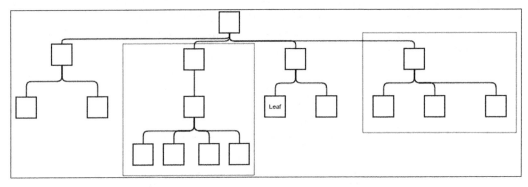

Examplesubtrees

Now, if you think about it, each node not only stores references to the children, but also sort of holds references to entire subtrees rooted at the child nodes. So, the depth-first traversal algorithm is nothing but the following steps:

1. Process the value in the current node.

2. For each child node of the current node, recursively traverse the entire subtree rooted at the child node.

The following method does exactly this:

```
protected void traverseDepthFirst(OneArgumentStatement<E> processor,
Node<E> current){
    processor.doSomething(current.value);
    current.children.forEach((n)-> traverseDepthFirst(processor, n));
}
```

The method takes a lambda and a node to traverse. All this method does is first run the lambda on the current value and then call itself recursively on each of the subtrees. Now, we can write a wrapper method without the parent node argument:

```
public void traverseDepthFirst(OneArgumentStatement<E> processor){
    traverseDepthFirst(processor, getRoot());
}
```

It is still not clear, though, why this way of traversing is called a depth-first traversal. If you think about the order in which the nodes are processed, you can see that since the complete subtree root at any child node must be entirely processed before the next child is processed, the depth of the tree will be covered before the breadth.

We have used a recursive function to do our depth-first search. Alternatively, we can use a stack to do the trick:

```
public void traverseDepthFirstUsingStack(
    OneArgumentStatement<E> processor){

    Stack<Node<E>> stack = new StackImplLinkedList<>();
    stack.push(getRoot());
    while(stack.peek()!=null){
        Node<E> current = stack.pop();
        processor.doSomething(current.value);
        current.children.forEach((n)->stack.push(n));
    }
}
```

Let's see what is happening in the preceding piece of code. We first push the root into the stack and go in a loop that continues until all the stack elements have been cleared. Every time we pop a node, we process it and push all its children into the stack. Now, since the stack is **last in first out** (**LIFO**), all these children will be popped and processed before any other node can be processed. However, the moment the first of these children is popped, its children will be pushed into the stack and would be processed before anything else is processed. This will go on until we hit the leaf nodes, which would not have any more children. This, in effect, is almost the same as the recursive version.

There is a slight difference between the outputs of this code and the recursive version, although both are indeed depth-first. However, please note that in the case of the recursive version, the child that is near the head of the linked list is processed first. In the case of the stack version, we push the children in the same order, but since the stack is LIFO, we pop the children in the reverse order. To reverse this order, we can store the list of children in the opposite order in a temporary list before pushing them into the stack, as shown in the following code:

```
public void traverseDepthFirstUsingStack(
    OneArgumentStatement<E> processor){

    Stack<Node<E>> stack = new StackImplLinkedList<>();
    stack.push(getRoot());
    while(stack.peek()!=null){
        Node<E> current = stack.pop();
```

```
            processor.doSomething(current.value);
            LinkedList<Node<E>> reverseList = new LinkedList<>();
            current.children.forEach((n)->reverseList.appendFirst(n));
            reverseList.forEach((n)->stack.push(n));
        }
    }
```

The list is reversed by storing in a temporary list, called `reverseList`, by appending the elements to its beginning. Then, the elements are pushed into the stack from `reverseList`.

The breadth-first traversal

Breadth-first traversal is the opposite of the depth-first traversal, in the sense that depth-first traversal processes children before siblings and breadth-first traversal processes the nodes of the same level before it processes any node of the succeeding level. In other words, in a breadth-first traversal, the nodes are processed level by level. This is simply achieved by taking the stack version of the depth-first traversal and replacing the stack with a queue. That is all that is needed for it:

```
public void traverseBreadthFirst(OneArgumentStatement<E> processor){
    Queue<Node<E>> queue = new QueueImplLinkedList<>();
    queue.enqueue(getRoot());
    while(queue.peek()!=null){
        Node<E> current = queue.dequeue();
        processor.doSomething(current.value);
        current.children.forEach((n)->queue.enqueue(n));
    }
}
```

Note that everything else remains exactly the same as that of the depth-first traversal. We still take one element from the queue, process its value and then enqueue the children.

To understand why the use of a queue lets us process nodes level by level, we need the following analysis:

- Root is pushed in the beginning, so root is dequeued first and processed.

- When the root is processed, the children of root, that is the nodes in level 1, get enqueued. This means the level 1 nodes would be dequeued before any further levels are dequeued.

- When any node in level 1 is dequeued next, its children, which are the nodes of level 2, will all get enqueued. However, since all the nodes in level 1 are enqueued in the previous step, the nodes of level 2 will not be dequeued before the nodes of level 1 are dequeued. When all the nodes of level 1 are dequeued and processed, all the level 2 nodes would be enqueued because they are all children of level 1 nodes.

- This means all the level 2 nodes would be dequeued and processed before any nodes of higher levels are processed. When all the level 2 nodes are already processed, all the level 3 nodes would be enqueued.

- In a similar manner, in all further levels, all the nodes in a particular level will be processed before all the nodes of the next level are processed. In other words, the nodes will be process level by level.

The tree abstract data type

Now that we have some idea of the tree, we can define the tree ADT. A tree ADT can be defined in multiple ways. We will check out two. In an imperative setting, that is, when trees are mutable, we can define a tree ADT as having the following operations:

- Get the root node
- Given a node, get its children

This is all that is required to have a model for a tree. We may also include some appropriate mutation methods.

The recursive definition for the tree ADT can be as follows:

- A tree is an ordered pair containing the following:

    ○ a value

    ○ a list of other trees, which are meant to be it's subtrees

We can develop a tree implementation in exactly the same way as it is defined in the functional tree ADT:

```
public class FunctionalTree<E> {
    private E value;
    private LinkedList<FunctionalTree<E>> children;
```

As defined in the ADT, the tree is an ordered pair of a value and a list of other trees, as follows:

```
public FunctionalTree(E value, LinkedList
                          <FunctionalTree<E>> children) {
    this.children = children;
    this.value = value;
}


public  LinkedList<FunctionalTree<E>> getChildren() {
    return children;
}


public E getValue() {
    return value;
}


public void traverseDepthFirst(OneArgumentStatement<E> processor){
    processor.doSomething(value);
    children.forEach((n)-> n.traverseDepthFirst(processor));
}


}
```

The implementation is quite simple. The depth-first traversal can be achieved using recursive calls to the children, which are indeed subtrees. A tree without any children needs to have an empty list of children. With this, we can create the functional version of the same tree that we had created for an imperative version:

```
public static void main(String [] args){
    LinkedList<FunctionalTree<Integer>> emptyList =
      LinkedList.emptyList();

    FunctionalTree<Integer> t1 = new FunctionalTree<>(5, emptyList);
    FunctionalTree<Integer> t2 = new FunctionalTree<>(9, emptyList);
    FunctionalTree<Integer> t3 = new FunctionalTree<>(6, emptyList);

    FunctionalTree<Integer> t4 = new FunctionalTree<>(2, emptyList);
    FunctionalTree<Integer> t5 = new FunctionalTree<>(5,
        emptyList.add(t1));
    FunctionalTree<Integer> t6 = new FunctionalTree<>(9,
        emptyList.add(t3).add(t2));
    FunctionalTree<Integer> t7 = new FunctionalTree<>(6, emptyList);
    FunctionalTree<Integer> t8 = new FunctionalTree<>(2, emptyList);
```

```
FunctionalTree<Integer> t9 = new FunctionalTree<>(5,
    emptyList.add(t6).add(t5).add(t4));
FunctionalTree<Integer> t10 = new FunctionalTree<>(1,
    emptyList.add(t8).add(t7));

FunctionalTree<Integer> tree = new FunctionalTree<>(1,
    emptyList.add(t10).add(t9));
```

At the end, we can do a depth-first traversal to see if it outputs the same tree as before:

```
tree.traverseDepthFirst(System.out::print);
}
```

Binary tree

A binary tree is a tree that has a maximum of two children per node. The two children can be called the left and the right child of a node. The following figure shows an example of a binary tree:

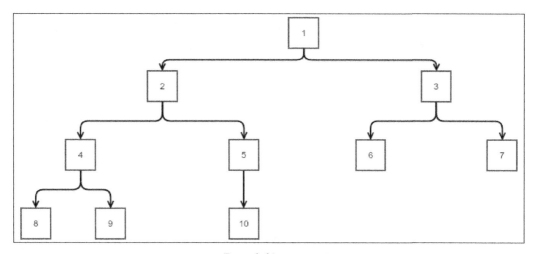

Example binary tree

This particular tree is important mostly because of its simplicity. We can create a BinaryTree class by inheriting the general tree class. However, it will be difficult to stop someone from adding more than two nodes and will take a lot of code just to perform the checks. So, instead, we will create a BinaryTree class from scratch:

```
public class BinaryTree<E>  {
```

The Node has a very obvious implementation just like the generic tree:

```java
public static class Node<E>{
    private E value;
    private Node<E> left;
    private Node<E> right;
    private Node<E> parent;
    private BinaryTree<E> containerTree;

    protected Node(Node<E> parent,
    BinaryTree<E> containerTree, E value) {
        this.value = value;
        this.parent = parent;
        this.containerTree = containerTree;
    }

    public E getValue(){
        return value;
    }

}
```

Adding the root is exactly the same as that for a generic tree, except for the fact that we don't check for the existence of the root. This is just to save space; you can implement as required:

```java
private Node<E> root;

public void addRoot(E value){
    root = new Node<>(null, this,  value);
}

public Node<E> getRoot(){
    return root;
}
```

The following method lets us add a child. It takes a Boolean parameter that is true when the child to be added is the left child and false otherwise:

```java
public Node<E> addChild(Node<E> parent, E value, boolean left){
    if(parent == null){
        throw new NullPointerException("Cannot add node to
                                        null parent");
    }else if(parent.containerTree != this){
        throw new IllegalArgumentException
                ("Parent does not belong to this tree");
    }else {
```

```
        Node<E> child = new Node<E>(parent, this, value);
        if(left){
            parent.left = child;
        }else{
            parent.right = child;
        }
        return child;
    }
}
```

We now create two wrapper methods for specifically adding either the left or the right child:

```
public Node<E> addChildLeft(Node<E> parent, E value){
    return addChild(parent, value, true);
}

public Node<E> addChildRight(Node<E> parent, E value){
    return addChild(parent, value, false);
}

}
```

Of course, the traversal algorithms for a generic tree would also work for this special case. However, for a binary tree, the depth-first traversal can be of three different types.

Types of depth-first traversals

The depth-first traversal of a binary tree can be of three types according to when the parent node is processed with respect to when the child subtrees are processed. The orders can be summarized as follows:

- Pre-order traversal:
    1. Process the parent.
    2. Process the left subtree.
    3. Process the right subtree.

- In-order traversal:
    1. Process the left subtree.
    2. Process the parent.
    3. Process the right subtree.

- Post-order traversal:

    1. Process the left subtree.

    2. Process the right subtree.

    3. Process the parent.

These different traversal types will produce a slightly different ordering when traversing:

```
public static enum DepthFirstTraversalType{
    PREORDER, INORDER, POSTORDER
}

public void traverseDepthFirst(OneArgumentStatement<E> processor,
                    Node<E> current, DepthFirstTraversalType tOrder)
{
    if(current==null){
        return;
    }
    if(tOrder == DepthFirstTraversalType.PREORDER){
        processor.doSomething(current.value);
    }
    traverseDepthFirst(processor, current.left, tOrder);
    if(tOrder == DepthFirstTraversalType.INORDER){
        processor.doSomething(current.value);
    }
    traverseDepthFirst(processor, current.right, tOrder);
    if(tOrder == DepthFirstTraversalType.POSTORDER){
        processor.doSomething(current.value);
    }
}
```

We have created an enum DepthFirstTraversalType to pass to the traverseDepthFirst method. We process the current node according to its value. Note that the only thing that changes is when the processor is called to process a node. Let's create a binary tree and see how the results differ in the case of each ordering:

```
public static void main(String [] args){
    BinaryTree<Integer> tree = new BinaryTree<>();
    tree.addRoot(1);
    Node<Integer> n1 = tree.getRoot();
    Node<Integer> n2 = tree.addChild(n1, 2, true);
    Node<Integer> n3 = tree.addChild(n1, 3, false);
    Node<Integer> n4 = tree.addChild(n2, 4, true);
    Node<Integer> n5 = tree.addChild(n2, 5, false);
    Node<Integer> n6 = tree.addChild(n3, 6, true);
    Node<Integer> n7 = tree.addChild(n3, 7, false);
```

```
Node<Integer> n8 = tree.addChild(n4, 8, true);
Node<Integer> n9 = tree.addChild(n4, 9, false);
Node<Integer> n10 = tree.addChild(n5, 10, true);

tree.traverseDepthFirst(System.out::print, tree.getRoot(),
 DepthFirstTraversalType.PREORDER);
System.out.println();

tree.traverseDepthFirst(System.out::print, tree.getRoot(),
 DepthFirstTraversalType.INORDER);
System.out.println();

tree.traverseDepthFirst(System.out::print, tree.getRoot(),
 DepthFirstTraversalType.POSTORDER);
System.out.println();
}
```

We have created the same binary tree as shown in the previous figure. The following is the output of the program. Try to relate how the positions are getting affected:

```
1 2 4 8 9 5 10 3 6 7
8 4 9 2 10 5 1 6 3 7
8 9 4 10 5 2 6 7 3 1
```

You can take a note of the following points while matching the program output:

- In the case of a pre-order traversal, in any path starting from the root to any leaf, a parent node will always be printed before any of the children.

- In the case of an in-order traversal, if we look at any path from the root to a particular leaf, whenever we move from the parent to the left child, the parent's processing is postponed. But whenever we move from the parent to the right child, the parent is immediately processed.

- In the case of a post-order traversal, all the children are processed before any parent is processed.

Non-recursive depth-first search

The depth-first search we have seen for the general tree is pre-order in the sense that the parent node is processed before any of the children are processed. So, we can use the same implementation for the pre-order traversal of a binary tree:

```
public void traversePreOrderNonRecursive(
    OneArgumentStatement<E> processor) {
    Stack<Node<E>> stack = new StackImplLinkedList<>();
    stack.push(getRoot());
```

```
        while (stack.peek()!=null){
            Node<E> current = stack.pop();
            processor.doSomething(current.value);
            if(current.right!=null)
                stack.push(current.right);
            if(current.left!=null)
                stack.push(current.left);
        }
    }
```

 We have to check whether the children are null. This is because the absence of children is expressed as null references instead of an empty list, as in the case of a generic tree.

Implementation of the in-order and post-order traversals is a bit tricky. We need to suspend processing of the parent node even when the children are expanded and pushed to the stack. We can achieve this by pushing each node twice. Once, we push it when it is first discovered due to its parent being expanded, and the next time we do it when its own children are expanded. So, we must remember which of these pushes caused it to be in the stack when it's popped. This is achieved using an additional flag, which is then wrapped up in a class called StackFrame. The in-order algorithm is as follows:

```
public void traverseInOrderNonRecursive(
    OneArgumentStatement<E> processor) {
    class StackFame{
        Node<E> node;
        boolean childrenPushed = false;

        public StackFame(Node<E> node, boolean childrenPushed) {
            this.node = node;
            this.childrenPushed = childrenPushed;
        }
    }
    Stack<StackFame> stack = new StackImplLinkedList<>();
    stack.push(new StackFame(getRoot(), false));
    while (stack.peek()!=null){
        StackFame current = stack.pop();
        if(current.childrenPushed){
            processor.doSomething(current.node.value);
        }else{
            if(current.node.right!=null)
                stack.push(new StackFame(current.node.right, false));
            stack.push(new StackFame(current.node, true));
```

```
                if(current.node.left!=null)
                    stack.push(new StackFame(current.node.left, false));
            }
        }
    }
```

Note that the stack is LIFO, so the thing that needs to be popped later must be pushed earlier. The post-order version is extremely similar:

```
public void traversePostOrderNonRecursive(OneArgumentStatement<E>
processor) {
    class StackFame{
        Node<E> node;
        boolean childrenPushed = false;

        public StackFame(Node<E> node, boolean childrenPushed) {
            this.node = node;
            this.childrenPushed = childrenPushed;
        }
    }
    Stack<StackFame> stack = new StackImplLinkedList<>();
    stack.push(new StackFame(getRoot(), false));
    while (stack.peek()!=null){
        StackFame current = stack.pop();
        if(current.childrenPushed){
            processor.doSomething(current.node.value);
        }else{
            stack.push(new StackFame(current.node, true));
            if(current.node.right!=null)
                stack.push(new StackFame(current.node.right, false));

            if(current.node.left!=null)
                stack.push(new StackFame(current.node.left, false));
        }
    }
}
```

Note that the only thing that has changed is the order of pushing the children and the parent. Now we write the following code to test these out:

```
public static void main(String [] args){
    BinaryTree<Integer> tree = new BinaryTree<>();
    tree.addRoot(1);
    Node<Integer> n1 = tree.getRoot();
    Node<Integer> n2 = tree.addChild(n1, 2, true);
    Node<Integer> n3 = tree.addChild(n1, 3, false);
```

```
Node<Integer> n4 = tree.addChild(n2, 4, true);
Node<Integer> n5 = tree.addChild(n2, 5, false);
Node<Integer> n6 = tree.addChild(n3, 6, true);
Node<Integer> n7 = tree.addChild(n3, 7, false);
Node<Integer> n8 = tree.addChild(n4, 8, true);
Node<Integer> n9 = tree.addChild(n4, 9, false);
Node<Integer> n10 = tree.addChild(n5, 10, true);

tree.traverseDepthFirst((x)->System.out.print(""+x),
    tree.getRoot(), DepthFirstTraversalType.PREORDER);
System.out.println();
tree.traverseDepthFirst((x)->System.out.print(""+x),
    tree.getRoot(), DepthFirstTraversalType.INORDER);
System.out.println();
tree.traverseDepthFirst((x)->System.out.print(""+x),
    tree.getRoot(), DepthFirstTraversalType.POSTORDER);
System.out.println();

System.out.println();
tree.traversePreOrderNonRecursive((x)->System.out.print(""+x));
System.out.println();
tree.traverseInOrderNonRecursive((x)->System.out.print(""+x));
System.out.println();
tree.traversePostOrderNonRecursive((x)->System.out.print(""+x));
System.out.println();

}
```

We preserved the recursive versions as well so that we can compare the output, which is as follows:

```
1 2 4 8 9 5 10 3 6 7
8 4 9 2 10 5 1 6 3 7
8 9 4 10 5 2 6 7 3 1

1 2 4 8 9 5 10 3 6 7
8 4 9 2 10 5 1 6 3 7
8 9 4 10 5 2 6 7 3 1
```

The first three lines are the same as the last three, showing that they produce the same result.

Summary

In this chapter, you learned what a tree is. We started out with an actual implementation and then designed an ADT out of it. You also learned about a binary tree, which is just a tree with a maximum of two children per node. We also saw different traversal algorithms for a generic tree. They are depth-first and breadth-first traversals. In the case of a binary tree, a depth-first traversal can be done in three different ways: pre-order, in-order, and post-order. Even in the case of a generic tree, we can find equivalents of the pre-order and post-order traversals for a depth-first traversal. However, it is difficult to point to any particular equivalent of an in-order traversal as it is possible to have more than two children.

In the next chapter, we will see the use of a binary tree in searching, and we will see some other ways of searching as well.

8
More About Search – Search Trees and Hash Tables

In the previous chapters, we had a look at both binary search and trees. In this chapter, we will see how they are related and how this helps us create some more flexible, searchable data structures. We will also look at a different kind of searchable structure called a hash table. The reason for using these structures is that they allow mutation and still remain searchable. Basically, we need to be able to insert and delete elements from the data structures with ease while still being able to conduct a search efficiently. These structures are relatively complicated, so we need to take a step-by-step approach toward understanding it.

We'll cover the following topics in this chapter:

- Binary search trees
- Balanced binary search trees
- Hash tables

Binary search tree

You already know what binary search is. Let's go back to the sorted array from an earlier chapter and study it again. If you think about binary search, you know you need to start from the middle of the sorted array. Depending on the value to be searched, either we return if the middle element is the search item, or move to the left or right based on whether the search value is greater than or less than the middle value. After this, we continue the same process recursively. This means the landing points in each step are quite fixed; they are the middle values. We can draw all the search paths as in the next figure. In each step, the arrows connect to the mid points of both the right half and left half, considering the current position. In the bottom part, we disassemble the array and spread out the elements while keeping the sources and targets of the arrows similar. As one can see, this gives us a binary tree. Since each edge in this tree moves from the midpoint of one step to the midpoint of the next step in the binary search, the same search can be performed in the tree by simply following its edges. This tree is quite appropriately called a binary search tree. Each level of this tree represents a step in binary search:

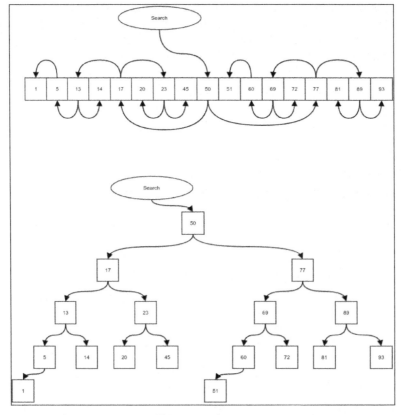

Binary search tree

Say we want to search for item number **23**. We start from the original midpoint, which is the root of the tree. The root has the value **50**. **23** is less than **50**, so we must check the left-hand side; in the case of our tree, follow the left edge. We arrive at the value **17**. **23** is greater than **17**, so we must follow the right edge and arrive at the value **23**. We just found the element we have been searching for. This algorithm can be summarized as follows:

1. Start at the root.

2. If the current element is equal to the search element, we are done.

3. If the search element is less than the current element, we follow the left edge and start again from 2.

4. If the search element is greater than the current element, we follow the right edge and start again from 2.

To code this algorithm, we must first create a binary search tree. Create a `BinarySearchTree` class extending the `BinaryTree` class and then put your algorithm inside it:

```
public class BinarySearchTree<E extends Comparable<E>> extends
BinaryTree<E> {

    protected Node<E> searchValue(E value, Node<E> root){
        if(root==null){
            return null;
        }
        int comp = root.getValue().compareTo(value);
        if(comp == 0){
            return root;
        }else if(comp>0){
            return searchValue(value, root.getLeft());
        }else{
            return  searchValue(value, root.getRight());
        }
    }
}
```

Now wrap the method so that you don't need to pass the root. This method also checks whether the tree is an empty tree and fails the search if that is the case:

```
public Node<E> searchValue(E value){
    if(getRoot()==null){
        return null;
    }else{
```

```
            return searchValue(value, getRoot());
        }
    }
    ...


}
```

So what exactly is the point of modifying an array in a binary tree? After all, are we not doing the same exact search still? Well, the point is that when we have this in a tree form, we can easily insert new values in the tree or delete some values. In the case of an array, insertion and deletion have linear time complexity and cannot go beyond the preallocated array size.

Insertion in a binary search tree

Insertion in a binary search tree is done by first searching for the value to be inserted. This either finds the element or ends the search unsuccessfully, where the new value is supposed to be if it were in that position. Once we reach this position, we can simply add the element to the tree. In the following code, we rewrite the search again because we need access to the parent node once we find the empty spot to insert our element:

```
protected Node<E> insertValue(E value, Node<E> node){
    int comp = node.getValue().compareTo(value);
    Node<E> child;
    if(comp<=0){
        child = node.getRight();
        if(child==null){
            return addChild(node,value,false);
        }else{
            return insertValue(value, child);
        }
    }else if(comp>0){
        child = node.getLeft();
        if(child==null){
            return addChild(node,value,true);
        }else{
            return insertValue(value, child);
        }
    }else{
        return null;
    }
}
```

We can wrap this up into a method that does not need a starting node. It also makes sure that when we insert into an empty tree, we just add a root:

```
public Node<E> insertValue(E value){
    if(getRoot()==null){
        addRoot(value);
        return getRoot();
    }else{
        return insertValue(value, getRoot());
    }
}
```

Suppose in our earlier tree, we want to insert the value **21**. The following figure shows the search path using arrows and how the new value is inserted:

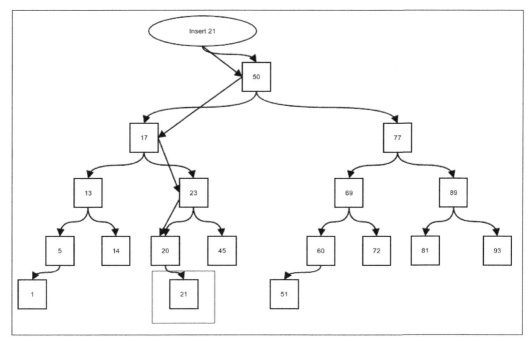

Insertion of a new value into a binary tree

Now that we have the means to insert elements in the tree, we can build the tree simply by a successive insertion. The following code creates a random tree with 20 elements and then does an in-order traversal of it:

```
BinarySearchTree<Integer> tree = new BinarySearchTree<>();
for(int i=0;i<20;i++){
    int value = (int) (100*Math.random());
```

```
        tree.insertValue(value);
    }
    tree.traverseDepthFirst((x)->System.out.print(""+x),
        tree.getRoot(), DepthFirstTraversalType.INORDER);
```

If you run the preceding code, you will always find that the elements are sorted. Why is this the case? We will see this in the next section.

What to do if the element inserted is the same as the element already present in the search tree? It depends on that particular application. Generally, since we search by value, we don't want duplicate copies of the same value. For simplicity, we will not insert a value if it is already there.

Invariant of a binary search tree

An invariant is a property that stays the same irrespective of the modifications made in the structure it is related to. An in-order traversal of a binary search tree will always result in the traversal of the elements in a sorted order. To understand why this happens, let's consider another invariant of a binary tree: all descendants of the left child of a node have a value less than or equal to the value of the node, and all descendants of the right child of a node have a value greater than the value of the node. It is understandable why this is true if you think about how we formed the binary search tree using the binary search algorithm. This is why when we see an element bigger than our search value, we always move to the left child. This is because all the values that are descendants of the right child are bigger than the left child so there is no point investing time in checking them. We will use this to establish that an in-order traversal of a binary search tree will traverse elements in a sorted order of the values in the nodes.

We will use induction to argue for this. Suppose we have a tree with only one node. In this case, any traversal could be easily sorted. Now let's consider a tree with only three elements, as shown in the following figure:

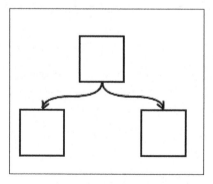

A binary search tree with three nodes

An in-order traversal of this tree will first process the left child, then the parent, and finally, the right child. Since the search tree guarantees that the left child has a value that is less than or equal to the parent and the right child has a value greater than or equal to the value of the parent, the traversal is sorted.

Now let's consider our general case. Suppose this invariant we discussed is true for trees with maximum *h-levels*. We will prove that, in such a case, it is also true for trees with maximum *h+1* levels. We will consider a general search tree, as shown in the following figure:

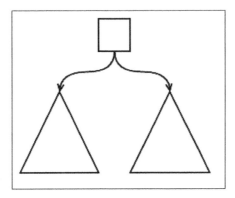

A general binary search tree

The triangles represent subtrees with maximum *n* levels. We assume that the invariant holds true for subtrees. Now, an in-order traversal would first traverse the left subtree in sorted order, then the parent, and finally, the right subtree in the same order. The sorted order traversal of the subtrees is implied by the assumption that the invariant holds true for these subtrees. This will result in the order *[traversal of left descendants in sorted order][traversal of parents][traversal of right descendants in sorted order]*. Since the left descendants are all less than or equal to the parent and right descendants are all greater than or equal to the parent, the order mentioned is actually a sorted order. So a tree of the maximum level *h+1* can be drawn, as shown in the preceding figure, with each sub-tree having *n* levels maximum. If this the case and the invariant is true for all trees with level *h*, it must also be true for trees with level *h+1*.

We already know that the invariant is true for trees with maximum level 1 and 2. However, it must be true for trees with maximum level 3 as well. This implies it must be true for trees with maximum level 4 and so on up to infinity. This proves that the invariant is true for all *h* and is universally true.

Deletion of an element from a binary search tree

We are interested in all the modifications of a binary search tree where the resultant tree will remain a valid binary search tree. Other than insertion, we need to be able to carry out deletion as well. That is to say, we need to be able to remove an existing value from the tree:

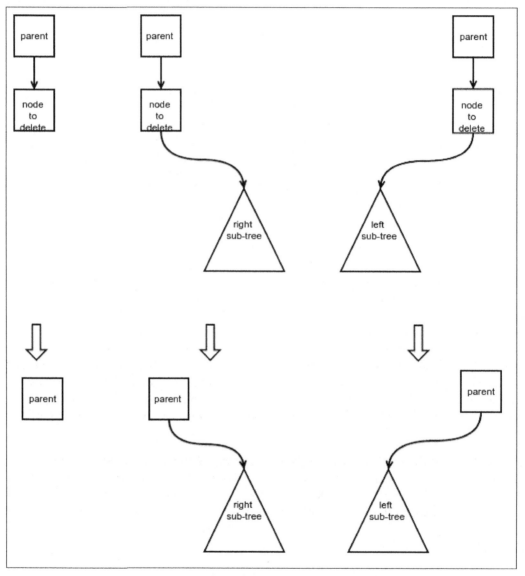

Three simple cases of deletion of nodes

The main concern is to know what to do with the children of the deleted node. We don't want to lose those values from the tree, and we still want to make sure the tree remains a search tree. There are four different cases we need to consider. The relatively easier three cases are shown in the preceding figure. Here's a brief description of these cases:

- The first case is where there is no child. This is the easiest case; we just delete the node.

- The second case is where there is only a right subtree. In this case, the subtree can take the place of the deleted node.

- The third case is very similar to the second case, except it is about the left subtree.

The fourth case is, of course, when both the children are present for the node to be deleted. In this case, none of the children can take the place of the node that is to be deleted as the other one would also need to be attached somewhere. We resolve this by replacing the node that needs to be deleted by another node that can be a valid parent of both the children. This node is the least node of the right subtree. Why is this the case? It is because if we delete this node from the right subtree, the remaining nodes of the right subtree would be greater than or equal to this node. And this node is also, of course, greater than all the nodes of the left subtree. This makes this node a valid parent.

The next question is this: what is the least node in the right subtree? Remember that when we move to the left child of a node, we always get a value that is less than or equal to the current node. Hence, we must keep traversing left until we find no more left child. If we do this, we will reach the least node eventually. The least node of any subtree cannot have any left child, so it can be deleted using the first case or the second case of deletion. The delete operation of the fourth case is thus used to:

- Copy the value of the least node in the right subtree to the node to be deleted

- Delete the least node in the right subtree

To write the deletion code, we need to first add a few methods to our `BinaryTree` class, which is meant for deleting nodes and rewriting node values. The method `deleteNodeWithSubtree` simply deletes a node along with all its descendants. It simply forgets about all the descendants. It also has certain checks to confirm the validity of the input. Deletion of a root, as usual, must be handled separately:

```
public void deleteNodeWithSubtree(Node<E> node){
    if(node == null){
        throw new NullPointerException("Cannot delete to
            null parent");
    }else if(node.containerTree != this){
```

```
            throw new IllegalArgumentException(
                "Node does not belong to this tree");
        }else {
            if(node==getRoot()){
                root=null;
                return;
            }else{
                Node<E> partent = node.getParent();
                if(partent.getLeft()==node){
                    partent.left = null;
                }else{
                    partent.right = null;
                }
            }
        }
    }
}
```

Now we add another method to the `BinaryTree` class for rewriting the value in a node. We don't allow this class to use public methods in the `node` class to maintain encapsulation:

```
public void setValue(Node<E> node, E value){
    if(node == null){
        throw new NullPointerException("Cannot add node to
            null parent");
    }else if(node.containerTree != this){
        throw new IllegalArgumentException(
                "Parent does not belong to this tree");
    }else {
        node.value = value;
    }
}
```

The preceding code is self-explanatory. Finally, we write a method to replace a node's child with another node from the same tree. This is useful for cases 2 and 3:

```
public Node<E> setChild(Node<E> parent, Node<E> child,
    boolean left){
    if(parent == null){
        throw new NullPointerException("Cannot set node
            to null parent");
    }else if(parent.containerTree != this){
        throw new IllegalArgumentException(
            "Parent does not belong to this tree");
    }else {
        if(left){
```

```
                        parent.left = child;
                    }else{
                        parent.right = child;
                    }
                    if(child!=null) {
                        child.parent = parent;
                    }
                    return child;
                }
            }
```

Finally, we add a method to `BinarySearchTree` to find the least node in the subtree. We walk keeping to the left until there is no more child on the left-hand side:

```
protected Node<E> getLeftMost(Node<E> node){
    if(node==null){
        return null;
    }else if(node.getLeft()==null){
        return node;
    }else{
        return getLeftMost(node.getLeft());
    }
}
```

Now we can implement our deletion algorithm. First, we create a `deleteNode` method that deletes a node. We can then use this method to delete a value:

```
private Node<E> deleteNode(Node<E> nodeToBeDeleted) {

    boolean direction;
    if(nodeToBeDeleted.getParent()!=null
        && nodeToBeDeleted.getParent().getLeft()==nodeToBeDeleted){
        direction = true;
    }else{
        direction = false;
    }
```

Case 1: There are no children. In this case, we can simply delete the node:

```
if(nodeToBeDeleted.getLeft()==null &&
    nodeToBeDeleted.getRight()==null){
    deleteNodeWithSubtree(nodeToBeDeleted);
    return nodeToBeDeleted;
}
```

Case 2: There is only a right child. The right child can take the place of the deleted node:

```
else if(nodeToBeDeleted.getLeft()==null){
    if(nodeToBeDeleted.getParent() == null){
        root = nodeToBeDeleted.getRight();
    }else {
        setChild(nodeToBeDeleted.getParent(),
        nodeToBeDeleted.getRight(), direction);
    }
     return nodeToBeDeleted;
}
```

Case 3: There is only a left child. The left child can take the place of the deleted node:

```
else if(nodeToBeDeleted.getRight()==null){
    if(nodeToBeDeleted.getParent() == null){
        root = nodeToBeDeleted.getLeft();
    }else {
        setChild(nodeToBeDeleted.getParent(),
        nodeToBeDeleted.getLeft(), direction);
    }
    return nodeToBeDeleted;
}
```

Case 4: Both left child and right child are present. In this case, first we copy the value of the leftmost child in the right subtree (or the successor) to the node that needs to be deleted. Once we do this, we delete the leftmost child in the right subtree:

```
else{
  Node<E> nodeToBeReplaced = getLeftMost(
    nodeToBeDeleted.getRight());
    setValue(nodeToBeDeleted, nodeToBeReplaced.getValue());
    deleteNode(nodeToBeReplaced);
    return nodeToBeReplaced;
}
}
```

The process of deleting a node turned out to be a little more complicated, but it is not difficult. In the next section, we will discuss the complexity of the operations of a binary search tree.

Complexity of the binary search tree operations

The first operation we will consider is the search operation. It starts at the root and moves down one level every time we move from one node to either of its children. The maximum number of edges we have to traverse during the search operation must be equivalent to the maximum height of the tree—that is, the maximum distance between any node and root. If the height of the tree is h, then the complexity of search is $O(h)$.

Now what is the relation between the number of nodes n of a tree and the height h of a tree? It really depends on how the tree is built. Any level would require at least one node in it, so in the worst case scenario, $h = n$ and the search complexity is $O(n)$. What is our best case? Or rather, what do we want h to be in relation to n? In other words, what is the minimum h, given a particular n. To answer this, we first ask, what is the maximum n we can fit in a tree with height h?

The root is just a single element. The children of the root make a complete level adding two more nodes for a tree of height 2. In the next level, we will have two children for any node in this level. So the next level or level three has a total of $2 X 2 = 4$ nodes. It can be easily seen that the level h of the tree has a total of $2^{(h-1)}$ nodes. The total number of nodes that a tree of height h can then have is as follows:

```
n = 1 + 2 + 4+ ... + 2 (h-1) = 2h - 1
=> 2h = (n+1)
=> h = lg (n+ 1)
```

This is our ideal case where the complexity of the search is $O(lg\ n)$. This kind of a tree where all the levels are full is called a balanced binary tree. Our aim is to maintain the balanced nature of the tree even when insertion or deletion is carried out. However, in general, the tree would not remain balanced in the case of an arbitrary order of insertion of elements.

Insertion simply requires searching the element; once this is done, adding a new node is just a constant time operation. Therefore, it has the same complexity as that of a search. Deletion actually requires a maximum of two searches (in the fourth case), so it also has the same complexity as that of a search.

Self-balancing binary search tree

A binary search tree that remains balanced to some extent when insertion and deletion is carried out is called a self-balancing binary search tree. To create a balanced version of an unbalanced tree, we use a peculiar operation called **rotation**. We will discuss rotation in the following section:

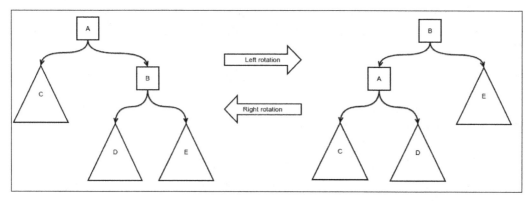

Rotation of a binary search tree

This figure shows the rotation operation on nodes **A** and **B**. Left rotation on **A** creates the right image, and right rotation on **B** creates the left image. To visualize a rotation, first think about pulling out the subtree **D**. This subtree is somewhere in the middle. Now the nodes are rotated in either the left or right direction. In the case of the left rotation, the right child becomes the parent and the parent becomes the left child of the original child. Once this rotation is done, the **D** subtree is added to the right child's position of the original parent. The right rotation is exactly the same but in the opposite direction.

How does it help balance a tree? Notice the left-hand side of the diagram. You'll realize that the right side looks heavier, however, once you perform left rotation, the left-hand side will appear heavier. Actually, a left rotation decreases the depth of the right subtree by one and increases that of the left subtree by one. Even if, originally, the right-hand side had a depth of 2 when compared to the left-hand side, you could fix it using left rotation. The only exception is the subtree **D** since the root of **D** remains at the same level; its maximum depth does not change. A similar argument will hold true for the right rotation as well.

Rotation keeps the search-tree property of the tree unchanged. This is very important if we are going to use it to balance search trees. Let's consider the left rotation. From the positions, we can conclude the following inequalities:

- Each node in **C ≤ A**

- A ≤ B

- **A** ≤ Each node in **D ≤ B**

- **B** ≤ Each node in **E**

After we perform the rotation, we check the inequalities the same way and we find they are exactly the same. This proves the fact that rotation keeps the search-tree property unchanged. A very similar argument can be made for the right rotation as well. The idea of the algorithm of a rotation is simple: first take the middle subtree out, do the rotation, and reattach the middle subtree. The following is the implementation in our BinaryTree class:

```
protected void rotate(Node<E> node, boolean left){
```

First, let's do some parameter value checks:

```
if(node == null){
    throw new IllegalArgumentException("Cannot rotate
        null node");
}else if(node.containerTree != this){
    throw  new IllegalArgumentException(
        "Node does not belong to the current tree");
}
Node<E> child = null;
Node<E> grandchild = null;
Node<E> parent = node.getParent();
boolean parentDirection;
```

The child and grandchild we want to move depend on the direction of the rotation:

```
if(left){
    child = node.getRight();
    if(child!=null){
        grandchild = child.getLeft();
    }
}else{
    child = node.getLeft();
    if(child!=null){
        grandchild = child.getRight();
    }
}
```

The root node needs to be treated differently as usual:

```
if(node != getRoot()){
    if(parent.getLeft()==node){
        parentDirection = true;
    }else{
        parentDirection = false;
    }
    if(grandchild!=null)
        deleteNodeWithSubtree(grandchild);
    if(child!=null)
        deleteNodeWithSubtree(child);
        deleteNodeWithSubtree(node);
    if(child!=null) {
        setChild(parent, child, parentDirection);
        setChild(child, node, left);
    }
    if(grandchild!=null)
        setChild(node, grandchild, !left);
}else{
    if(grandchild!=null)
        deleteNodeWithSubtree(grandchild);
    if(child!=null)
        deleteNodeWithSubtree(child);
        deleteNodeWithSubtree(node);
    if(child!=null) {
        root = child;
        setChild(child, node, left);
    }
    if(grandchild!=null)
        setChild(node, grandchild, !left);
        root.parent = null;
    }
}
```

We now can look at our first self-balancing binary tree called the AVL tree.

AVL tree

AVL tree is our first self-binary search tree. The idea is simple: keep every subtree as balanced as possible. An ideal scenario would be for both the left and right subtrees, starting from every node, to have exactly the same height. However, since the number of nodes are not in the form of 2^p-1, where p is a positive integer, we cannot always achieve this. Instead, we allow a little bit of wiggle room. It's important that the difference between the height of the left subtree and the right subtree must not be greater than one. If, during any insert or delete operation, we happen to break this condition, we will apply rotations to fix this. We only have to worry about a difference of two between the heights as we are only thinking of insertion and deletion of one element at a time, and inserting one element or deleting it cannot change the height by more than one. Therefore, our worst case is that there was already a difference of one and the new addition or deletion created one more difference requiring a rotation.

The simplest kind of rotation is shown in the following figure. The triangles represent subtrees of equal heights. Notice that the height of the left subtree is two less than the height of the right subtree:

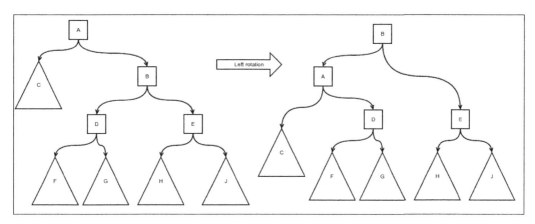

AVL tree – simple rotation

So we do a left rotation to generate the subtree of the structure, as shown in the preceding diagram. You can see that the heights of the subtrees follow our condition. The simple right rotation case is exactly the same, just in the opposite direction. We must do this for all the ancestors of the node that were either inserted or deleted as the heights of subtrees rooted by these nodes were the only ones affected by it. Since rotations also cause heights to change, we must start from the bottom and walk our way up to the root while doing rotations.

There is one more kind of case called a double rotation. Notice that the height of the subtree rooted by the middle grandchild does not change due to the rotation. So, if this is the reason for the imbalance, a simple rotation will not fix it. It is shown in the following figure:

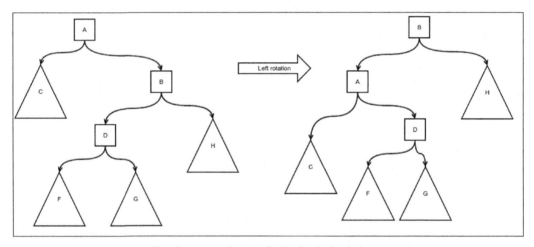

Simple rotation does not fix this kind of imbalance

Here, the subtree that received an insertion is rooted by **D** or a node is deleted from the subtree **C**. In the case of an insertion, notice that there would be no rotation on **B** as the left subtree of **B** has a height of only one more than that of its right subtree. **A** is however unbalanced. The height of the left subtree of **A** is two less than that of its right subtree. However, if we do a rotation on **A**, as shown in the preceding figure, it does not fix the problem; only the left-heavy condition is transformed into a right-heavy condition. To resolve this, we need a double rotation, as shown in the next figure. First, we do an opposite direction rotation of the middle grandchild so that it is not unbalanced in the opposite direction. A simple rotation after this will fix the imbalance.

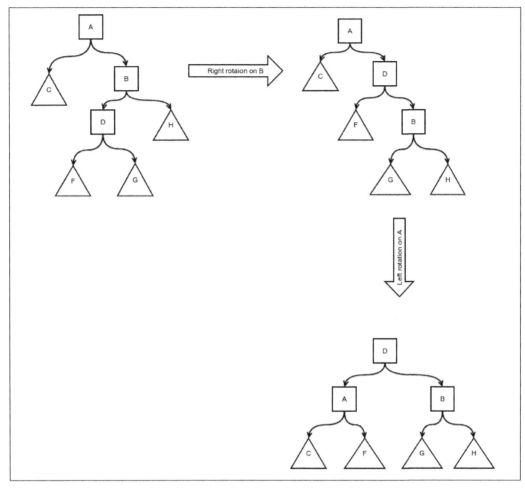

AVL tree double rotation

So we create an AVL tree class, and we add an extra field to the Node class to store the height of the subtree rooted by it:

```
public class AVLTree<E extends Comparable<E>>
        extends BinarySearchTree<E>{
    public static class Node<E extends Comparable<E>>
            extends BinaryTree.Node{
        protected int height = 0;
        public Node(BinaryTree.Node parent,
                    BinaryTree containerTree, E value) {
            super(parent, containerTree, value);
        }
    }
```

We must override the `newNode` method to return our extended node:

```
@Override
protected BinaryTree.Node<E> newNode(
  BinaryTree.Node<E> parent, BinaryTree<E> containerTree, E value) {
    return new Node(parent, containerTree, value);
}
```

We use a utility method to retrieve the height of a subtree with a null check. The height of a null subtree is zero:

```
private int nullSafeHeight(Node<E> node){
    if(node==null){
        return 0;
    }else{
        return node.height;
    }
}
```

First, we include a method to compute and update the height of the subtree rooted by a node. The height is one more than that of the maximum height of its children:

```
private void nullSafeComputeHeight(Node<E> node){
    Node<E> left = (Node<E>) node.getLeft();
    Node<E> right = (Node<E>) node.getRight();
    int leftHeight = left==null? 0 : left.height;
    int rightHeight = right==null? 0 :right.height;
    node.height =  Math.max(leftHeight, rightHeight)+1;
}
```

We also override the `rotate` method in `BinaryTree` to update the height of the subtrees after the rotation:

```
@Override
protected void rotate(BinaryTree.Node<E> node, boolean left) {
    Node<E> n = (Node<E>) node;
    Node<E> child;
    if(left){
        child = (Node<E>) n.getRight();
    }else{
        child = (Node<E>) n.getLeft();
    }
    super.rotate(node, left);
    if(node!=null){
        nullSafeComputeHeight(n);
    }
    if(child!=null){
        nullSafeComputeHeight(child);
```

```
            }
        }
```

With the help of these methods, we implement the rebalancing of a node all the way up to the root, as described in the preceding code. The rebalancing bit is done by checking the difference in the height of the left and right subtrees. If the difference is 0, 1, or -1, nothing needs to be done. We simply move up the tree recursively. When the height difference is 2 or -2, this is when we need to rebalance:

```
    protected void rebalance(Node<E> node){
        if(node==null){
            return;
        }
        nullSafeComputeHeight(node);
        int leftHeight = nullSafeHeight((Node<E>) node.getLeft());
        int rightHeight = nullSafeHeight((Node<E>) node.getRight());
        switch (leftHeight-rightHeight){
            case -1:
            case 0:
            case 1:
                rebalance((Node<E>) node.getParent());
                break;
            case 2:
                int childLeftHeight = nullSafeHeight(
                        (Node<E>) node.getLeft().getLeft());
                int childRightHeight = nullSafeHeight(
                        (Node<E>) node.getLeft().getRight());
                if(childRightHeight > childLeftHeight){
                    rotate(node.getLeft(), true);
                }
                Node<E> oldParent = (Node<E>) node.getParent();
                rotate(node, false);
                rebalance(oldParent);
                break;
            case -2:
                childLeftHeight = nullSafeHeight(
                        (Node<E>) node.getRight().getLeft());
                childRightHeight = nullSafeHeight(
                        (Node<E>) node.getRight().getRight());
                if(childLeftHeight > childRightHeight){
                    rotate(node.getRight(), false);
                }
                oldParent = (Node<E>) node.getParent();
                rotate(node, true);
                rebalance(oldParent);
                break;
        }
    }
```

Once the rotation is implemented, implementing the insert and delete operations is very simple. We first do a regular insertion or deletion, followed by rebalancing. A simple insertion operation is as follows:

```
@Override
    public BinaryTree.Node<E> insertValue(E value) {
        Node<E> node = (Node<E>) super.insertValue(value);
        if(node!=null)
            rebalance(node);
            return node;
    }
```

The delete operation is also very similar. It only requires an additional check confirming that the node is actually found and deleted:

```
@Override
    public BinaryTree.Node<E> deleteValue(E value) {
        Node<E> node = (Node<E>) super.deleteValue(value);
        if(node==null){
            return null;
        }
        Node<E> parentNode = (Node<E>) node.getParent();
        rebalance(parentNode);
        return node;
    }
```

Complexity of search, insert, and delete in an AVL tree

The worst case of an AVL tree is when it has maximum imbalance. In other words, the tree is worst when it reaches its maximum height for a given number of nodes. To find out how much that is, we need to ask the question differently, given a height h: what is the minimum number of nodes (n) that can achieve this? Let the minimum number of nodes required to achieve this be $f(h)$. A tree of height h will have two subtrees, and without any loss of generality, we can assume that the left subtree is higher than the right subtree. We would like both these subtrees to also have a minimum number of nodes. So the height of the left subtree would be $f(h-1)$. We want the height of the right subtree to be minimum, as this would not affect the height of the entire tree. However, in an AVL tree, the difference between the heights of two subtrees at the same level can differ by a maximum of one. The height of this subtree is $h-2$. So the number of nodes in the right subtree is $f(h-2)$. The entire tree must also have a root, hence the total number of nodes:

```
f(h) = f(h-1) + f(h-2) + 1
```

It almost looks like the formula of the Fibonacci sequence, except for the *+1* part. Our starting values are 1 and 2 because *f(1) = 1* (only the root) and *f(2) = 2* (just one child). This is greater than the starting values of the Fibonacci sequence, which are 1 and 1. One thing is of course clear that the number of nodes would be greater than the corresponding Fibonacci number. So, the following is the case:

```
f(h) ≥ F_h where F_h is the h^th Fibonacci number.
```

We know that for a large enough *h*, $F_h \approx \varphi F_{h-1}$ holds true; here φ is the golden ratio *(1 + √5)/2*. This means $F_h = C \varphi^h$, where C is some constant. So, we have the following:

```
f(h) ≥ C φ^h
=>n ≥ C  φ^h
=> log_φ n ≥  h +  log_φ C
=> h = O(  log_φ n) = O(lg n)
```

This means even the worst height of an AVL tree is logarithmic, which is what we wanted. Since an insertion processes one node in each level until it reaches the insertion site, the complexity of an insertion is *O(lg n)*; it is the same for performing search and delete operations, and it holds true for the same reason.

Red-black tree

An AVL tree guarantees logarithmic insertion, deletion, and search. But it makes a lot of rotations. In most applications, insertions are randomly ordered and so are deletions. So, the trees would sort of balance out eventually. However, since the AVL tree is too quick to rotate, it may make very frequent rotations in opposite directions even when it would be unnecessary, had it been waiting for the future values to be inserted. This can be avoided using a different approach: knowing when to rotate a subtree. This approach is called a red-black tree.

In a red-black tree, the nodes have a color, either black or red. The colors can be switched during the operations on the node, but they have to follow these conditions:

- The root has to be black

- A red node cannot have a black child

- The black height of any subtree rooted by any node is equal to the black height of the subtree rooted by the sibling node

Now what is the black height of a subtree? It is the number of black nodes found from the root to the leaf. When we say *leaf*, we really mean null children, which are considered black and allow a parent to be red without violating rule 2. This is the same no matter which path we take. This is because of the third condition. So the third condition can also be restated as this: the number of black nodes in the path from the root of any subtree to any of its leaves is the same, irrespective of which leave we choose.

For ease of manipulation, the null children of the leaves are also considered sort of half nodes; null children are always considered black and are the only ones really considered as leaves as well. So leaves don't contain any value. But they are different from the conventional leaves in other red-black trees. New nodes can be added to the leaves but not in a red-black tree; this is because the leaves here are null nodes. So we will not draw them out explicitly or put them in the code. They are only helpful to compute and match black heights:

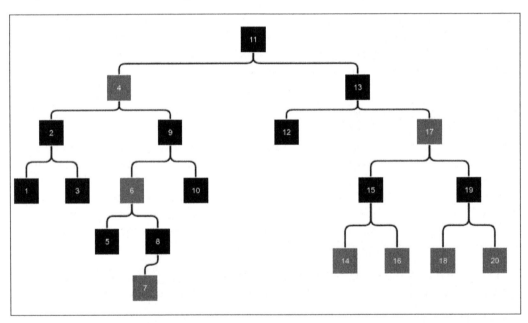

An example of a red-black tree

In our example of the red-black tree of height 4, the null nodes are black, which are not shown (in print copy, the light-colored or gray nodes are red nodes and dark-colored nodes are black nodes).

Both insertion and deletion are more complicated than the AVL tree, as there are more cases that we need to handle. We will discuss this in the following sections.

Insertion

Insertion is done in the same way we do it with BST. After an insertion is complete, the new node is colored red. This preserves the black height, but it can result in a red node being a child of another red node, which would violate condition 2. So we do some manipulation to fix this. The following two figures show four cases of insertions:

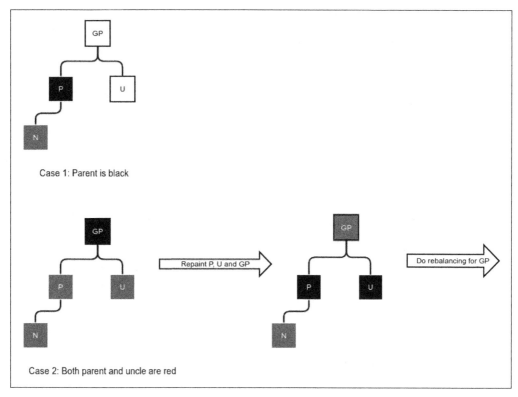

Case 1 and 2 of red-black tree insertion

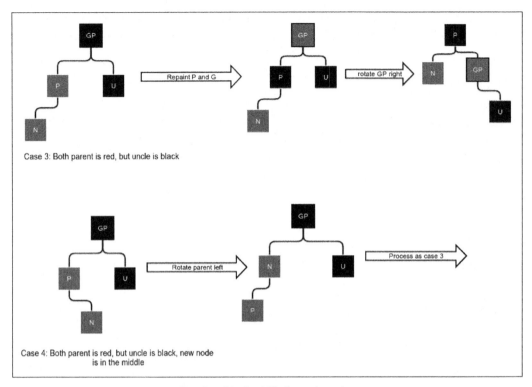

Case 3 and 4 of red-black tree insertion

Let's discuss the insertions case by case. Notice that the trees in the diagram look black and unbalanced. But this is only because we have not drawn the entire tree; it's just a part of the tree we are interested in. The important point is that the black height of none of the nodes change because of whatever we do. If the black height must be increased to fit the new node, it must be at the top level; so we simply move it up to the parent. The four cases are as follows:

1. The parent is black. In this case, nothing needs to be done as it does not violate any of the constraints.

2. Both parent and uncle are red. In this case, we repaint parent, uncle, and grandparent and the black heights are still unchanged. Notice now that no constraints are violated. If, however, the grandparent is the root, keep it black. This way, the entire tree's black height is increased by 1.

3. The parent is red and uncle is black. The newly added node is on the same side of the parent as the parent is of the grandparent. In this case, we make a rotation and repaint. We first repaint the parent and grandparent and then rotate the grandparent.

4. This is the case that is similar to case 3, except the newly added node is on the opposite side of the parent as the parent is of the grandparent. Case 3 cannot be applied here because doing so will change the black height of the newly added node. In this case, we rotate the parent to make it the same as case 3.

5. Note that all the cases can happen in the opposite direction, that is, in mirror image. We will handle both the cases the same way.

Let's create our `RedBlackTree` class extending the `BinarySearchTree` class. We have to again extend the `Node` class and include a flag to know whether the node is black:

```java
public class RedBlackTree<E extends Comparable<E>> extends
BinarySearchTree<E>{
    public static class Node<E> extends BinaryTree.Node<E>{
        protected int blackHeight = 0;
        protected boolean black = false;
        public Node(BinaryTree.Node parent,
                    BinaryTree containerTree, E value) {
            super(parent, containerTree, value);
        }
    }

    @Override
    protected  BinaryTree.Node<E> newNode(
      BinaryTree.Node<E> parent, BinaryTree<E> containerTree, E value) {
        return new Node(parent, containerTree, value);
    }
...
}
```

We now add a utility method that returns whether a node is black. As explained earlier, a null node is considered black:

```java
protected boolean nullSafeBlack(Node<E> node){
    if(node == null){
        return true;
    }else{
        return node.black;
    }
}
```

Now we're ready to define the method of rebalancing after we do an insertion. This method works as described in the four cases earlier. We maintain a `nodeLeftGrandChild` flag that stores whether the parent is the left child of the grand parent or its right child. This helps us find the uncle and also rotate in the correct direction:

```
protected void rebalanceForInsert(Node<E> node){
    if(node.getParent() == null){
        node.black = true;
    }else{
        Node<E> parent = (Node<E>) node.getParent();
        if(parent.black){
            return;
        }else{
            Node<E> grandParent = (Node<E>) parent.getParent();
            boolean nodeLeftGrandChild = grandParent
                                         .getLeft()== parent;

            Node<E> uncle = nodeLeftGrandChild?
                (Node<E>) grandParent.getRight()
                : (Node<E>) grandParent.getLeft();
            if(!nullSafeBlack(uncle)){
                if(grandParent!=root)
                    grandParent.black = false;
                uncle.black = true;
                parent.black = true;
                rebalanceForInsert(grandParent);
        }else{
            boolean middleChild = nodeLeftGrandChild?
                parent.getRight() == node:parent.getLeft()
                == node;
            if (middleChild){
                rotate(parent, nodeLeftGrandChild);
                node = parent;
                parent = (Node<E>) node.getParent();
            }
            parent.black = true;
            grandParent.black = false;
            rotate(grandParent, !nodeLeftGrandChild);
        }
        }
    }
}
```

The insertion is now done as follows:

```
@Override
public BinaryTree.Node<E> insertValue(E value) {
    Node<E> node = (Node<E>) super.insertValue(value);
    if(node!=null)
        rebalanceForInsert(node);
    return node;
}
```

Deletion

Deletion starts with a normal binary search tree deletion. If you remember, this always involves deletion of a node with at most one child. Deletion of an internal node is done by first copying the value of the leftmost node of the right subtree and deleting it. So we will consider only this case:

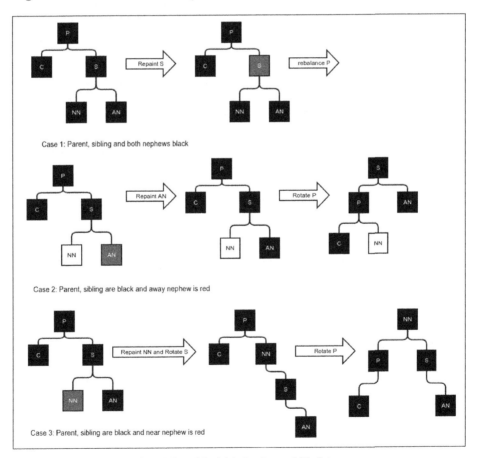

Case 1, 2, and 3 of deletion in a red-black tree

After the deletion is done, the parent of the deleted node either has no child or has one child, which was originally its grandchild. During the insertion, the problem we needed to solve was a red child of a red parent. In a deletion process, this cannot happen. But it can cause the black height to change.

One simple case is that if we delete a red node, the black height does not change anything, so we don't have to do anything. Another simple case is that if the deleted node were black and the child red, we can simply repaint the child black in order to restore the black height.

A black child cannot really happen because that would mean the original tree was black and unbalanced, as the deleted node had a single black child. But since recursion is involved, a black child can actually arise while moving up the path with recursive rebalancing. In the following discussion, we only look at cases where the deleted node was black and the child was also black (or null child, which is considered black). Deletion is done as per the following cases, as shown in the figures *Case 1 and 2 and 3 of deletion in a red-black tree* and *Case 4, 5 and 6 of deletion from a red-black tree*:

1. The first case we have is when the parent, sibling, and both the nephews are black. In this case, we can simply repaint the sibling to red, which will make the parent black and balanced. However, the black height of the whole subtree will reduce by one; hence, we must continue rebalancing from the parent.

2. This is the case when the parent and sibling are black, but the away nephew is red. In this case, we cannot repaint the sibling as this would cause the red sibling to have a red child, violating constraint 2. So we first repaint the red nephew to black and then rotate to fix the black height of the nephew while fixing the black height of the child.

3. When the near nephew is red instead of the away nephew, the rotation does not restore the black height of the near nephew that has been repainted. So, we repaint NN but do a double rotation instead.

4. Now consider what happens when the sibling is red. We first repaint the parent and sibling using opposite colors and rotating P. But this does not change the black height of any node; it reduces the case to case 5 or 6, which we will discuss now. So we simply call the rebalancing code again recursively.

5. We are now done with all the cases where the parent was black. This is a case where the parent is red. In this case, we consider the near nephew to be black. Simply rotating the parent fixes the black height.

6. Our final case is when the parent is red and the near nephew is red. In this case, we recolor the parent and do a double rotation. Notice that the top node remains red. This is not a problem because the original top node, which is the parent node, was also red and hence its parent must be black.

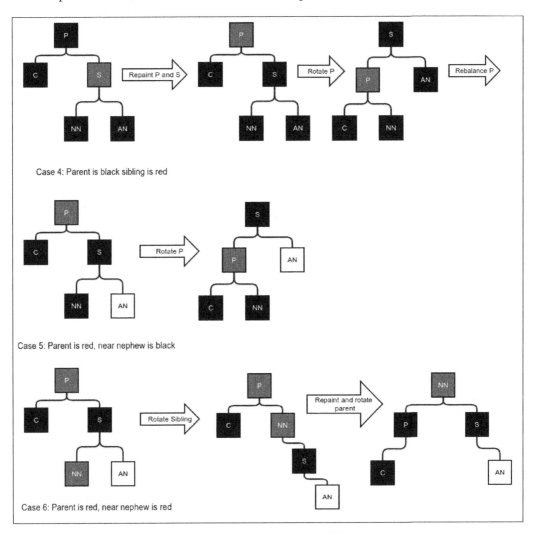

Case 4, 5, and 6 of deletion from a red-black tree

Now we can define the `rebalanceForDelete` method coding all the preceding cases:

```
protected void rebalanceForDelete(Node<E> parent, boolean
    nodeDirectionLeft){
    if(parent==null){
        return;
```

```
        }
        Node<E> node = (Node<E>) (nodeDirectionLeft?
          parent.getLeft(): parent.getRight());
        if(!nullSafeBlack(node)){
            node.black = true;
            return;
        }

        Node<E> sibling = (Node<E>) (nodeDirectionLeft?
          parent.getRight(): parent.getLeft());


        Node<E> nearNephew = (Node<E>) (nodeDirectionLeft?
          sibling.getLeft():sibling.getRight());

        Node<E> awayNephew = (Node<E>) (nodeDirectionLeft?
          sibling.getRight():sibling.getLeft());

        if(parent.black){
            if(sibling.black){
                if(nullSafeBlack(nearNephew) && nullSafeBlack(
                    awayNephew)){
                    sibling.black = false;
                    if(parent.getParent()!=null){
                        rebalanceForDelete (
                            (Node<E>) parent.getParent(),
                            parent.getParent().getLeft() == parent);
                    }
                }else if(!nullSafeBlack(awayNephew)){
                    awayNephew.black = true;
                    rotate(parent, nodeDirectionLeft);
                }else{
                    nearNephew.black = true;
                    rotate(sibling, !nodeDirectionLeft);
                    rotate(parent, nodeDirectionLeft);
                }

            }else{
                parent.black = false;
                sibling.black = true;
                rotate(parent, nodeDirectionLeft);
                rebalanceForDelete(parent, nodeDirectionLeft);
            }
        }else{
```

```
        if(nullSafeBlack(nearNephew)){
            rotate(parent, nodeDirectionLeft);
        }else{
            parent.black = true;
            rotate(sibling, !nodeDirectionLeft);
            rotate(parent, nodeDirectionLeft);
        }
    }

}
```

Now we override the `deleteValue` method to invoke rebalancing after the deletion. We only need to rebalance if the deleted node was black. We first check that. Then, we need to figure out whether the deleted child was a left child of the parent or the right child. After that, we can invoke the `rebalanceForDelete` method:

```
@Override
public BinaryTree.Node<E> deleteValue(E value) {
    Node<E> node = (Node<E>) super.deleteValue(value);

    if(node !=null && node.black && node.getParent()!=null){
        Node<E> parentsCurrentChild = (Node<E>) (
          node.getLeft() == null ? node.getRight():
          node.getLeft());
        if(parentsCurrentChild!=null){
            boolean isLeftChild = parentsCurrentChild
            .getParent().getLeft() == parentsCurrentChild;
            rebalanceForDelete(
                    (Node<E>) node.getParent(), isLeftChild);
        }else{
            boolean isLeftChild = node.getParent()
                                    .getRight()!=null;
            rebalanceForDelete(
                    (Node<E>) node.getParent(), isLeftChild);
        }

    }
    return node;
}
```

The worst case of a red-black tree

What is the worst possible red-black tree? We try to find out the same way we did in the case of the AVL tree. This one is a little more complicated, though. To understand the worst tree, we must take into account the black height. To fit the minimum number of nodes n into height h, we need to first choose a black height. Now it is desirable to have as few black nodes as possible so that we don't have to include black nodes for balancing the black height in the siblings of the nodes we are trying to stretch the height with. Since a red node cannot be the parent of another, we must have alternate black nodes. We consider height *h* and an even number so that the black height is *h/2 = l*. For simplicity, we don't count the black null nodes for either the height or the black height. The next figure shows some examples of the worst trees:

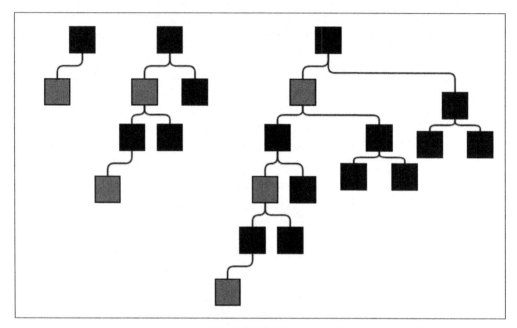

Worst red-black trees

The general idea is, of course, to have one path with the maximum possible height. This path should be stuffed with the maximum number of red nodes and the other paths filled with the least number of nodes, that is, with only black nodes. The general idea is shown in the next figure.

The number of nodes in a full black tree of height *l-1* is of course $2^{l-1} - 1$. So, if the number of nodes for height *h = 2l* is *f(l)*, then we have the recursive formula:

```
f(1) = f(1-1) + 2 ( 21-1 - 1) + 2
=> f(1) = f(1-1) + 21
```

Now, from the preceding figure, we can already see that $f(1) = 2$, $f(2) = 6$, and $f(3) = 14$. It looks like the formula should be $f(l) = 2^{l+1} - 2$. We already have the base cases. If we can prove that if the formula is true for l, then it is also true for $l+1$, we would be able to prove the formula for all l by induction. This is what we will try to do:

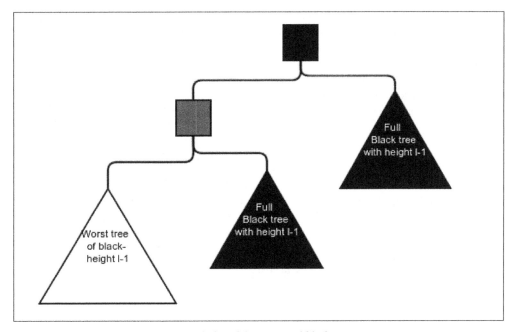

General idea of the worst red-black tree

We already have $f(l+1) = f(l) + 2l+1$ and we also assume $f(l) = 2l+1-2$. So this is the case: $f(l+1) = 2l+1-2 + 2l+1 = 2l+2-2$. Hence, if the formula holds true for l, it also holds true for $l+1$; therefore, it is proved by induction.

So the minimum number of nodes is as follows:

```
n = f(l)  =   2l+2-2.
=> lg n = lg ( 2l+2-2)
=> lg n >  lg ( 2l+1)
=> lg n > l+1
=> l + 1< lg n
=> l < lg n
=> l = O (lg n)
```

Therefore, a red-black tree has a guaranteed logarithmic height; from this, it is not hard to derive that the search, insertion, and deletion operations are all logarithmic.

Hash tables

A hash table is a completely different kind of searchable structure. The idea starts from what is called a hash function. It is a function that gives an integer for any value of the desired type. For example, the hash function for strings must return an integer for every string. Java requires every class to have a hashcode() method. The object class has one method implemented by default, but we must override the default implementation whenever we override the equals method. The hash function holds the following properties:

- Same values must always return the same hash value. This is called consistency of the hash. In Java, this means if x and y are two objects and x.equals(y) is true, then x.hashcode() == y.hashcode().

- Different values may return the same hash, but it is preferred that they don't.

- The hash function is computable in constant time.

A perfect hash function will always provide a different hash value for different values. However, such a hash function cannot be computed in constant time in general. So, we normally resort to generating hash values that look seemingly random but are really complicated functions of the value itself. For example, hashcode of the String class looks like this:

```
public int hashCode() {
    int h = hash;
     if (h == 0 && value.length > 0) {
        char val[] = value;

        for (int i = 0; i < value.length; i++) {
            h = 31 * h + val[i];
        }
         hash = h;
    }
    return h;
}
```

Notice that it is a complicated function that is computed from constituent characters.

A hash table keeps an array of buckets indexed by the hash code. The bucket can have many kinds of data structures, but here, we will use a linked list. This makes it possible to jump to a certain bucket in constant time and then the bucket is kept small enough so that the search within the bucket, even a linear search, will not cost that much.

Let's create a skeleton class for our hash table:

```
public class HashTable<E> {
    protected LinkedList<E> [] buckets;
    protected double maximumLoadFactor;
    protected int totalValues;
    public HashTable(int initialSize, double maximumLoadFactor){
        buckets = new LinkedList[initialSize];
        this.maximumLoadFactor = maximumLoadFactor;
    }
    ...
}
```

We accept two parameters. InitialSize is the initial number of buckets we want to start with, and our second parameter is the maximum load factor.

What is load factor? Load factor is the average number of values per bucket. If the number of buckets is *k* and the total number of values in it is *n*, then load factor is *n/k*.

Insertion

Insertion is done by first computing the hash and picking up the bucket in that index. Now firstly, the bucket is searched linearly for the value. If the value is found, insertion is not carried out; otherwise, the new value is added to the end of the bucket.

First we create a function for inserting in a given array of buckets and then using it to perform the insertion. This would be useful when you are dynamically growing your hash table:

```
protected boolean insert(E value, int arrayLength,
                            LinkedList<E>[] array) {
    int hashCode = value.hashCode();
    int arrayIndex = hashCode % arrayLength;
    LinkedList<E> bucket = array[arrayIndex];
    if(bucket == null){
        bucket = new LinkedList<>();
        array[arrayIndex] = bucket;
    }
    for(E element: bucket){
        if(element.equals(value)){
            return false;
        }
    }
    bucket.appendLast(value);
    totalValues++;
    return true;
}
```

Note that effective hash code is computed by taking the remainder of the actual hash code divided by the number of buckets. This is done to limit the number of hash code.

There is one more thing to be done here and that is rehashing. Rehashing is the process of dynamically growing the hash table as soon as it exceeds a predefined load factor (or in some cases due to other conditions, but we will use load factor in this text). Rehashing is done by creating a second array of buckets of a bigger size and copying each element to the new set of buckets. Now the old array of buckets is discarded. We create this function as follows:

```java
protected void rehash(){
    double loadFactor = ((double)(totalValues))/buckets.length;
    if(loadFactor>maximumLoadFactor){
        LinkedList<E> [] newBuckets = new LinkedList[
                            buckets.length*2];
        totalValues = 0;
        for(LinkedList<E> bucket:buckets){
            if(bucket!=null) {
                for (E element : bucket) {
                    insert(element, newBuckets.length,
                        newBuckets);
                }
            }
        }
        this.buckets = newBuckets;
    }
}
```

Now we can have our completed `insert` function for a value:

```java
public boolean insert(E value){
    int arrayLength = buckets.length;
    LinkedList<E>[] array = buckets;
    boolean inserted = insert(value, arrayLength, array);
    if(inserted)
        rehash();
    return inserted;
}
```

The complexity of insertion

It is easy to see that the insert operation is almost constant time unless we have to rehash it; in this case, it is $O(n)$. So how many times do we have to rehash it? Suppose the load factor is l and the number of buckets is b. Say we start from an `initialSize` B. Since we are doubling every time we rehash, the number of buckets will be $b = B.2^R$; here R is the number of times we rehashed. Hence, the total number of elements can be represented as this: $n = bl = Bl.\ 2^R$. Check this out:

```
lg n = R + lg(Bl) .
=> R = ln n - lg (Bl) = O(lg n)
```

There must be about `lg n` number of rehashing operations, each with complexity of `O(n)`. So the average complexity for inserting n elements is `O(n lg n)`. Hence, the average complexity for inserting each element is `O(lg n)`. This, of course, would not work if the values are all clustered together in a single bucket that we are inserting into. Then, each insert would be `O(n)`, which is the worst case complexity of an insertion.

Deletion is very similar to insertion; it involves deletion of elements from the buckets after they are searched.

Search

Search is simple. We compute the hash code, go to the appropriate bucket, and do a linear search in the bucket:

```
public E search(E value){
    int hash = value.hashCode();
    int index = hash % buckets.length;
    LinkedList<E> bucket = buckets[index];
    if(bucket==null){
        return null;
    }else{
        for(E element: bucket){
            if(element.equals(value)){
                return element;
            }
        }
        return null;
    }
}
```

Complexity of the search

The complexity of the search operation is constant time if the values are evenly distributed. This is because in this case, the number of elements per bucket would be less than or equal to the load factor. However, if all the values are in the same bucket, search is reduced to a linear search and it is $O(n)$. So the worst case is linear. The average case of search is constant time in most cases, which is better than that of binary search trees.

Choice of load factor

If the load factor is too big, each bucket would hold a lot of values that would output a bad linear search. But if the load factor is too small, there would be a huge number of unused buckets causing wastage of space. It is really a compromise between search time and space. It can be shown that for a uniformly distributed hash code, the fraction of buckets that are empty can be approximately expressed as e^{-l}, where l is the load factor and e is the base of a natural logarithm. If we use a load factor of say 3, then the fraction of empty buckets would be approximately $e^{-3} = 0.0497$ or 5 percent, which is not bad. In the case of a non-uniformly distributed hash code (that is, with unequal probabilities for different ranges of values of the same width), the fraction of empty buckets would always be greater. Empty buckets take up space in the array, but they do not improve the search time. Therefore, they are undesirable.

Summary

In this chapter, we saw a collection of searchable and modifiable data structures. All of these allowed you to insert new elements or delete elements while still remaining searchable and that too quite optimally. We saw binary search trees in which a search follows the paths of the tree from the root. Binary search trees can be modified optimally while still remaining searchable if they are of the self-balancing type. We studied two different kinds of self-balancing trees: AVL trees and red-black trees. Red-black trees are less balanced than AVL trees, but they involve a fewer number of rotations than AVL trees. In the end, we went through the hash table, which is a different kind of searchable structure. Although the worst case complexity of search or insertion is $O(n)$, hash tables provide constant time search and average time insertion ($O(lg\ n)$) in most cases. If a hash table does not keep growing, the average insertion and deletion operations will also be constant time.

In the next chapter, we will see some more important general purpose data structures.

9
Advanced General Purpose Data Structures

In this chapter, we will take a look at some more interesting data structures that are commonly used. We will start with the concept of a priority queue. We will see some efficient implementations of a priority queue. In short, we will cover the following topics in this chapter:

- Priority queue ADT
- Heap
- Binomial forest
- Sorting using a priority queue and heap

Priority queue ADT

A priority queue is like a queue in that you can enqueue and dequeue elements. However, the element that gets dequeued is the one with the minimum value of a feature, called its priority. We will use a comparator to compare elements and learn which one has the lowest priority. We will use the following interface for the priority queue:

```
public interface PriorityQueue<E> {
    E checkMinimum();
    E dequeueMinimum();
    void enqueue(E value);
}
```

We require the following set of behaviors from the methods:

- checkMinimum: This method must return the next value to be dequeued without dequeuing it. If the queue is empty, it must return null.

- dequeueMinimum: This must dequeue the element with the minimum priority and return it. It should return null when the queue is empty.

- enqueue: This should insert a new element in the priority queue.

We would also like to do these operations as efficiently as possible. We will see two different ways to implement it.

Heap

A heap is a balanced binary tree that follows just two constraints:

- The value in any node is less than the value in either of the children. This property is also called the heap property.

- The tree is as balanced as possible — in the sense that any level is completely filled before a single node is inserted in the next level.

The following figure shows a sample heap:

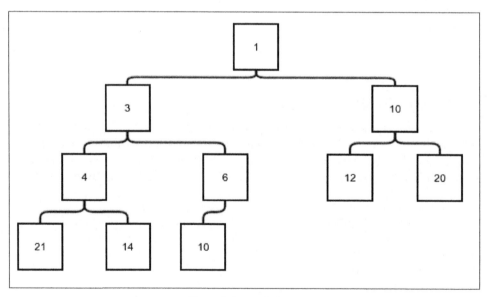

Figure 1. A sample heap

It would not be really clear until we actually discuss how to insert elements and remove the least element. So let's jump into it.

Insertion

The first step of insertion is to insert the element in the next available position. The next available position is either another position in the same level or the first position in the next level; of course, this applies when there is no vacant position in the existing level.

The second step is to iteratively compare the element with its parent and keep switching until the element is bigger than the parent, thus restoring the constraints. The following figure shows the steps of an insertion:

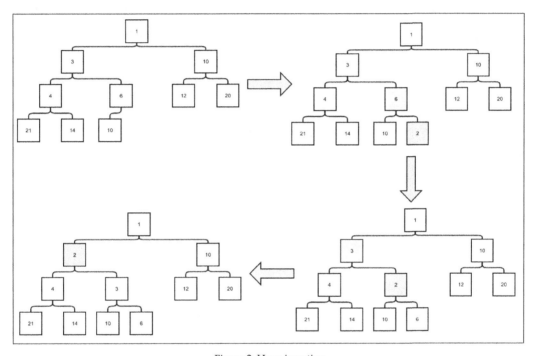

Figure 2. Heap insertion

The gray box represents the current node, and the yellow box represents the parent node, whose value is larger than the current node. First, the new element is inserted in the next available spot. It must be swapped until the constraint is satisfied. The parent is **6**, which is bigger than **2**, so it is swapped. If the parent is **3**, which is also larger than **2**, it is swapped. If the parent is **1**, which is less than **2**, we stop and the insertion is complete.

Removal of minimum elements

The constraint that the parent is always less than or equal to the children guarantees that the root is the element with the least value. This means the removal of the least element leads only to the removal of the top element. However, the empty space of the root must be filled, and elements can only be deleted from the last level to maintain the constraint **2**. To ensure this, the last element is first copied to the root and then removed. We must now iteratively move the new root element downward until the constraint **1** is satisfied. The following figure shows an example of a delete operation:

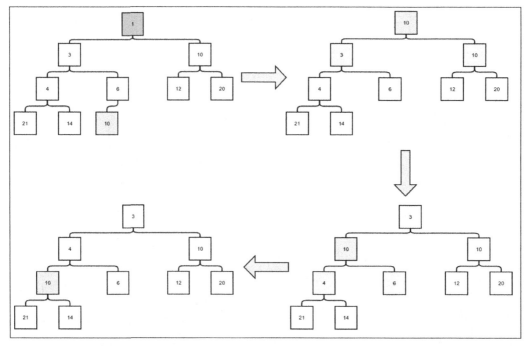

Heap deletion

There is one question though, since any parent can have two children: which one should we compare and swap with? The answer is simple. We need the parent to be less than both the children; this means we must compare and swap with the minimum value of the children.

Analysis of complexity

First, let's check out the height of a heap for a given number of nodes. The first layer contains just the root. The second layer contains a maximum of two nodes. The third layer contains four. Indeed, if any layer contains m elements, the next layer will contain, at the maximum, the children of all these m elements. Since each node can have two children, the maximum number of elements in the next layer will be 2m. This shows that the number of elements in layer l is 2^{l-1}. So, a full heap of height h will have total $1+2+4+...+2^{h-1} = 2^h-1$ nodes. Therefore, a heap of height h can have maximum $2^{h+1}-1$ nodes. What is the minimum number of nodes in a heap of height h. Well, since only the last level can have unfilled positions, the heap must be full, except the last layer. The last layer can have one node minimum. So, the minimum number of nodes in a heap of height h is $(2^{h-1}-1) + 1 = 2^{h-1}$. Hence, if the number of nodes is n, then we have this:

```
2^{h-1} ≤ n ≤ 2^h -1
=>   h-1 ≤ lg n ≤ lg(2^h -1) <lg( 2^h)
=> h-1 ≤ lg n < h
```

We also have the following:

```
2^{h-1} ≤ n ≤ 2^h -1
=> 2^h≤ n ≤ 2^{h+1} -1
=>h ≤ lg (2n)< h+1
```

Combining the preceding two expressions, we get this:

```
lg n < h ≤ lg (2n)
=> h = θ(lg n)
```

Now, let's assume that adding a new element to the end of the heap is a constant time operation or $\theta(lg\ n)$. We will see that this operation can be made this efficient. Now we deal with the complexity of a trickle up operation. Since in each compare-and-swap operation, we only compare with the parent and never backtrack, the maximum number of swaps that can happen in a trickle up operation equals the height of the heap h. Hence, the insertion is $O(lg\ n)$. This means that the insert operation itself is $O(lg\ n)$.

Similarly, for the trickle down operation, we can only do as many swaps as the height of the heap. So trickling down is also $O(lg\ n)$. Now if we assume that removing the root node and copying the last element to the root is at the maximum $O(lg\ n)$, we can conclude that the delete operation is also $O(lg\ n)$.

Serialized representation

A heap can be represented as a list of numbers without any blanks in the middle. The trick is to list the elements in order after each level. Positions from 1 through n for an n element heap adopt the following conventions:

- For any element at index j, the parent is at index $j/2$, where '$/$' represents an integer division. This means divide j by two and ignore the remainder if any.

- For any element at index j, the children are $j*2$ and $j*2+1$. One can verify that this is the same as the first formula written the other way round.

The representation of our example tree is shown in the following figure. We have just flattened the process of writing a tree one entire level before another. We retained the tree edges, and one can see that the parent-child relationships work as described previously:

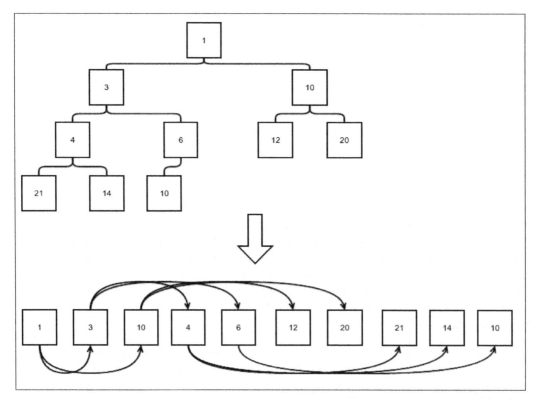

Array representation of a heap

With the knowledge of the array-based storage function of a heap, we can proceed to implement our heap.

Array-backed heap

An array-backed heap is a fixed-sized heap implementation. We start with a partial implementation class:

```
public class ArrayHeap<E> implements PriorityQueue<E>{

    protected E[] store;

    protected Comparator<E> comparator;
    int numElements = 0;
    public ArrayHeap(int size, Comparator<E> comparator){
        store = (E[]) new Object[size];
        this.comparator = comparator;
}
```

Given any index of the array (starting from 0), find the index of the parent element. It involves converting the index to 1 based form (so add 1), dividing by 2, and then converting it back to 0 (so subtract 1):

```
    protected int parentIndex(int nodeIndex){
        return ((nodeIndex+1)/2)-1;
    }
```

Find the index of the left child using this:

```
    protected int leftChildIndex(int nodeIndex){
        return (nodeIndex+1)*2 -1;
    }
```

Swap the elements in the two indexes provided using this:

```
    protected void swap(int index1, int index2){
        E temp = store[index1];
        store[index1] = store[index2];
        store[index2] = temp;
    }
    ...
}
```

To implement the insertion, first implement a method that would trickle the value up until constraint 1 is satisfied. We compare the current node with the parent, and if the value of the parent is larger, then do a swap. We keep moving upwards recursively:

```
    protected void trickleUp(int position){
        int parentIndex = parentIndex(position);
```

```
        if(position> 0 && comparator.compare(store[parentIndex],
            store[position])>0){
            swap(position, parentIndex);
            trickleUp(parentIndex);
        }
    }
```

Now we can implement the insertion. The new element is always added to the end of the current list. A check is done to ensure that when the heap is full, an appropriate exception is thrown:

```
    public void insert(E value){
        if(numElements == store.length){
            throw new NoSpaceException("Insertion in a full heap");
        }
        store[numElements] = value;
        numElements++;
        trickleUp(numElements-1);
    }
```

Similarly, for deletion, we first implement a trickle down method that compares an element with its children and makes appropriate swaps until constraint 1 is restored. If the right child exists, the left child must also exist. This happens because of the balanced nature of a heap. In this case, we must compare only with a minimum of two children and swap them if it is necessary. When the left child exists but the right child does not, we only need to compare it with one element:

```
    protected void trickleDown(int position){
        int leftChild = leftChildIndex(position);
        int rightChild = leftChild+1;
        if(rightChild<numElements) {
            if (comparator.compare(store[leftChild],
                store[rightChild]) < 0) {
                if (comparator.compare(store[leftChild],
                    store[position]) < 0) {
                    swap(position, leftChild);
                    trickleDown(leftChild);
                }
            } else {
                if (comparator.compare(store[rightChild],
                    store[position]) < 0) {
                    swap(position, rightChild);
                    trickleDown(rightChild);
                }
            }
        }else if(leftChild<numElements){
```

```
        if (comparator.compare(store[leftChild],
            store[position]) < 0) {
                swap(position, leftChild);
                trickleDown(leftChild);
        }
    }
}
```

With the `trickleDown` method available, removing the minimum element is simple. We first save the current root as the minimum element, then copy the last element to the root position. We then call the `trickleDown` method to restore constraint 1:

```
public E removeMin(){
    if(numElements==0){
        return null;
    }else{
        E value  = store[0];
        store[0] = store[numElements-1];
        numElements--;
        trickleDown(0);
        return value;
    }
}
```

Now we only have to use it as an implementation of the priority queue. So we implement the relevant methods using our `insert` and `removemin`:

```
@Override
public E checkMinimum() {
if(numElements==0){
return null;
}else{
return store[0];
}
}

    @Override
    public E dequeueMinimum() {
        return removeMin();
    }

    @Override
    public void enqueue(E value) {
        insert(value);
    }
```

This completes our array-based heap implementation. It has the same problem as our array-based queue implementation, that is, we need to know its maximum size beforehand. Next, we will have an implementation of a heap that has an implementation in the form of a linked binary tree.

Linked heap

A linked heap is an actual binary tree where every node holds references to its children. We first create a skeleton structure for our heap:

```
public class LinkedHeap<E> implements PriorityQueue<E>{

    protected static class Node<E>{
        protected E value;
        protected Node<E> left;
        protected Node<E> right;
        protected Node<E> parent;
        public Node(E value, Node<E> parent){
            this.value = value;
            this.parent = parent;
        }
    }
    ...
}
```

To keep track of the next position, each position is given a number, just like we did in our array-based representation. We have the same calculation for the index of the parent and children. But, in this case, looking up the value at a particular index requires a traversal from the root to that node. We create a method to do this. Note that since we are not using an array, the position starts from 1. We start by finding the parent node recursively. The parent node is of course the node at the position that is half the value of the children. The remainder, when divided by 2, is the bit that tells us whether the node is to the left or right of the parent. We return the node accordingly:

```
protected Node<E> findNodeAtPostion(int position){
    if(position == 1){
        return root;
    }else{
        int side = position % 2;
        int parentPosition = position / 2;
        Node<E> parent = findNodeAtPostion(parentPosition);
        switch (side){
            case 0:
                return parent.left;
```

```
            case 1:
                return parent.right;
        }
    }
    return null;
}
```

Next, we turn to swapping. In the case of an array-based heap, we could swap the values between any two indexes. However, this general implementation would require multiple traversals in this case. We only need to swap the values between a node and its parent. The swapWithParent takes the parent node as an argument. Another argument is to know whether the current node is the left or right child of the parent and switch references appropriately:

```
protected void swapWithParent(Node<E> parent, boolean left){
    Node<E> node = left? parent.left:parent.right;
    Node<E> leftChild = node.left;
    Node<E> rightChild = node.right;
    Node<E> sibling = left? parent.right:parent.left;
    Node<E> grandParent = parent.parent;
    parent.left = leftChild;
    if(leftChild!=null){
        leftChild.parent = parent;
    }
    parent.right = rightChild;
    if(rightChild!=null){
        rightChild.parent = parent;
    }
    parent.parent = node;
    if(left){
        node.right = sibling;
        node.left = parent;
    }else{
        node.left = sibling;
        node.right = parent;
    }
    node.parent = grandParent;
    if(sibling!=null)
        sibling.parent = node;

    if(parent == root){
        root = node;
    }else{
        boolean parentLeft = grandParent.left==parent;
        if(parentLeft){
```

```
                grandParent.left = node;
            }else{
                grandParent.right = node;
            }
        }
    }
```

Insertion

Insertion involves inserting a new element at the end first and then trickling it in the upward direction. First, we create a trickle up method, similar to the one in the `ArrayHeap` class:

```
protected void trickleUp(Node<E> node){
    if(node==root){
        return;
    }else if(comparator.compare(node.value, node.parent.value)<0){
        swapWithParent(node.parent, node.parent.left == node);
        trickleUp(node);
    }
}
```

Now, we implement the insert method. If the tree is empty, we just have to add a root. Otherwise, the position of the new element is *(numElements+1)*. In this case, it's parent must be *((numElements+1)/2)*. Whether it should be the left or right child of its parent is determined by the value of *((numElements+1)%2)*. A new node is then created and added to the parent as a child. Finally, `numElements` is incremented to keep track of the number of elements:

```
public void insert(E value){

    if(root==null){
        root = new Node<>(value, null);
    }else{
        Node<E> parent = findNodeAtPostion((numElements+1)/2);
        int side = (numElements+1)%2;
        Node<E> newNode = new Node<>(value, parent);
        switch (side){
            case 0:
                parent.left = newNode;
                break;
            case 1:
                parent.right = newNode;
                break;
        }
```

```
            trickleUp(newNode);
        }
        numElements++;
    }
```

Removal of the minimal elements

Similar to the array-based heap, we need to implement a trickle down method. Since the left child must exist if the right child does, if the left child is null, the node does not have any child. But, if the right child is null and the left child is not, we only need to compare the current node's value with that of the left child. Otherwise, compare and swap with the child that has the minimum value:

```
protected void trickleDown(Node<E> node){
    if(node==null){
        return;
    }
    if(node.left == null){
        return;
    }else if(node.right == null){
        if(comparator.compare(node.left.value, node.value)<0){
            swapWithParent(node, true);
            trickleDown(node);
        }
    }else{
        if(comparator.compare(node.left.value,
           node.right.value)<0){
            if(comparator.compare(node.left.value, node.value)<0){
                swapWithParent(node, true);
                trickleDown(node);
            }
        }else{
            if(comparator.compare(node.right.value, node.value)<0){
                swapWithParent(node, false);
                trickleDown(node);
            }
        }
    }

}
```

Now we can implement the method to remove the minimum element. If the root is null, it means the queue is empty. If the last element is the root, there is only one element and we just remove and return it. Otherwise, we copy the value of the root to a temporary variable, then copy the value of the last element to the root, and finally, trickle down the root:

```java
public E removeMin(){
    if(root==null){
        return null;
    }
    Node<E> lastElement = findNodeAtPostion(numElements);
    if(lastElement==root){
        root = null;
        numElements--;
        return lastElement.value;
    }
    E value = root.value;
    root.value = lastElement.value;
    Node<E> parent = lastElement.parent;
    if(parent.left==lastElement){
        parent.left = null;
    }else{
        parent.right=null;
    }
    numElements--;
    trickleDown(root);
    return value;
}
```

Finally, we implement the methods required to make it a valid priority queue:

```java
@Override
public E checkMinimum() {
    return root==null? null : root.value;
}

@Override
public E dequeueMinimum() {
    return removeMin();
}

@Override
public void enqueue(E value) {
    insert(value);
}
```

This completes our priority queue implementation using heaps. We will now introduce a different way of implementing a priority queue. It is called a binomial forest, which comprises our next section.

Complexity of operations in ArrayHeap and LinkedHeap

We have already seen that if we can append an element to the end of a heap in at most *O(lg n)*, where n is the number of elements already in the heap, we can perform both insertion and removal of the minimum element *θ(lg n)* times. In the case of `ArrayHeap`, insertion of a new element implies just setting the value of an element in an array at a known index. This is a constant time operation. So, in `ArrayHeap`, both the insertion and removal of minimum element are *θ(lg n)*. Checking the minimum element is just the check the value at index zero of the array and hence is constant time.

In the case of `LinkedHeap`, insertion of a new element at the end involves traversing the tree to the end position. Since the height of the tree is *θ(lg n)*, this operation is also *θ(lg n)*. This means, the insertion and deletion operation in `LinkedHeap` is also *θ(lg n)*. Checking the minimum element means just checking the value at the root, and this operation is constant time.

Binomial forest

A binomial forest is a very interesting data structure. But, to discuss it, we need to first start with a binomial tree. A binomial tree is a tree in which a combination of two smaller binomial trees of the same size are combined in a particular way:

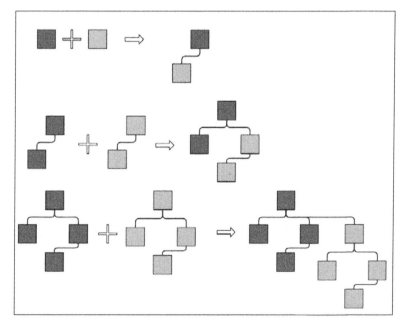

Binomial tree

The preceding figure shows how binomial trees combine to create larger binomial trees. In the first row, two binomial trees of height 1 combine to create a new binomial tree of height 2. In the second row, two binomial trees of height 2 combine to create a new binomial tree of height 3. In the final example, two binomial trees of height 3 combine to create a binomial tree of height 4, and it continues. The two trees that are combined together are not treated symmetrically. Instead, the root of one becomes the parent of the other. The next figure shows one more step in the sequence and then shows a different way to look at a binomial tree. In the last row, I have highlighted the subtrees differently. Notice how:

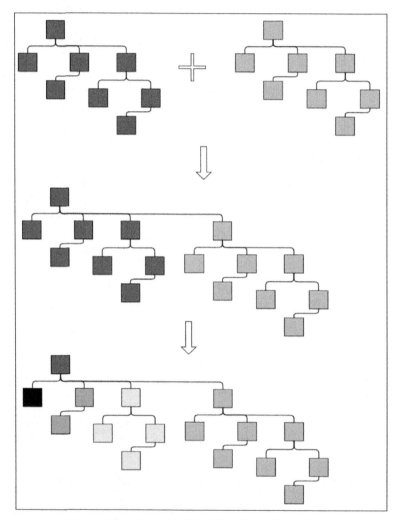

Figure 6. The other way of thinking about a binomial tree

Each subtree is a binomial tree. Not only that, the first subtree is a binomial tree of height 1, the second one of height 2, third one of height 3, and so on. So, another way of thinking about a binomial tree is that it is a root and a sequence of subtrees that are binomial trees of consecutive heights up to one less than the height of the entire tree. Both these views are required in our discussion. The first view is needed when analyzing the idea and the second when implementing it.

Why call it a binomial tree?

Remember the choose function we discussed in *Chapter 4, Detour - Functional Programming*? There, I pointed out that it is also called the binomial coefficient. Let's see how it is related to a binomial tree. Suppose we have a binomial tree of height h and we want to find out the number of nodes at level l. Let's assume that for a tree of height h, the number of nodes is *f(t,r)*, where *t=h-1* and *r = l-1*. The reason for taking a variable that is one less than the height and level will become clearer a little later. Basically, *t* is the height of the tree that starts from *0* instead of *1*, and *r* is the level that starts from zero. Now this tree is obviously a tree of only one element or it is made up of two trees of height *h-1 = t*:

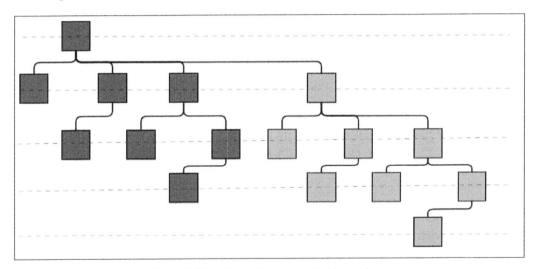

Figure 7. The rationale for naming it a binomial tree

We will call these two subtrees this: red subtree and green subtree. This is because they are colored this way in the preceding figure. The levels are highlighted using dashed lines. It is clear from the picture that the nodes at the level r in the complete tree is either at level r in the red tree or at level $r-1$ in the green tree. Both the red and green trees are trees of height $h-1$. This means the following: $f(t,r) = f(t-1,r) + f(t-1,r-1)$. This equation is the same as what we have for the choose function we have already discussed. The only thing we have to check is the boundary conditions. The top level (that is $t=0$) always has only one node, so $f(t,0) = 1$. We also know that the number of levels in the tree has to be less than or equal to the height of the tree, so we have $f(t,r) = 0$ if $t < r$. So, $f(t,t) = f(t-1,t) + f(t-1,t-1) = 0 + f(t-1,t-1) = f(t-1,t-1)$ for any t. In the same way, $f(t-1,t-1) = f(t-2,t-2) = f(t-3,t-3) = \ldots = f(0,0) = 1$ (because $f(t,0) = 1$). Therefore, all the conditions of the choose function are satisfied; hence we can see $f(t,r) = choose(t,r) = choose(h-1, l-1)$. Since the *choose* function is also called the binomial coefficient, this gives the binomial tree its name.

Number of nodes

What is the number of nodes n in a binomial tree of height h? When $h=1$, we only have one node. A tree of height 2 is made up of two trees of height 1, a tree of height 3 is made up of two trees of height 2, and so on. So, for the increment of 1 in height, the number of nodes must be twice as much as the original number. That is, when $h=1, n=1$; $h=2, n=2$; $h=3, n=4$,... In general, this should be the case: $n = 2^{h-1} = 2^t$. Here t is the height starting from zero.

Notice also that we can say that the number of nodes n in a tree is the sum of the number of nodes in each level, which is *choose(t, r)*, where r is the level starting from 0 to t. The two formulas must be equal, so the sum *choose(t, 0)* + *choose(t, 1)* + *choose(t, 2)* + ... + *choose(t, t)* equals 2^t. This is a proof of this relationship. There are other proofs as well, but this is a valid proof too.

The heap property

Of course, with only this structure, we have no way of making sure of having some easy way of figuring out the minimum element. So, we also enforce the heap property on a binomial tree:

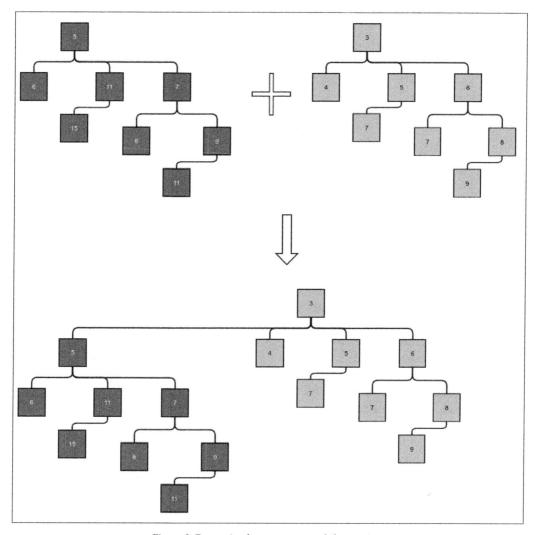

Figure 8. Preserving heap property while merging.

This is the property: the value of any node is smaller than the value of each of its children. When merging two trees to make one, the only thing we need to do to preserve the heap property is to use the heap with the lesser value at its top node as the top subtree and the one with the higher value at its top node as the subordinate subtree. This is shown in the preceding figure. The red tree happens to have a higher value in the root node than that of the green tree. Hence, the red tree must be the subordinate tree. The heap property ensures that the root of any binomial tree holds the minimum element.

Binomial forest

So how do we make a queue out of this? Firstly, note that any tree will have nodes with at least the power of 2. But, in a queue, we want an arbitrary number of elements. So we store these elements in more than one tree. Any number can be expressed as the sum of the power of 2 because any number can be expressed in binary form. Suppose we need to store 20 nodes. The number 20 in binary is 10100. So we need two binomial trees: one with height 5 and 16 nodes and one with height 3 and four nodes. A queue is built using a collection of binomial trees to store the nodes. Hence it is called a binomial forest.

Before we discuss how to insert new elements and remove the minimum element, we need to understand how to merge two binomial forests. We have already seen that the numbers of elements are represented according to binary form. Just write the number in binary form, and if 1 exists, it means there is a tree of height that is equal to one plus its position from right to left. When we merge two forests, the number of elements of the merged forest is the sum of the number of elements in the forests that need to be merged. This means the result will have trees of sizes where the binary representation of the sum will have the number 1. We can find this binary representation by performing a binary addition of the binary representations of the node's source number. For example, let's merge two forests: one with 12 elements and one with 10 elements. Their binary representations will be 1100 and 1010, respectively. If we do a binary addition, we have 1100 + 1010 = 10110. This means the original trees had trees of heights 3, 5 and 4, 5 and the result must have trees of heights 3, 4, and 6. The merge happens the same way we do a binary addition. The trees are stored in sequence, and we have empty places that represent zeros in the binary representation. While merging, each tree represents a bit and it has the number of nodes that the bit represents. We take the corresponding bit from each forest and also consider a carry. All these trees must either be empty or have exactly the same number of nodes. Then, we merge them to create the resulting bits.

To do any binary addition, we have input of three bits for each bit: one from each of the input and a carry. We need to compute both the output bit and the next carry. Similarly, while merging two trees, we need to compute the output tree and the carry tree from the given input trees (two) and a carry tree. Once the merging is done, inserting and removing min is simple.

The insert simply merges a forest with a single tree using a single node. Removing the minimum element is a little more complicated operation. The first step is to find out the minimum. We know every tree has the minimum element at its root. So we need to walk through all the trees while comparing the root elements to find the minimum element and the tree that has it. Removing it is simply taking the root off, leaving a list of subtrees that make a forest of consecutive heights of trees. Therefore, we can merge the subtrees in the main forest to complete the removal process.

Let's see the implementation. First, we create a skeleton class. A binomial tree has a root, which contains a value and a list of subtrees. The list of subtrees is like a dense forest. The list of trees in the forest is stored in a linked list. We use `DoublyLinkedList` because we need to remove the last element:

```
public class BinomialForest<E> implements PriorityQueue<E>{

    protected Comparator<E> comparator;
    protected static class BinomialTree<E>{
        E value;
        LinkedList<BinomialTree<E>> subTrees = new LinkedList<>();
        public BinomialTree(E value){
            this.value = value;
        }
    }

    public BinomialForest(Comparator<E> comparator){
        this.comparator = comparator;
    }



    DoublyLinkedList<BinomialTree<E>> allTrees =
      new DoublyLinkedList<>();
    ...
}
```

As discussed earlier, we will start with the merge operation now. First we need to merge two trees, which we will use to merge two forests. Merging two trees is a simple constant time operation. Merging with a null tree does not change the tree. The two trees being merged should be of the same size. We need to simply compare the root elements. The tree with the smaller value in its root will get the other as a child:

```
    protected BinomialTree<E> merge(BinomialTree<E> left,
      BinomialTree<E> right){

        if(left==null){
            return right;
        }else if(right==null){
            return left;
        }
        if(left.subTrees.getLength() != right.subTrees.getLength()){
            throw new IllegalArgumentException(
                    "Trying to merge two unequal trees of sizes " +
```

```
                    left.subTrees.getLength() + " and " +
                       right.subTrees.getLength());
        }
        if(comparator.compare(left.value, right.value)<0){
            left.subTrees.appendLast(right);
            return left;
        }else{
            right.subTrees.appendLast(left);
            return right;
        }
    }
```

Since we want to check the minimum element in constant time, just like in a heap, we will store the minimum element in a state variable. We will also store its position in the allTrees list:

```
        BinomialTree<E> minTree = null;
        int minTreeIndex = -1;
```

We will define a method to find out and update the variables. Since the smallest element in any tree is the root, we only have to go through the root to find the minimum element:

```
        protected void updateMinTree(){
            if(allTrees.getLength()==0){
                minTree = null;
                minTreeIndex = -1;
            }
            E min = null;
            int index = 0;
            for(BinomialTree<E> tree:allTrees){
                if(tree==null){
                    index++;
                    continue;
                }
                if(min == null || comparator.compare(min, tree.value)>0){
                    min = tree.value;
                    minTree = tree;
                    minTreeIndex = index;
                }
                index++;
            }
        }
```

To implement the merging of two forests, we need to first implement how to compute the output and carry the tree out of the two input trees and a carry tree. These methods are fairly simple. We need to understand that both the input and the carry must be of the same size if they are not null. The height of the output must be the same as the height of the output, and the height of the carry must be one more than the height of the input:

```
protected BinomialTree<E> computeOutputWithoutCarry(
BinomialTree<E> lhs, BinomialTree<E> rhs, BinomialTree<E> carry){
    if(carry==null){
        if(lhs==null){
            return rhs;
        }else if(rhs==null){
            return lhs;
        }else{
            return null;
        }
    }else{
        if(lhs==null && rhs==null){
            return carry;
        }else if(lhs == null){
            return null;
        }else if(rhs == null){
            return null;
        }else{
            return carry;
        }
    }
}
protected BinomialTree<E>  computeCarry(
    BinomialTree<E> lhs, BinomialTree<E> rhs, BinomialTree<E> carry)
{
    if(carry==null){
        if(lhs!=null && rhs!=null){
            return merge(lhs, rhs);
        }else{
            return null;
        }
    }else{
        if(lhs==null && rhs==null){
            return null;
        }else if(lhs == null){
            return merge(carry, rhs);
        }else if(rhs == null){
```

```
                    return merge(carry, lhs);
              }else{
                    return merge(lhs, rhs);
              }
        }
    }
```

We also need to enhance the `ListIterator` class in our imperative `LinkedList` implementation so that we can modify the value of any node while iterating through it. We use the following implementation to do this:

```java
public class ListIterator implements Iterator<E> {
    protected Node<E> nextNode = first;
    protected Node<E> currentNode = null;
    protected Node<E> prevNode = null;

    @Override
    public boolean hasNext() {
        return nextNode != null;
    }

    @Override
    public E next() {
        if (!hasNext()) {
            throw new IllegalStateException();
        }
        prevNode = currentNode;
        currentNode = nextNode;
        nextNode = nextNode.next;
        return currentNode.value;
    }

    @Override
    public void remove() {
        if(currentNode==null || currentNode == prevNode){
            throw new IllegalStateException();
        }
        if(currentNode==first){
            first = nextNode;
        }else{
            prevNode.next = nextNode;
        }
        currentNode=prevNode;

    }
```

```
        public void setValue(E value){
            currentNode.value = value;
        }


    }
```

With these methods available, we can implement the merging of two forests or two lists of trees:

```
    protected void merge(LinkedList<BinomialTree<E>> rhs){
        LinkedList<BinomialTree<E>>.ListIterator lhsIter
            = (LinkedList<BinomialTree<E>>.ListIterator)allTrees
            .iterator();
        Iterator<BinomialTree<E>> rhsIter = rhs.iterator();
        BinomialTree<E> carry = null;
        while(lhsIter.hasNext() || rhsIter.hasNext()){
            boolean lhsHasValue = lhsIter.hasNext();
            BinomialTree<E> lhsTree = lhsHasValue?
                lhsIter.next():null;
            BinomialTree<E> rhsTree = rhsIter.hasNext()?
                rhsIter.next():null;
            BinomialTree<E> entry = computeOutputWithoutCarry(
                lhsTree, rhsTree, carry);
            carry = computeCarry(lhsTree, rhsTree, carry);
            if(lhsHasValue) {
                lhsIter.setValue(entry);
            }else{
                this.allTrees.appendLast(entry);
            }
        }
        if(carry!=null){
            this.allTrees.appendLast(carry);
        }
        updateMinTree();
    }
```

The `Insert` method is very simple to implement with the merge available. Just merge a list containing one tree with the value 1:

```
    public void insert(E value){
        BinomialTree<E> newTree = new BinomialTree<E>(value);
        DoublyLinkedList<BinomialTree<E>> newList
                = new DoublyLinkedList<>();
        newList.appendLast(newTree);
        merge(newList);
    }
```

Removal of the minimum element is a little more complex. It involves removing the tree with the minimum value and then considering its root as the minimum element. Once this is done, the subtrees need to be merged with the original forest. If the last tree is being removed, we must actually remove it from the list. This is the same as not writing a leading zero in binary representation. Otherwise, we only set the value to null so that we know it is a zero bit:

```java
public E removeMin() {
    if (allTrees.getLength()==0) {
        return null;
    }
    E min = minTree.value;
    if (minTreeIndex==allTrees.getLength()-1) {
        allTrees.removeLast();
    } else {
        allTrees.setValueAtIndex(minTreeIndex, null);
    }
    merge(minTree.subTrees);
    return min;
}
```

Finally, we can implement the methods required to use it as a priority queue:

```java
@Override
public E dequeueMinimum() {
    return removeMin();
}

@Override
public void enqueue(E value) {
    insert(value);
}

@Override
public Iterator<E> iterator() {
    return null;
}
```

This completes our implementation of a binomial queue.

Complexity of operations in a binomial forest

We already know that the number of nodes in a binomial tree of height h is $2h\text{-}1$. The question is, if we want to store n elements, what should be the maximum height of the trees in the forest? We have seen that the trees we need are as per the binary expression of the integer n. The most significant bit of the binary representation of n is the floor of $(lg\ n)$, that is the greatest integer less than or equal to $lg\ n$. We will write this as $lg\ n$. The height of the tree representing this bit is $1 + lg\ n$. The length of the list holding the trees in the forest is also $1 + lg\ n = \theta(lg\ n)$. Both in the case of an insertion and removal of a new element, a merge operation is involved. The merge operation is constant time for each pair of input trees and one carry. So, the number of operations for a merge operation of two forests is this: *constant times the number of trees in the largest forest* $= \theta(lg\ n)$, where n is the number of trees in the largest forest.

At the time of insertion, we just merge a new forest of only one tree and one element. So this operation is $\theta(lg\ n)$, where n is the number of elements in the original forest.

The removal process involves two steps. The first is to remove the minimum element. This involves a constant time operation, which is used to remove the tree with the minimum element, and a merge operation, which is $\theta(lg\ n)$, as seen already. The second step/operation is to update the tree with the minimum element. This involves scanning the roots of all the trees; therefore, it is $\theta(lg\ n)$, just like the merge operation. So, as a whole, the removal process is also $\theta(lg\ n)$.

Checking the minimum element is of course constant time, as we have it referenced already.

Sorting using a priority queue

Since a priority queue always returns the minimum element, if we insert all input elements and then keep dequeuing them, they would be dequeued in sorted order. This can be used to sort a list of elements. In our example, we will add a new method called the `LinkedList` implementation. This implementation sorts the elements using `PriorityQueue`. First insert all the elements into the priority queue. Then, dequeue the elements and append them back to the linked list:

```
public void sort(Comparator<E> comparator){
    PriorityQueue<E> priorityQueue = new LinkedHeap<E>(comparator);

    while (first!=null){
        priorityQueue.enqueue(getFirst());
        removeFirst();
    }
```

```
    while (priorityQueue.checkMinimum()!=null){
        appendLast(priorityQueue.dequeueMinimum());
    }
}
```

Both enqueue and dequeue have $\theta(lg\ n)$ complexity, and we have to enqueue and dequeue each of the elements. We have already seen this: $lg\ 1 + lg\ 2 + \dots + lg\ n = \theta(n\ lg\ n)$. So, the enqueueing and dequeueing of the elements is $\theta(n\ lg\ n)$, which means the sort is $\theta(n\ lg\ n)$, which is asymptotically optimal.

In-place heap sort

We can use an array-based heap implementation to do an in-place sort of the elements of an array. The trick is to use the same array for backing the heap. In the beginning, we simply insert the elements in the heap from the beginning of the array. We achieve this by replacing the array in the heap, except the one that is passed. Since the heap also uses the space from the beginning, it does not overwrite the elements we are still to insert. While dequeuing the elements, we start saving them from the end of the array, as this is the part that is being freed up by the heap. This means we want the largest element to be dequeued first. This is achieved by simply using a comparator that is the opposite of the one that is passed. We add this static method to our `ArrayHeap` class:

```
public static <E> void heapSort(E[] array, Comparator<E> comparator){

    ArrayHeap<E> arrayHeap = new ArrayHeap<E>(0,
        (a,b) -> comparator.compare(b,a));


    arrayHeap.store = array;

    for(int i=0;i<array.length;i++){
        arrayHeap.insert(array[i]);
    }

    for(int i=array.length-1;i>=0;i--){
        array[i] = arrayHeap.removeMin();
    }
}
```

This is actually a sort using a priority queue as shown before, except that here we are sharing the array with the priority queue. Hence, this sort is also $\theta(n\ lg\ n)$, just as before.

Summary

In this chapter, we discussed priority queues and their implementation. Priority queues are important data structures that are used in a lot of problems. We saw two implementations of a priority queue, a heap, and a binomial forest. We also saw how to use priority queues for sorting, which is asymptotically optimal. A variation of this allowed us to sort an array in place using an array-based heap.

In the next chapter, we will discuss the concept of graphs, which are very useful, almost ubiquitous ADTs, and data structures that are used in many real-life applications.

10
Concepts of Graph

A graph is a generalization of a tree. In a tree, every node has one parent. In a graph, a node can have multiple parents. The most common way to think about a graph is as a set of vertices and edges. Vertices are like points and edges are like lines that connect the points. In the generic notion of a graph, there is no restriction on which vertices can be connected by edges. This allows graphs to model a versatile category of real-life concepts. The Internet, for example, is a graph where the vertices are the web pages and the edges the hyperlinks between the pages. A social networking site, such as Facebook, has a graph of profiles in which the vertices are the profiles and the edges the friendships between the profiles. Each software has a graph of dependencies, called a dependency graph, in which the vertices are the different software libraries used and the edges the dependencies between the software libraries. There is no end to examples of graphs. In this chapter, we will discuss the following topics:

- Different types of graphs
- The ADT graph
- Representation of graphs in memory
- Traversal of a graph
- Cycle detection
- Spanning trees
- Minimum spanning trees

What is a graph?

A graph is a collection of vertices and edges that connect the vertices. *Figure 1* gives a visual representation of an example of a graph. There are a few features to note here, which we will discuss next:

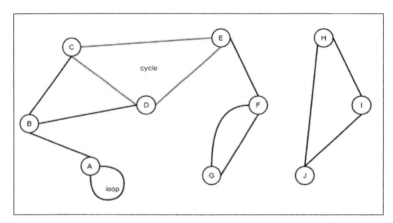

Figure 1: Example of an undirected graph

- **Undirected graph**: An undirected graph is a graph in which the edges have no direction, as shown in *Figure 1*.

- **Directed graph**: This is a graph in which the edges have a direction.

- **Path**: A path is a sequence of edges that connects a set of vertices that are distinct from one another, except the first and the last vertices as they may be the same. For example, in *Figure 1*, the edges **AB**, **BD**, and **DE** represent a path. It can also be described as the **ABDE** path, which does not repeat its vertices. In the case of a directed graph, the edges must traverse only in the specified direction to form the sequence of edges required to make a path.

- **Cycle**: A cycle is a path with at least two vertices involved; it starts and ends on the same vertex. For example, in *Figure 1*, the path **DCED** is a cycle.

- **Loop**: A loop is an edge that connects a node to itself. In *Figure 1*, vertex **A** has a loop.

- **Subgraph**: The subgraph of a graph is another type of graph where all the edges and vertices are the same as the edges and vertices of the original graph. For example, in *Figure 1*, the nodes **A**, **B**, and **C** along with the edges **AB** and **BC** represent a subgraph.

- **Connected graph**: A connected graph is a graph in which there exists a path that starts from any arbitrary vertex and ends in any arbitrary, but different vertex. The graph in *Figure 1* is not connected. But, the subgraph with vertices **H**, **I**, and **J** and the edges **HI**, **IJ**, and **JH** represent a connected subgraph:

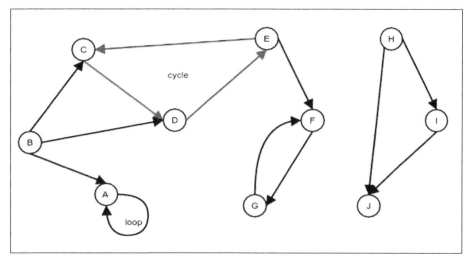

Figure 2. Example directed graph

- **Tree**: A tree is a connected but undirected graph with no cycles and loops.
  Figure 3 shows an example of a tree. Note that this is slightly different from
  the tree we have studied earlier. This tree does not have any particular root.
  The nodes in this tree do not have any particular parent, and any node can
  act as a root:

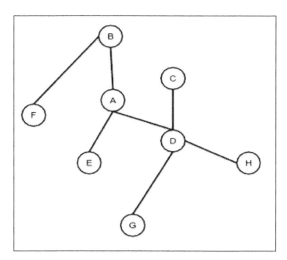

Figure 3. Example tree

- **Forest**: A forest is an unconnected, undirected graph with no cycles or loops.
  You can think of a forest as a collection of trees. A single tree is also a forest.
  In other words, a forest is a collection of zero or more trees.

- **Complete graph**: A complete graph is an undirected graph that has the maximum number of edges, given a certain number of vertices. It also has constraints as per which there can only be one edge between two given vertices, with no loops. *Figure 4* shows an example of a complete graph. For a complete graph with the set of vertices V and the set of edges E, $|E| = |V|$ $(|V| - 1)/2$. It is easy to see why this is the case. Each vertex will have an edge between itself and other $|V| - 1$ nodes. That makes a total of $|V| (|V| - 1)$ edges. However, in this approach, each edge is counted twice, once for each of its two vertices. So, the actual number of edges in a complete graph is $|V| (|V| - 1)/2$:

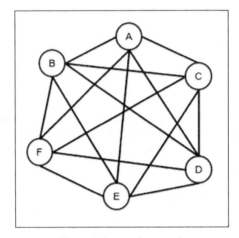

Figure 4. A complete graph

The graph ADT

We will now define what a data structure representing a graph should do. Later, we will discuss the different implementations of this ADT. A graph must support the following operations:

- **Add Vertex**: This adds a new vertex
- **Remove Vertex**: This removes a vertex
- **Add edge**: This adds a new edge; in our graph, we will allow a maximum of one edge between two vertices for simplicity
- **Remove edge**: This removes an edge
- **Adjacent**: This checks whether the two given vertices are adjacent to each other, that is, whether there is an edge between the given nodes

- **Neighbors**: This returns a list of vertices that are adjacent to the given vertex
- **Get Vertex Value**: This gets the value stored in a vertex
- **Set Vertex Value**: This stores a value in a vertex
- **Get Edge Value**: This gets the value stored in an edge
- **Set Edge Value**: This sets the value stored in an edge
- **Is undirected**: This returns whether the graph is undirected
- **Get all vertices**: This returns a self-balancing binary search tree containing all the vertices
- **Max Vertex ID**: This returns the highest ID of the vertices

Our algorithms will depend on the above operations being available in a graph data structure. The following Java interface is a realization of this ADT:

```
public interface Graph<V, E> {
    int addVertex();
    void removeVertex(int id);
    void addEdge(int source, int target);
    void removeEdge(int source, int target);
    boolean isAdjacent(int source, int target);
    LinkedList getNeighbors(int source);
    void setVertexValue(int vertex, V value);
    V getVertexValue(int vertex);
    void setEdgeValue(int source, int target, E value);
    E getEdgeValue(int source, int target);
    boolean isUndirected();
    BinarySearchTree<Integer> getAllVertices();
    int maxVertexID();
}
```

We identify each vertex by an ID; edges are identified by a source vertex and a target vertex. In the case of an undirected graph, the source and target could be interchanged. But, in the case of a directed graph, they are noninterchangeable.

Now that we have an ADT, we would like to have an implantation. To implement a graph data structure, we need to choose a representation in memory.

Representation of a graph in memory

A graph can be represented mainly in three different ways: adjacency matrix, adjacency list, and incidence matrix.

Adjacency matrix

An adjacency matrix is a matrix, a table of values, where each value represents an edge and both the rows are the columns that represent the vertices. The values in a matrix can be the members of the entry. The values of the edges can be stored in the matrix itself. There could also be a special value for representing the absence of an edge. The following image shows an adjacency matrix for the graph in *Figure 1*, where the value of the edge represents the number of edges between the corresponding vertices:

$$
\begin{vmatrix}
2 & 1 & 0 & 0 & 0 & 0 & 0 & 0 & 0 & 0 \\
1 & 0 & 1 & 1 & 0 & 0 & 0 & 0 & 0 & 0 \\
0 & 1 & 0 & 1 & 0 & 0 & 0 & 0 & 0 & 0 \\
0 & 1 & 1 & 0 & 1 & 0 & 0 & 0 & 0 & 0 \\
0 & 0 & 1 & 1 & 0 & 1 & 0 & 0 & 0 & 0 \\
0 & 0 & 0 & 0 & 1 & 0 & 2 & 0 & 0 & 0 \\
0 & 0 & 0 & 0 & 0 & 2 & 0 & 0 & 0 & 0 \\
0 & 0 & 0 & 0 & 0 & 0 & 0 & 0 & 1 & 1 \\
0 & 0 & 0 & 0 & 0 & 0 & 0 & 1 & 0 & 1 \\
0 & 0 & 0 & 0 & 0 & 0 & 0 & 1 & 1 & 0
\end{vmatrix}
$$

The following things can be noted about an adjacency matrix:

- Rows are used to represent the sources and columns to represent the targets of the edges
- In the case of an undirected graph, the source and target are indistinguishable, so the adjacency matrix is symmetric

The following code provides an implementation of the graph ADT with the adjacency matrix. We use a two-dimensional array to store the matrix. The ID of any vertex is directly used as the index of the array. This is true for both the array to store the values stored within the vertices and the values stored in the edges, or even the existence of the edges. When we remove a vertex, we don't free its space; we do this so that the IDs of the newer vertices don't get shifted. This improves lookup performance but is wasteful in terms of resources:

```
public class AdjacencyMatrixGraphWithSparseVertex<V,E>
implements Graph<V, E> {

    private static class NullEdgeValue{};
```

We create two special objects to signify an edge and a vertex; these objects do not yet hold a value. A null reference refers to the edge or vertex that does not exist:

```
private NullEdgeValue nullEdge = new NullEdgeValue();
private NullEdgeValue nullVertex = new NullEdgeValue();

Object [][] adjacencyMatrix = new Object[0][];
Object[] vertexValues = new Object[0];
```

A flag determines whether the graph is undirected:

```
boolean undirected;

public AdjacencyMatrixGraphWithSparseVertex(boolean undirected){
    this.undirected = undirected;
}
```

Adding a vertex involves creating a new matrix and an array of vertex values and copying all the older values into it:

```
@Override
public int addVertex() {
    int numVertices = adjacencyMatrix.length;
    Object [][] newAdjacencyMatrix = new Object[numVertices+1][];
    for(int i=0;i<numVertices;i++){
        newAdjacencyMatrix[i] = new Object[numVertices+1];
        System.arraycopy(adjacencyMatrix[i],0,
            newAdjacencyMatrix[i], 0, numVertices);
    }
    newAdjacencyMatrix[numVertices] = new Object[numVertices+1];
    adjacencyMatrix = newAdjacencyMatrix;
    Object [] vertexValuesNew = new Object[vertexValues.length+1];
    System.arraycopy(vertexValues,0, vertexValuesNew, 0,
                    vertexValues.length);
    vertexValuesNew[vertexValues.length] = nullVertex;
    vertexValues = vertexValuesNew;
    return numVertices;
}
```

Since we don't free any space, removing a vertex simply involves setting values to null. Note that removing a vertex has to be accompanied by the removal of all the associated edges, which is done in a loop:

```
@Override
public void removeVertex(int id) {
    vertexValues[id] = null;
    for(int i=0;i<adjacencyMatrix.length;i++){
        adjacencyMatrix[id][i] = null;
        adjacencyMatrix[i][id] = null;
    }
}
```

Adding an edge involves setting a particular position in the adjacency matrix. If the graph is undirected, there will be two updates. This is because the source and target could be interchanged and the adjacency matrix is always symmetric:

```
@Override
public void addEdge(int source, int target) {
    if(adjacencyMatrix[source][target] == null){
        adjacencyMatrix[source][target] = nullEdge;
        if(undirected){
            adjacencyMatrix[target][source] = nullEdge;
        }
    }else{
        throw new IllegalArgumentException("Edge already exists");
    }
}
```

The following operation is the simplest of all as it involves setting only one edge to null. In the case of an undirected graph, there would be a corresponding update that would interchange the source and target:

```
@Override
public void removeEdge(int source, int target) {
    adjacencyMatrix[source][target] = null;
    if(undirected){
        adjacencyMatrix[target][source] = null;
    }
}
```

The following is a trivial operation of checking the adjacency matrix:

```
@Override
public boolean isAdjacent(int source, int target) {
    return adjacencyMatrix[source][target] != null;
}
```

For any given source, find all the edges in the same row of the matrix and add them to a linked list that we can return. Note that in a directed graph, it traverses the edges only in the forward direction:

```
@Override
public LinkedList getNeighbors(int source) {
    LinkedList<Integer> neighborList = new LinkedList<>();
    for(int i=0;i<adjacencyMatrix.length;i++){
        if(adjacencyMatrix[source][i]!=null){
            neighborList.appendLast(i);
        }
    }
    return neighborList;
}
```

We store all the values of the vertices in a different array:

```
@Override
public void setVertexValue(int vertex, V value) {
    vertexValues[vertex] = value;
}

@Override
public V getVertexValue(int vertex) {
    if(vertexValues[vertex]!=nullVertex)
        return (V)vertexValues[vertex];
    else
        throw new IllegalArgumentException("Vertex "+vertex
            +" does not exist");
}
```

The values stored in the edges can be stored in the adjacency matrix itself:

```
@Override
public void setEdgeValue(int source, int target, E value) {
    adjacencyMatrix[source][target] = value;
    if(undirected){
        adjacencyMatrix[target][source] = value;
    }
}

@Override
public E getEdgeValue(int source, int target) {
    if(adjacencyMatrix[source][target] != nullEdge) {
```

```
                return (E) adjacencyMatrix[source][target];
            }else {
                return null;
            }
        }

    @Override
        public boolean isUndirected() {
            return undirected;
        }

    @Override
        public BinarySearchTree<Integer> getAllVertices() {
            BinarySearchTree<Integer> allVertices = new RedBlackTree<>();
            for(int i=0;i<vertexValues.length;i++){
                if(vertexValues[i]!=null){
                    allVertices.insertValue(i);
                }
            }
            return allVertices;
        }

    @Override
        public int maxVertexID() {
            return vertexValues.length-1;
        }
}
```

Complexity of operations in a sparse adjacency matrix graph

Now let's analyze the complexity of the operations we have already discussed:

- **Add vertex**: Adding a vertex requires us to create a new two-dimensional array with length and w the complexities of the idth $|V|$ and then copy the entire old content to the new array. Here, $|V|$ represents the cardinality of the set V of the vertices. What is the size of the adjacency matrix then? It's a square matrix whose length or width equals $|V|$, so its size is $|V|^2$. Hence, adding a new edge has this complexity: $\theta(|V|^2)$.

- **Remove Vertex**: Removing a vertex involves removing all the edges that correspond to the given vertex. The maximum number of edges that can be associated with a single vertex is $|V|$, which is the length of a row or column in the adjacency matrix. We must set all the values in the row and column containing the vertex being deleted, so the number of values that need to be changed is calculated as $2|V| - 1$. The "minus one" part comes from the fact that the row and column have one edge in common, the edge representing a loop on the node that is being deleted. The common edge is counted twice, both in the row and the column. So one of them must be stopped. Therefore, the complexity of this operation is $\theta(2|V| - 1) = \theta(|V|)$.

- **Add edge and Remove edge**: Adding an edge is as simple as setting a special value at a single entry in the adjacency matrix. It has this complexity: $\theta(1)$. Removing an edge is just setting null at the same position.

- **Adjacent**: This operation involves checking whether an edge exists between the given source and target. It checks one entry in the adjacency matrix, hence this complexity: $\theta(1)$.

- **Neighbors**: This operation requires reading all the values in the row of an adjacency matrix. So it requires reading $|V|$ values and possibly adding them to a linked list. Therefore, the complexity of this operation is $\theta(|V|)$.

- **Setting and getting values at vertices and edges**: These operations require reading/setting a single value into/from the adjacency matrix. These operations are all $\theta(1)$.

- **Get all vertices**: This involves scanning through all the vertices and inserting them in a binary search tree. So this operation is $\theta(|V| \ lg \ |V|)$.

More space-efficient adjacency-matrix-based graph

The trouble with the above graph implementation is that we are unable to recover any space when vertices are deleted. The problem with recovering space is that it changes the indexes of the vertices that are added later. To avoid this, we can choose to have an ID of a vertex that is separate from its index position in the arrays. If we do this, we need to be able to search the index of a vertex with the given ID. This mapping can be done with a self-balancing binary search tree, which is what we are going to do here.

First, we create a separate class that represents a graph vertex. The idea is to allow a comparison to exist on the ID of a vertex. Different graph implementations can then extend this class to accommodate additional data in the graph vertex:

```java
public class GraphVertex<V> implements Comparable<GraphVertex<V>>{
    int id;
    V value;

    public GraphVertex(int id, V value) {
        this.id = id;
        this.value = value;
    }

    public int getId() {
        return id;
    }

    public void setId(int id) {
        this.id = id;
    }

    public V getValue() {
        return value;
    }

    public void setValue(V value) {
        this.value = value;
    }

    @Override
    public boolean equals(Object o) {
        if (this == o) return true;
        if (o == null || getClass() != o.getClass()) return false;
        GraphVertex<?> that = (GraphVertex<?>) o;
        return id == that.id;
    }

    @Override
    public int hashCode() {
        return id;
    }


    @Override
    public int compareTo(GraphVertex<V> o) {
        return id - o.id;
    }
}
```

With this class available, we can implement our adjacency-matrix-based graph implementation with a dense vertex and edge representation:

```
public class AdjacencyMatrixGraphWithDenseVertex<V,E> implements
Graph<V, E> {
```

First, we extend the `GraphVertex` class to include an `addition` field that stores the index of a vertex in the adjacency matrix as well as in the array meant for storing the values of the vertices:

```
class Vertex extends GraphVertex<V>{
    int internalIndex;

    public Vertex(int id, V value, int internalIndex) {
        super(id, value);
        this.internalIndex = internalIndex;
    }

    public int getInternalIndex() {
        return internalIndex;
    }

    public void setInternalIndex(int internalIndex) {
        this.internalIndex = internalIndex;
    }
}
```

The `nextId` variable is used to store the next ID that would be used:

```
private int nextId;
```

Special values to represent empty vertices and edges:

```
private static class NullValue {};
private NullValue nullEdge = new NullValue();

Object [][] adjacencyMatrix = new Object[0][];
```

The following is the binary search tree that stores the vertices with their indexes in the arrays:

```
RedBlackTree<GraphVertex<V>> vertices = new RedBlackTree<>();
boolean undirected;

public AdjacencyMatrixGraphWithDenseVertex(boolean undirected){
    this.undirected = undirected;
}
```

The process of adding involves the same operations as before apart from the extra operation of generating a new ID and storing an entry in the search tree:

```
@Override
public int addVertex() {
    int id = nextId++;
    int numVertices = adjacencyMatrix.length;
    Object [][] newAdjacencyMatrix = new Object[numVertices+1][];
    for(int i=0;i<numVertices;i++){
        newAdjacencyMatrix[i] = new Object[numVertices+1];
        System.arraycopy(adjacencyMatrix[i],0,
        newAdjacencyMatrix[i], 0, numVertices);
    }
    newAdjacencyMatrix[numVertices] = new Object[numVertices+1];

    vertices.insertValue(new Vertex(id, null,
                        adjacencyMatrix.length));
    adjacencyMatrix = newAdjacencyMatrix;
    return numVertices;
}
```

The removal of a vertex now actually involves creating a smaller adjacency matrix and copying all the edges, except the ones associated with the vertex that is being deleted:

```
@Override
public void removeVertex(int id) {
    BinaryTree.Node<GraphVertex<V>> node = vertices.searchValue(
    new GraphVertex<V>(id, null));
    if(node!=null){
        int internalId = ((Vertex)(node.getValue())))
                        .getInternalIndex();
        int numVertices = adjacencyMatrix.length;
        Object [][] newAdjacencyMatrix = new Object[
                                    numVertices-1][];
```

First, copy all the rows before the one for the vertex being deleted:

```
for(int i=0;i<internalId;i++){
    newAdjacencyMatrix[i] = new Object[numVertices-1];
    System.arraycopy(adjacencyMatrix[i],0,
    newAdjacencyMatrix[i], 0, internalId);
```

```
        System.arraycopy(adjacencyMatrix[i],internalId+1,
        newAdjacencyMatrix[i], internalId,
        numVertices-internalId-1);
    }
```

Then, copy all the rows after the one for the vertex being deleted:

```
    for(int i=internalId+1;i<numVertices;i++){
        newAdjacencyMatrix[i-1] = new Object[numVertices-1];
        System.arraycopy(adjacencyMatrix[i],0,
        newAdjacencyMatrix[i-1], 0, internalId);
        System.arraycopy(adjacencyMatrix[i],internalId+1,
        newAdjacencyMatrix[i-1], internalId,
        numVertices-internalId-1);
    }
    adjacencyMatrix = newAdjacencyMatrix;
```

Now adjust all the indexes of the vertices added after the one that is deleted. We do this by traversing the tree in preorder and updating only when appropriate:

```
    vertices.traverseDepthFirstNonRecursive((gv)->{
        if(((Vertex)gv).getInternalIndex()>internalId)
            ((Vertex)gv).setInternalIndex(((
                Vertex)gv).getInternalIndex()-1);
    }, BinaryTree.DepthFirstTraversalType.PREORDER);
    vertices.deleteValue(new GraphVertex<>(id, null));
}else{
    throw new IllegalArgumentException("Vertex with id "+id
    +" does not exist");
}
}
```

Adding an edge involves setting an entry in the adjacency matrix. However, before doing this, we need to look up the index of the vertex:

```
@Override
public void addEdge(int source, int target) {
    BinaryTree.Node<GraphVertex<V>> sNode = vertices.searchValue(
            new GraphVertex<V>(source, null));
    BinaryTree.Node<GraphVertex<V>> tNode = vertices.searchValue(
            new GraphVertex<V>(target, null));
    if(sNode!=null && tNode!=null) {
        int s = ((Vertex)(sNode.getValue())).getInternalIndex();
        int t = ((Vertex)(tNode.getValue())).getInternalIndex();
```

```
            if(adjacencyMatrix[s][t] == null){
                adjacencyMatrix[s][t] = nullEdge;
                if(undirected){
                    adjacencyMatrix[t][s] = nullEdge;
                }
            }else{
                throw new IllegalArgumentException("Edge
                already exists");
            }
        }else{
            throw new IllegalArgumentException("Non-existent ID");
        }


    }
```

This is the same as adding an edge, other than the fact that we change the corresponding entry in the adjacency matrix to null:

```
    @Override
    public void removeEdge(int source, int target) {
        BinaryTree.Node<GraphVertex<V>> sNode = vertices.searchValue(
                new GraphVertex<V>(source, null));
        BinaryTree.Node<GraphVertex<V>> tNode = vertices.searchValue(
                new GraphVertex<V>(target, null));
        if(sNode!=null && tNode!=null) {
            int s = ((Vertex)(sNode.getValue())).getInternalIndex();
            int t = ((Vertex)(tNode.getValue())).getInternalIndex();
            adjacencyMatrix[s][t] = null;
        }else{
            throw new IllegalArgumentException("Non-existent ID");
        }


    }
```

Checking whether two vertices are adjacent involves looking up a value in the adjacency matrix like before. But again, we must first look up the indexes of the vertices:

```
    @Override
    public boolean isAdjacent(int source, int target) {
        BinaryTree.Node<GraphVertex<V>> sNode = vertices.searchValue(
                new GraphVertex<V>(source, null));
        BinaryTree.Node<GraphVertex<V>> tNode = vertices.searchValue(
                new GraphVertex<V>(target, null));
        if(sNode!=null && tNode!=null) {
            int s = ((Vertex)(sNode.getValue())).getInternalIndex();
            int t = ((Vertex)(tNode.getValue())).getInternalIndex();
```

```
                return adjacencyMatrix[s][t] != null;
            }else{
                throw new IllegalArgumentException("Non-existent ID");
            }


    }
```

Getting the list of neighbors is a little trickier. We don't have a search mechanism that lets us search by index to look up the ID. So instead of reading a row in the adjacency matrix, we simply preorder traverse the search tree and check whether there is an edge for the vertex in the adjacency matrix. We add a vertex only when there is an edge between the source vertex and the vertex in question:

```
    @Override
    public LinkedList<Integer> getNeighbors(int source) {
        BinaryTree.Node<GraphVertex<V>> node = vertices.searchValue(
                        new GraphVertex<V>(source, null));
        if(node!=null){
            LinkedList<Integer> neighborsList = new LinkedList<>();
            int sourceInternalIndex = ((Vertex)
            node.getValue()).getInternalIndex();
            vertices.traverseDepthFirstNonRecursive((gv)->{
                int targetInternalIndex = ((Vertex) gv)
                .getInternalIndex();
                if(adjacencyMatrix[sourceInternalIndex]
                   [targetInternalIndex]!=null)
                    neighborsList.appendLast(gv.getId());
            }, BinaryTree.DepthFirstTraversalType.INORDER);
            return neighborsList;
        }else{
            throw new IllegalArgumentException("Vertex with
                id "+source+" does not exist");
        }


    }
```

The process of setting and getting values into/from the edges and vertices is the same as before, except that we need to look up the index from the ID of the vertex before using it:

```
    @Override
    public void setVertexValue(int vertex, V value) {
        BinaryTree.Node<GraphVertex<V>> node =
                vertices.searchValue(
                        new GraphVertex<V>(vertex, null));
        if(node!=null){
            node.getValue().setValue(value);
```

```
        }else{
            throw new IllegalArgumentException("Vertex with
            id "+vertex+" does not exist");
        }
    }


    @Override
    public V getVertexValue(int vertex) {
        BinaryTree.Node<GraphVertex<V>> node =
                vertices.searchValue(
                        new GraphVertex<V>(vertex, null));
        if(node!=null){
            return node.getValue().getValue();
        }else{
            throw new IllegalArgumentException("Vertex with
            id "+vertex+" does not exist");
        }
    }


    @Override
    public void setEdgeValue(int source, int target, E value) {
        BinaryTree.Node<GraphVertex<V>> sNode = vertices.searchValue(
                new GraphVertex<V>(source, null));
        BinaryTree.Node<GraphVertex<V>> tNode = vertices.searchValue(
                new GraphVertex<V>(target, null));
        if(sNode!=null && tNode!=null) {
            int s = ((Vertex)(sNode.getValue())).getInternalIndex();
            int t = ((Vertex)(tNode.getValue())).getInternalIndex();
            adjacencyMatrix[s][t] = value;
            if (undirected) {
                adjacencyMatrix[t][s] = value;
            }
        }else{
            throw new IllegalArgumentException("Non-existent ID");
        }
    }


    @Override
    public E getEdgeValue(int source, int target) {
        BinaryTree.Node<GraphVertex<V>> sNode = vertices.searchValue(
                new GraphVertex<V>(source, null));
        BinaryTree.Node<GraphVertex<V>> tNode = vertices.searchValue(
                new GraphVertex<V>(target, null));
        if(sNode!=null && tNode!=null) {
```

```
            int s = ((Vertex)(sNode.getValue())).getInternalIndex();
            int t = ((Vertex)(tNode.getValue())).getInternalIndex();
            return (E) adjacencyMatrix[s][t];
        }else{
            throw new IllegalArgumentException("Non-existent ID");
        }
    }

    @Override
    public boolean isUndirected() {
        return undirected;
    }

    @Override
    public BinarySearchTree<Integer> getAllVertices() {
        BinarySearchTree<Integer> allVertices = new RedBlackTree<>();
        vertices.traverseDepthFirstNonRecursive(
          (v) -> allVertices.insertValue(v.getId()),
            BinaryTree.DepthFirstTraversalType.PREORDER);
        return allVertices;
    }
    @Override
    public int maxVertexID() {
        return nextId-1;
    }
}
```

Complexity of operations in a dense adjacency-matrix-based graph

The following are the complexities of the operations we just discussed in a dense adjacency-matrix-based graph:

- **Add vertex**: Addition still has the same $\theta(|V|^2)$ operation for creating a new adjacency matrix and copying all the old values. The additional operation of inserting a new vertex in the search tree is $\theta(lg\ |V|)$. So the entire operation is still $\theta(|V|^2)$.

- **Remove vertex**: The removal of a vertex here follows the same operation of recreating an adjacency matrix and copying all the old values, which is $\theta(|V|^2)$. The operation of removing a vertex from the search tree is $\theta(lg\ |V|)$. So the entire operation is $\theta(|V|^2)$.

- **Add edge and remove edge**: The operation of updating an entry in the adjacency matrix is still $\theta(1)$. However, now we need to have two lookups in the search tree to figure out the indexes of the source and target. Both these searches are $\theta(lg \, |V|)$. So the entire operation is $\theta(lg \, |V|)$.

- **Adjacent**: This is also $\theta(lg \, |V|)$ due to the same reason mentioned in the preceding bullet point.

- **Neighbors**: Traversing the search tree is $\theta(|V|)$, and for each of the vertices thus traversed, we create a constant number of operations. Looking up the index of the source vertex is $\theta(lg \, |V|)$. Hence, the entire operation is still $\theta(|V|)$.

- **Setting and getting values at vertices and edges**: These operations require a fixed number of lookups (one or two) and then a constant time operation for setting or getting the appropriate value. The lookups are $\theta(lg \, |V|)$, so the entire operations are also $\theta(lg \, |V|)$.

- **Get all vertices**: Just like the previous implementation, this operation is $\theta(|V| \, lg \, |V|)$.

Adjacency list

An adjacency list is a more space-efficient graph representation of sparse graphs. A sparse graph is a graph that has a very few edges as compared to the number of edges in a complete graph with the same number of vertices. A complete graph has $|V| \, (\, |V| - 1)/2 = \theta \, (|V|^2)$ edges, and the memory space required to store a graph as an adjacency matrix is also $\theta \, (|V|^2)$. So, in the case of a dense (almost complete) graph, it makes sense to store it as an adjacency matrix. However, this is not true for a sparse graph.

In an adjacency list representation, vertices are stored in an array or some other data structure, and edges are stored along with the vertices in some list or some other structure. First, we will consider an adjacency-list-based representation where the vertices are stored in an array indexed by their IDs, as in the case of a sparse adjacency matrix representation. It has the same problem: we cannot reduce the size of the array of vertices when a vertex is deleted. However, in this case, the list of edges are deleted, and this makes it way more space-efficient than what we encountered in an adjacency matrix:

```
public class AdjacencyListGraphWithSparseVertex<V,E> implements
Graph<V,E> {
    boolean undirected;

    public AdjacencyListGraphWithSparseVertex(boolean undirected) {
        this.undirected = undirected;
    }
```

The `Edge` class stores the details of the target and the value of an edge originating from a vertex. The vertex stores a collection of the associated edges. We make the edge comparable based of the ID of the target so that we can store them in a binary search tree to easily look it up based on the ID:

```
class Edge implements Comparable<Edge>{
        E value;
        int target;
```

To improve the performance of the `getNeighbors` operation, we store a list of neighbors in the node. We store a pointer in the node that corresponds to the target of this node in the `targetNode` state variable:

```
        DoublyLinkedList.DoublyLinkedNode<Integer> targetNode;

        public Edge(int target) {
            this.target = target;
        }

        @Override
        public boolean equals(Object o) {
            if (this == o) return true;
            if (o == null || getClass() != o.getClass()) return false;

            Edge edge = (Edge) o;

            return target == edge.target;

        }

        @Override
        public int hashCode() {
            return target;
        }

        @Override
        public int compareTo(Edge o) {
            return target - o.target;
        }
    }
```

The `Vertex` class is used to store a vertex along with its associated edges. The edges are stored in a red black tree:

```
        class Vertex extends GraphVertex<V>{
            RedBlackTree<Edge>
                    edges = new RedBlackTree<>();
```

```
        DoublyLinkedList<Integer> neighbors =
          new DoublyLinkedList<>();
        public Vertex(int id, V value) {
            super(id, value);
        }
    }
```

The vertices are then stored in an array:

```
    Object[] vertices = new Object[0];
```

Adding a vertex does not require us to copy any edges; it just ensures that the vertices are copied to a newly created array of bigger size:

```
    @Override
    public int addVertex() {
        Object[] newVertices = new Object[vertices.length+1];
        System.arraycopy(vertices, 0, newVertices, 0,
                        vertices.length);
        newVertices[vertices.length] = new Vertex(
          vertices.length, null);
        vertices=newVertices;
        return newVertices.length-1;
    }
```

Removing a vertex requires that you first set the vertex to null at its position. However, you must also remove all the edges from all the other vertices for which the deleted vertex was the target:

```
    @Override
    public void removeVertex(int id) {
        Vertex sVertex = (Vertex) vertices[id];
        if(sVertex==null){
            throw new IllegalArgumentException("Vertex "+
              id +" does not exist");
        }
        LinkedList<Integer> neighbors = getNeighbors(id);
        Edge dummyEdgeForId = new Edge(id);
```

We must remove all the edges associated with the vertex being deleted:

```
        for(int t:neighbors){
            Edge e = ((Vertex)vertices[t]).edges.deleteValue(
                        dummyEdgeForId).getValue();
            ((Vertex)vertices[t]).neighbors.removeNode(e.targetNode);
        }
        vertices[id] = null;
    }
```

Adding an edge requires making corresponding entries in the vertices associated with it:

```
@Override
public void addEdge(int source, int target) {
    Vertex sVertex = (Vertex) vertices[source];
    Edge sEdge = sVertex.edges.insertValue(new
      Edge(target)).getValue();
    sEdge.targetNode = (DoublyLinkedList.DoublyLinkedNode<Integer>)
    sVertex.neighbors.appendLast(sEdge.target);
    if(undirected){
        Vertex tVertex = (Vertex) vertices[target];
        Edge tEdge = tVertex.edges.insertValue(
          new Edge(source)).getValue();
        tEdge.targetNode = (DoublyLinkedList
          .DoublyLinkedNode<Integer>)
        tVertex.neighbors.appendLast(tEdge.target);
    }
}
```

Removing an edge requires removing the corresponding entries in the associated vertices:

```
@Override
public void removeEdge(int source, int target) {
    Vertex sVertex = (Vertex) vertices[source];
    Edge deletedEdge = sVertex.edges.deleteValue(
      new Edge(target)).getValue();
    sVertex.neighbors.removeNode(deletedEdge.targetNode);
    if(undirected){
        Vertex tVertex = (Vertex) vertices[target];
        deletedEdge = tVertex.edges.deleteValue(
          new Edge(source)).getValue();
        tVertex.neighbors.removeNode(deletedEdge.targetNode);
    }
}
```

Checking adjacency involves looking up the source vertex first and then looking up an edge for the target in the corresponding red black tree:

```
@Override
public boolean isAdjacent(int source, int target) {
    Vertex sVertex = (Vertex) vertices[source];
    return sVertex.edges.searchValue(new Edge(target))!=null;
}
```

We have the list of neighbors precomputed, so we simply return this list:

```
@Override
public LinkedList<Integer> getNeighbors(int source) {s
    Vertex sVertex = (Vertex) vertices[source];
    return sVertex.neighbors;
}
```

The process of setting and getting the values of a vertex or an edge are self-explanatory:

```
@Override
public void setVertexValue(int vertex, V value) {
    Vertex sVertex = (Vertex) vertices[vertex];
    if(sVertex==null){
        throw new IllegalArgumentException("Vertex "+ vertex
        + "does not exist");
    }else{
        sVertex.setValue(value);
    }
}


@Override
public V getVertexValue(int vertex) {
    Vertex sVertex = (Vertex) vertices[vertex];
    if(sVertex==null){
        throw new IllegalArgumentException("Vertex "+ vertex
            + "does not exist");
    }else{
        return sVertex.getValue();
    }
}


@Override
public void setEdgeValue(int source, int target, E value) {
    Vertex sVertex = (Vertex) vertices[source];
    Vertex tVertex = (Vertex) vertices[target];
```

```
        if(sVertex==null){
            throw new IllegalArgumentException("Vertex "+ source
                + "does not exist");
        }else if(tVertex==null){
            throw new IllegalArgumentException("Vertex "+ target
                + "does not exist");
        }else{
            BinaryTree.Node<Edge> node = sVertex.edges.searchValue(
                new Edge(target));
            if(node==null){
                throw new IllegalArgumentException(
                    "Edge between "+ source + "and" + target
                    + "does not exist");

            }else{
                node.getValue().value = value;
            }
        }
    }


    @Override
    public E getEdgeValue(int source, int target) {
        Vertex sVertex = (Vertex) vertices[source];
        Vertex tVertex = (Vertex) vertices[target];
        if(sVertex==null){
            throw new IllegalArgumentException("Vertex "+ source
                + "does not exist");
        }else if(tVertex==null){
            throw new IllegalArgumentException("Vertex "+ target
                + "does not exist");
        }else{
            BinaryTree.Node<Edge> node =
                    sVertex.edges.searchValue(new Edge(target));
            if(node==null){
                throw new IllegalArgumentException(
                    "Edge between "+ source + "and" + target
                    + "does not exist");
            }else{
                return node.getValue().value;
            }
        }
    }
}
```

```java
@Override
public boolean isUndirected() {
    return undirected;
}

@Override
public BinarySearchTree<Integer> getAllVertices() {
    BinarySearchTree<Integer> allVertices = new RedBlackTree<>();
    for(int i=0;i<vertices.length;i++){
        if(vertices[i]!=null){
            allVertices.insertValue(i);
        }
    }
    return allVertices;
}

@Override
public int maxVertexID() {
    return vertices.length-1;
}
}
```

Complexity of operations in an adjacency-list-based graph

The following lists the complexities of the operations we have discussed in an adjacency-list-based graph:

- **Add vertex**: Addition of a vertex requires that you create a new array first and then copy all the vertices to it. So it is $\theta(|V|)$.

- **Remove Vertex**: The removal process does not change the array of the vertices. However, this operation involves checking each vertex to remove the edges which has the vertex being deleted as the target. So this operation is $\theta(|V|)$ as well.

- Add edge and remove edge: The first step of this operation is to look up the source vertex, which is constant time. The second step is to add or remove an edge in a red black tree, so it is $\theta(lg\ |V|)$. So the entire operation of adding/ deleting an edge is $\theta(lg\ |V|)$.

- **Adjacent**: The first step of this operation is to look up the source vertex, which is constant time. The second step is to look up the edge in a red black tree, so it is $\theta(lg\ |V|)$. So the entire operation of adding/deleting an edge is $\theta(lg\ |V|)$.

- **Neighbors**: Since the list of neighbors is precomputed, the complexity is the same as that for looking up a vertex, which is constant time.

- **Setting and Getting values at vertices**: These operations require looking up the vertex first, which is constant time. The second step is setting/getting the value. These operations are $\theta(1)$.

- **Setting and Getting values at edges**: These operations require looking up the source vertex first and then looking up the particular edge. The first is $\theta(1)$ and the second is $\theta(lg\ |V|)$. At the end, setting or getting the value of an edge is $\theta(l)$. Hence, the total operation is $\theta(lg\ |V|)$.

- **Get all vertices**: This operation is $\theta(\ |V|\ lg\ |V|\ )$, just like the previous implementations.

Adjacency-list-based graph with dense storage for vertices

Just as in the case of an adjacency-matrix-based graph, dense storage of vertices can be done using a search tree instead of an array. This allows us to recover space when we delete a vertex without affecting the IDs of the other vertices. Everything else remains the same as the array-based storage of the vertices:

```
public class AdjacencyListGraphWithDenseVertex<V,E> implements
Graph<V,E> {
```

The `nextId` variable stores the value that would be the ID of the next vertex that is inserted:

```
int nextId;
boolean undirected;
```

We have the `Edge` and `Vertex` class as before:

```
class Edge implements Comparable<Edge>{
    E value;
    int target;

    DoublyLinkedList.DoublyLinkedNode<Integer> targetNode;
    public Edge(int target) {
        this.target = target;
    }

    @Override
    public boolean equals(Object o) {
        if (this == o) return true;
```

```
            if (o == null || getClass() != o.getClass())
                return false;
            Edge edge = (Edge) o;
            return target == edge.target;
        }


        @Override
        public int hashCode() {
            return target;
        }


        @Override
        public int compareTo(Edge o) {
            return target - o.target;
        }
    }
    class Vertex extends GraphVertex<V>{
        RedBlackTree<Edge> edges = new RedBlackTree<Edge>();

        DoublyLinkedList<Integer> neighbors
                            = new DoublyLinkedList<>();
        public Vertex(int id, V value) {
            super(id, value);
        }
    }

    public AdjacencyListGraphWithDenseVertex(boolean undirected) {
        this.undirected = undirected;
    }
```

Now, instead of using an array to store the vertices, use a red black tree:

```
    RedBlackTree<GraphVertex<V>> vertices = new RedBlackTree<>();
```

Adding a new vertex means inserting a new one in the red black tree:

```
    @Override
    public int addVertex() {
        vertices.insertValue(new Vertex(nextId++, null));
        return nextId;
    }
```

The removal process, as before, involves not only removing the vertex but also going through all the other vertices and deleting every edge that has the vertex that is being deleted as the target:

```java
@Override
public void removeVertex(int id) {
    vertices.deleteValue(new GraphVertex<V>(id, null));
    vertices.traverseDepthFirstNonRecursive((gv)->{
            BinaryTree.Node<Edge> edgeNode = ((
                Vertex) gv).edges.deleteValue(new Edge(id));
            if(edgeNode!=null){
                Edge edge = edgeNode.getValue();
                ((Vertex) gv)
                    .neighbors.removeNode(edge.targetNode);
            }
        },
            BinaryTree.DepthFirstTraversalType.INORDER);
}
```

The first step is to find the source and the target node to confirm that they exist. After this, add an edge to the collection of edges of the source node. If the graph is undirected, add an edge to the collection of edges in the target node as well:

```java
@Override
public void addEdge(int source, int target) {
    BinaryTree.Node<GraphVertex<V>> sNode =
        vertices.searchValue(new GraphVertex<V>(source, null));
    BinaryTree.Node<GraphVertex<V>> tNode =
            vertices.searchValue(
                    new GraphVertex<V>(target, null));
    if(sNode == null){
        throw new IllegalArgumentException("Vertex ID "
            +source+" does not exist");
    }else if(tNode == null){
        throw new IllegalArgumentException("Vertex ID "
            +target+" does not exist");
    }else{
        Vertex sVertex = (Vertex) sNode.getValue();
        Vertex tVertex = (Vertex) tNode.getValue();
        Edge tEdge = new Edge(target);
        sVertex.edges.insertValue(tEdge);
        tEdge.targetNode = (DoublyLinkedList
            .DoublyLinkedNode<Integer>) sVertex.neighbors
            .appendLast(tVertex.getId());
```

```
        if(undirected) {
            Edge sEdge = new Edge(source);
            tVertex.edges.insertValue(sEdge);
            sEdge.targetNode = (DoublyLinkedList
                .DoublyLinkedNode<Integer>) tVertex.neighbors
                .appendLast(sVertex.getId());
        }
    }
}
```

The first step is the same as that of the previous one. After this, the edge is removed from the collection of the edges of the source node. If the graph is undirected, the edge is also removed from the collection of edges in the target node:

```
@Override
public void removeEdge(int source, int target) {
    BinaryTree.Node<GraphVertex<V>> sNode =
            vertices.searchValue(
                    new GraphVertex<V>(source, null));
    BinaryTree.Node<GraphVertex<V>> tNode =
            vertices.searchValue(
                    new GraphVertex<V>(target, null));
    if(sNode == null){
        throw new IllegalArgumentException("Vertex ID "
          +source+" does not exist");
    }else if(tNode == null){
        throw new IllegalArgumentException("Vertex ID "
          +target+" does not exist");
    }else{
        Vertex sVertex = (Vertex) sNode.getValue();
        Edge deletedEdge = sVertex.edges.deleteValue(
          new Edge(target)).getValue();
        sVertex.neighbors.removeNode(deletedEdge.targetNode);
        if(undirected) {
            Vertex tVertex = (Vertex) tNode.getValue();
            deletedEdge = tVertex.edges.deleteValue(
              new Edge(source)).getValue();
            tVertex.neighbors.removeNode(deletedEdge.targetNode);
        }
    }
}
```

The first step is the same as that of the previous one. After this, the edge with the correct target is looked up. If the edge is found, the vertices are adjacent:

```
@Override
public boolean isAdjacent(int source, int target) {
    BinaryTree.Node<GraphVertex<V>> sNode =
            vertices.searchValue(
                    new GraphVertex<V>(source, null));
    BinaryTree.Node<GraphVertex<V>> tNode =
            vertices.searchValue(
                    new GraphVertex<V>(target, null));
    if(sNode == null){
        throw new IllegalArgumentException("Vertex ID "
                                    +source+" does not exist");
    }else if(tNode == null){
        throw new IllegalArgumentException("Vertex ID "
                                    +target+" does not exist");
    }else{
        Vertex sVertex = (Vertex) sNode.getValue();
        return sVertex.edges.searchValue(
                            new Edge(target)) != null;


    }
}
```

We just look up the vertex and then return our precomputed list of neighbors:

```
@Override
public LinkedList<Integer> getNeighbors(int source) {
    BinaryTree.Node<GraphVertex<V>> sNode =
            vertices.searchValue(
                    new GraphVertex<V>(source, null));
    if(sNode == null){
        throw new IllegalArgumentException(
                "Vertex ID "+source+" does not exist");
    }else{
        Vertex sVertex = (Vertex) sNode.getValue();
        return  sVertex.neighbors;
    }
}
```

The process of setting and getting values is the same as before, except that we need to look up the vertex/vertices in the red black tree instead of the array before setting up the values:

```java
@Override
public void setVertexValue(int vertex, V value) {
    BinaryTree.Node<GraphVertex<V>> sNode =
            vertices.searchValue(
                    new GraphVertex<V>(vertex, null));
    if(sNode == null){
        throw new IllegalArgumentException("Vertex ID "
                        +vertex+" does not exist");
    }else{
        Vertex sVertex = (Vertex) sNode.getValue();
        sVertex.setValue(value);
    }
}


@Override
public V getVertexValue(int vertex) {
    BinaryTree.Node<GraphVertex<V>> sNode =
            vertices.searchValue(
                    new GraphVertex<V>(vertex, null));
    if(sNode == null){
        throw new IllegalArgumentException("Vertex ID "
                        +vertex+" does not exist");
    }else{
        Vertex sVertex = (Vertex) sNode.getValue();
        return sVertex.getValue();
    }
}


@Override
public void setEdgeValue(int source, int target, E value) {
    BinaryTree.Node<GraphVertex<V>> sNode =
            vertices.searchValue(
                    new GraphVertex<V>(source, null));
    BinaryTree.Node<GraphVertex<V>> tNode =
            vertices.searchValue(
                    new GraphVertex<V>(target, null));
    if(sNode == null){
        throw new IllegalArgumentException("Vertex ID "
                        +source+" does not exist");
    }else if(tNode == null){
        throw new IllegalArgumentException("Vertex ID "
                        +target+" does not exist");
```

```
        }else{
            Vertex sVertex = (Vertex) sNode.getValue();
            BinaryTree.Node<Edge> edgeNode =
                    sVertex.edges.searchValue(new Edge(target));
            if(edgeNode!=null) {
                edgeNode.getValue().value = value;
                if (undirected) {
                    Vertex tVertex = (Vertex) tNode.getValue();
                    edgeNode = tVertex.edges
                            .searchValue(new Edge(source));
                    edgeNode.getValue().value = value;
                }
            }else{
                throw new IllegalArgumentException(
                        "No edge exists between the vertices "
                        + source + " and " + target);
            }
        }
    }
}

@Override
public E getEdgeValue(int source, int target) {
    BinaryTree.Node<GraphVertex<V>> sNode =
            vertices.searchValue(
                    new GraphVertex<V>(source, null));
    BinaryTree.Node<GraphVertex<V>> tNode =
            vertices.searchValue(
                    new GraphVertex<V>(target, null));
    if(sNode == null){
        throw new IllegalArgumentException("Vertex ID
                            "+source+" does not exist");
    }else if(tNode == null){
        throw new IllegalArgumentException("Vertex ID
                            "+target+" does not exist");
    }else{
        Vertex sVertex = (Vertex) sNode.getValue();
        BinaryTree.Node<Edge> edgeNode =
                sVertex.edges.searchValue(new Edge(target));
        if(edgeNode!=null) {
            return edgeNode.getValue().value;

        }else{
            throw new IllegalArgumentException(
                    "No edge exists between the vertices "
                    + source + " and " + target);
```

```
            }
        }
    }

    @Override
    public boolean isUndirected() {
        return undirected;
    }

    @Override
    public BinarySearchTree<Integer> getAllVertices() {
        BinarySearchTree<Integer> allVertices
                              = new RedBlackTree<>();
        vertices.traverseDepthFirstNonRecursive(
                (v) -> allVertices.insertValue(v.getId()),
            BinaryTree.DepthFirstTraversalType.PREORDER);
        return allVertices;
    }

    @Override
    public int maxVertexID() {
        return nextId -1;
    }
}
```

Complexity of the operations of an adjacency-list-based graph with dense storage for vertices

The complexity of the operations of an adjacency-list-based graph is as follows:

- **Add vertex**: Addition of a vertex requires insertion of one in the red black tree. So this operation is $\theta(lg \, |V|)$.

- **Remove Vertex**: The removal process requires deletion of the vertex from the red black tree, which is $\theta(lg \, |V|)$. However, this operation involves checking each vertex to remove the edges which has the vertex being deleted as the target. So this operation is $\theta(|V|)$ as well.

- **Add edge and remove edge**: The first step of this operation is to look up the source vertex, which is $\theta(lg \, |V|)$. The second step is to add or remove an edge to/from a red black tree, so this is also $\theta(lg \, |V|)$. Therefore, the entire operation of adding/deleting an edge is $\theta(lg \, |V|)$.

- **Adjacent**: The first step of this operation is to look up the source vertex, which is $\theta(lg \mid V \mid)$. The second step is to look up the edge in a red black tree, which is $\theta(lg \mid V \mid)$ too. Therefore, the entire operation of adding/deleting an edge is $\theta(lg \mid V \mid)$.

- **Neighbors**: The list of neighbors is precomputed, so the complexity of this operation is the same as that of searching a vertex, which is $\theta(lg \mid V \mid)$.

- **Setting and getting values at vertices**: These operations require you to first look up the vertex, which is $\theta(lg \mid V \mid)$. The second step is to set/get the value. These operations are $\theta(lg \mid V \mid)$.

- **Setting and getting values at edges**: These operations require you to first look up the source vertex and then the particular edge. Both of these operations are $\theta(lg \mid V \mid)$. At the end, setting or getting the value of an edge is $\theta(l)$. Hence, the total operation is $\theta(lg \mid V \mid)$.

- **Get all vertices**: Here too, this operation is $\theta(\mid V \mid lg \mid V \mid)$.

Traversal of a graph

The traversal of a graph is the graph's equivalent of the traversal of a tree, as discussed in an earlier chapter. Just as in the case of a tree, we can traverse either breadth-first or depth-first. However, unlike a tree, a graph can reach all the vertices without going through the edges. This makes it necessary to consider the traversal of all the edges and vertices separately. Another thing is that a graph has no designated root, so we can start from any particular vertex. Finally, since a graph may not be connected, we may not be able to traverse all the vertices/edges, starting from one single vertex. This is achieved by performing the traversal repeatedly, starting each time from any vertex that has not been visited yet already. This is a simple extension of the basic breadth-first or depth-first traversal that we are going to discuss here.

First, let's discuss visiting vertices using both the breadth-first and depth-first search. It involves maintaining two collections of vertices: one that stores all the vertices that are discovered but are yet to be visited/explored and another that stores a Boolean array that checks whether a vertex has already been explored/visited.

The collection of vertices that are discovered but yet to be explored can be of two types: if it is a stack, we have a depth-first traversal, and if it is a queue, we have a breadth-first traversal.

To implement both depth-first and breadth-first searches in a single method, we need to create a super interface of our `Stack` and `Queue` interfaces. We will need to define three methods in it:

```
public interface OrderedStore<E> {
    void insert(E value);
    E pickFirst();
    E checkFirst();
}
```

Now implement these methods in the `Stack` and `Queue` interfaces as default methods to delegate to their appropriate methods:

```
public interface Stack<E> extends OrderedStore<E>{
    void push(E value);
    E pop();
    E peek();
    @Override
    default E checkFirst(){
        return peek();
    }

    @Override
    default void insert(E value){
        push(value);
    }

    @Override
    default E pickFirst(){
        return pop();
    }
}

public interface Queue<E> extends OrderedStore<E>{
    void enqueue(E value);
    E dequeue();
    E peek();

    @Override
    default E checkFirst(){
        return peek();
    }

    @Override
    default void insert(E value){
        enqueue(value);
```

```
    }

    @Override
    default E pickFirst(){
        return dequeue();
    }
}
```

This allows us to use the OrderedStore interface to hold both a stack and a queue. We also create a new functional interface that represents a lambda that takes two arguments and does not return anything:

```
public interface TwoArgumentStatement<E,F> {
    void doSomething(E e, F f);
}
```

We implement this search as a default method in the Graph interface itself.

```
enum TraversalType{
    DFT, BFT
}
```

In the beginning, we only insert the starting vertex to the collection of vertices that are not yet explored. Then, we loop until all the vertices that can be discovered in the search are processed and there are no more elements in the collection of vertices. We avoid processing each vertex from the collection of vertices if it has already been processed. Otherwise, we mark it as "being processed" and invoke the visitor on it. Finally, we expand this vertex by inserting all its neighbors to the collection of elements that have to be processed:

```
default void visitAllConnectedVertices(int startingNode,
TwoArgumentStatement<Integer, V> visitor, TraversalType type) {
        OrderedStore<Integer> toBeProcessed = null;
        boolean doneProcessing[] = new boolean[maxVertexID()+1];
        switch (type){
            case BFT:
                toBeProcessed = new QueueImplLinkedList<Integer>();
                break;
            case DFT:
                toBeProcessed = new StackImplLinkedList<Integer>();
                break;
        }

        toBeProcessed.insert(startingNode);
```

```
while(toBeProcessed.checkFirst()!=null){

    int currentVertex = toBeProcessed.pickFirst();
    if(doneProcessing[currentVertex]){
        continue;
    }

    doneProcessing[currentVertex] = true;
    visitor.doSomething(currentVertex,
                    getVertexValue(currentVertex));


    for(int neighbor:getNeighbors(currentVertex)){
        if(doneProcessing[neighbor]==false){
            toBeProcessed.insert(neighbor);
        }
    }
}
}
```

The process of traversal of edges is also very similar; we can follow either the breadth-first or depth-first traversal. In this case, the visitor needs access to both the source and target of the edges, which makes it necessary to store both of them in the stack or queue we use. For this purpose, we create a class named Edge. The class is comparable so that edges can be stored in a binary search tree for easy search ability:

```
class Edge implements Comparable<Edge>{
        int source;
        int target;

        public Edge(int source, int target) {
            this.source = source;
            this.target = target;
        }

        @Override
        public boolean equals(Object o) {
            if (this == o) return true;
            if (o == null || getClass() != o.getClass())
                return false;

            Edge edge = (Edge) o;

            if (source != edge.source) return false;
            return target == edge.target;
```

```
        }

        @Override
        public int hashCode() {
            int result = source;
            result = 31 * result + target;
            return result;
        }


        @Override
        public int compareTo(Edge o) {
            if(source!=o.source){
                return source - o.source;
            }else {
                return target - o.target;
            }
        }
    }
}
```

Now we can implement the process of traversal of edges using the breadth-first and depth-first traversal:

```
default void visitAllConnectedEdges(int startingNode,
ThreeArgumentStatement<Integer, Integer, E> visitor,
                                    TraversalType type){

    OrderedStore<Edge> toBeProcessed = null;
    boolean doneProcessing[] = new boolean[maxVertexID()+1];
    switch (type){
        case BFT: toBeProcessed = new QueueImplLinkedList<Edge>();
        break;
        case DFT: toBeProcessed = new StackImplLinkedList<Edge>();
        break;
    }
    toBeProcessed.insert(new Edge(-1, startingNode));
    while (toBeProcessed.checkFirst()!=null){
        Edge edge = toBeProcessed.pickFirst();
        LinkedList<Integer> neighbors = getNeighbors(edge.target);
        if(edge.source>=0) {
            visitor.doSomething(edge.source, edge.target,
              getEdgeValue(edge.source, edge.target));
        }
        if(doneProcessing[edge.target]){
            continue;
        }
```

```
        for(int target: neighbors){
            if(isUndirected() && doneProcessing[target]){
                continue;
            }
            Edge nextEdge = new Edge(edge.target, target);
            if(nextEdge.target!=edge.source)
                toBeProcessed.insert(nextEdge);
        }

        doneProcessing[edge.target] = true;
    }
}
```

Complexity of traversals

For each traversal, either all vertices or edges, all edges must be traversed. This is true even if you just want to visit the vertices. The actual complexity depends on the particular map implementation, so we will use that the complexity of the operation `getNeighbors` method is $\theta(g(|V|))$.

If you're visiting either the edges or vertices, ensure that each vertex is expanded only once. This operation is done $|V|$ times, each of which is $\theta(g(|V|))$. So the complexity, due to the expansion of the vertex, to find out the neighbors is $\theta(|V|g(|V|))$. When expanded, they are visited once, and for each edge, we have one neighbor. Some of these neighbors have been visited before; however, we need to perform constant time to verify this. So each vertex is visited once and each neighbor is checked once. This changes the complexity to $\theta(|V|g(|V|) + |E|)$. Since we have seen an implementation of a graph that has the constant time `getNeighbors` method, we can have a traversal in $\theta(|V| + |E|)$.

Cycle detection

One of the uses of a traversal is cycle detection. A connected undirected graph without any cycle is a tree. A directed graph without any cycle is called a directed acyclic graph (DAG). Cycle detection in graphs can be done in a very similar manner. In the case of an undirected graph, if we do a DFS and the same node is visited twice as the target of an edge, there is a cycle. Since the edge is undirected, we are satisfied if either the source or the target has not been seen before.

In the case of a directed graph, visiting the same node twice is not enough if you want to know whether there is a cycle; we should also consider the direction of the edges. This means while traversing the edges, we need to know whether we can reach the same node we started with. This requires us to remember the entire path while doing a DFS. This is why we use a recursive helper method to detect a cycle in a directed graph. We create the helper method for the directed cycle first. The checkDirectedCycleFromVertex method takes the path and binary search tree of the vertices. The list of vertices is the one that stores all the vertices, and the ones already visited must be removed so that they are not used as the starting point of cycle detection later. The list of integers is the path from the starting point in a depth-first traversal. If a vertex is repeated in the same path, it means a cycle exists:

```
default void checkDirectedCycleFromVertex(
        com.example.functional.LinkedList<Integer> path,
    BinarySearchTree<Integer> allVertices){
```

The head of the list is the deepest vertex in the path; we need to expand this:

```
        int top = path.head();
        allVertices.deleteValue(top);
        LinkedList<Integer> neighbors = getNeighbors(top);
```

Now if any neighbor is already present in the path, a cycle exists, which is what we check. If a cycle is found, we throw an instance of a custom exception:

```
        for(int n:neighbors){
            com.example.functional.LinkedList<Integer>
              pathPart = path;
            while (!pathPart.isEmpty()){
                int head = pathPart.head();
                if(head == n){
                    throw new CycleDetectedException(
                      "Cycle detected");
                }
                pathPart = pathPart.tail();
            }
            checkDirectedCycleFromVertex(path.add(n), allVertices);
        }
    }
```

Now we create the method for detection of cycles in either type of graph. Go through all the vertices as there might be unconnected parts of the graph. A directed graph may have connected vertices that cannot be reached from a particular starting vertex due to the directionality of the edges. However, once a vertex is visited in any traversal, it does not need to be visited again. This is taken care of by having all the vertices in a binary search tree and removing the ones that have been visited already:

```
default boolean detectCycle(){
```

First, we get a list of all the vertices. We get it directly by understanding how the vertices are stored inside the graphs:

```
BinarySearchTree<Integer> allVertices = getAllVertices();
try {
    if (isUndirected()) {
        while (allVertices.getRoot() != null) {
            int start = allVertices.getRoot().getValue();
            RedBlackTree<Integer> metAlready
                            = new RedBlackTree<>();
            metAlready.insertValue(start);
            allVertices.deleteValue(start);
            visitAllConnectedEdges(start, (s, t, v) -> {
                    if(metAlready.searchValue(t) == null) {
                        metAlready.insertValue(t);
                        allVertices.deleteValue(t);
                    }else if(metAlready.searchValue(s)== null){
                        metAlready.insertValue(s);
                        allVertices.deleteValue(s);
                    }else{
                        throw new CycleDetectedException(
                            "found "+t);
                    }
                }, TraversalType.DFT);
        }
    } else {
        while (allVertices.getRoot() != null) {
            checkDirectedCycleFromVertex(
                com.example.functional.LinkedList
                .<Integer>emptyList().add(allVertices
                .getRoot().getValue()), allVertices);
        }
    }
}catch (CycleDetectedException ex){
    return true;
}
return false;
}
```

Complexity of the cycle detection algorithm

First, let's check out the complexity of cycle detection in an undirected graph. The complexity of getAllVertices is $\Theta(|V| \lg |V|)$. Looking up a vertex in the search tree of vertices that have already been visited is $\Theta(\lg |V|)$. We do this twice for every edge. We also have to insert a new vertex in the metAlready search tree and delete a vertex from the allVertices search tree; the complexity of these operations for each edge is $\Theta(\lg |V|)$. So the total complexity is $\Theta(|E| \lg |V|)$.

Now let's consider the complexity of cycle detection in a directed graph. Here, we traverse each edge once. However, for each edge, we have to look through the entire path to know whether the current vertex is seen in the path. The path can potentially be of this length: $|V| - 1$. So when we check it for each edge, the complexity is $O(|E||V|)$; this is a lot higher than $O(|E| \lg |V|)$.

Spanning tree and minimum spanning tree

A spanning tree in a connected graph is a subgraph consisting of all the vertices and some edges. So, a subgraph is a tree; it is a connected graph with no loops or cycles. *Figure 5* shows an example of a spanning tree in a graph:

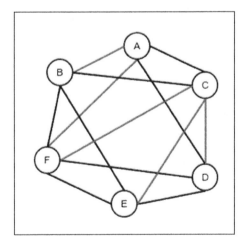

Figure 5. A spanning tree of a graph (shown in red)

A tree has minimum number of edges required to keep the vertices connected. Removing any edge from a tree will disconnect the graph. This can be useful in a map of roads that connect different places and has a minimal number of roads. With this motivation, we would really be interested in a spanning tree that has a minimum total length of roads. This may be important because constructing roads is a costly affair. Alternatively, we could design a bus route map for a city and have all the important places connected without creating too many routes; also, shorter routes are better. Such a spanning tree is called a minimum spanning tree. Finding a minimum spanning tree is an important problem. But before we discuss the algorithm, let's see some of the properties of a minimum spanning tree.

For any tree with vertices V and edges E, |V| = |E| + 1

First, let's consider this proposition: removing any edge from a tree will create two trees with no connection between them. Let's assume the opposite. We have a graph with two vertices A and B and an edge X between them. Let's assume that even if we remove X, the tree still remains connected. This means a path P exists between A and B even if you delete X. This means in the original graph, we can walk from A to B through P and use X to come back to A. This means the original graph has a cycle. But the original graph was assumed to be a tree, so this is impossible. Therefore, my original proposition that removing any edge from the tree will create two trees with no connection between them is true.

Now let's start with a graph G that has a set of edges E and vertices V. If we remove all the edges, we would of course be left with only V. These set of vertices without edges are actually single vertex trees with no connections between themselves.

We start with one tree, say G, and remove one edge. Now we have two trees. We can now remove another edge, and this will split one of these trees into two so we have three trees. This way, after the removal of each edge, we will have one more tree. Therefore, after the removal of all the edges, we will have $|E| + 1$ trees (because there was one tree before any edge was removed). These must be $|V|$ single vertex trees. So, it is either $|V| = |E| + 1$ or $|E| = |V| - 1$.

Any connected undirected graph has a spanning tree

Let's take an undirected graph. If there are loops and cycles. First, we simply delete all the loops. Consider A and B as two vertices that are neighbors and part of a cycle. This means if we walk through the edge from A to B, we can use another path: B to A (this is what makes it a cycle). So if we delete the B to A edge, we will still have a connected graph. We do this operation for every cycle. At the end of these operations, we will have a connected graph with no loops or cycles; this is a tree. This tree connects all the vertices, so it is a spanning tree.

Any undirected connected graph with the property |V| = |E| + 1 is a tree

Now let's check the reverse of the preceding theorem. Suppose there is a connected graph where $|V| = |E| + 1$. We assume it is not a tree. This graph must have a spanning tree, which is a subgraph, with fewer edges. This spanning tree will have the same number of vertices (because we never deleted any vertices) but fewer edges. Therefore, if the spanning tree has the set of edges E_1, we have $|E_1| | < |E|$ => $|E_1| | + 1 < |E| + 1$ => $|E_1| | + 1 < |V|$. But this is not possible because the new graph is a tree. So the original proposition that any undirected connected graph with the property $|V| = |E| + 1$ is a tree.

Cut property

Cut refers to a minimum set of edges that when removed would split a connected undirected graph into two separate connected graphs with no connections between them. There can be many cuts in a given graph.

The cut property can be defined as this: if an edge is an element of a cut and has a minimum cost associated with it within the cut, it is part of the minimum spanning tree of the graph. To check this out, first note that for any cut of an undirected connected graph, a spanning tree will always have exactly one member of the cut in it.

Let's have a cut X that divides the graph G into subgraphs H and J. Let G have a spanning tree called S. Since G is a connected graph and X is a cut, this means H and J are connected with each other. If X is empty, it means G was not connected; this is not possible. Now we have the Y subset of X where all the members of Y are part of the spanning tree S. If Y is empty, the vertices of H and J will be disconnected in S, so this is impossible. Now as a contradiction to $|Y| = 1$, let's assume $|Y| > 1$. This means there is more than one edge in S, between H and J. Let's pick two of them. Let the first is between vertex A in H and vertex B in J, and the second one between vertex C in H and vertex D in J. Now since the spanning tree S has all the vertices of H and J connected, there is a path from A to C and D to B in S outside of Y. So we have a cycle from A to C and C to D using one of our selected edges and we have D to B and B to A using the other selected edge. This means S has a cycle and hence S is not a tree, which is a contradiction. Therefore, $|Y| = 1$. Thus, the spanning tree has exactly one member of any cut in an undirected connected graph.

If S is the minimum spanning tree of G and X is a cut in G dividing G into H and J, S has exactly one member for X, as proved in the preceding section. Let it be any edge other than the one with minimum cost. Since S is a spanning tree, if we remove the edge that is in X, we will have two disconnected subtrees, which are spanning trees of H and J. If we insert any other edge from X now, this new edge will connect these subtrees back to the single spanning tree. This is because all the edges of X are between one vertex in H and another in J. So we can replace the edge in S that is a member of X along with the edge in X with minimum cost, and we can thus create another spanning tree of G. But the edges of the new tree will be the same as in S, except the one that has a lesser cost than the one in S. So the sum of the costs of edges of the new spanning tree must be lesser than that of S, which is a contradiction as S is a minimum spanning tree. Therefore, the minimum spanning tree S must have an edge with the least cost within the cut X.

Minimum spanning tree is unique for a graph that has all the edges whose costs are different from one another

Let's assume that we have a connected undirected graph G for which there are two different minimum spanning trees, namely S and T. Since S and T are different and have the same number of edges (because for a spanning tree, the calculation is $|V|$ = $|E| + 1$), there is an edge E in S that is not in T. Let this edge be there between the vertices A and B. Now let's create a partition of the set of vertices in G so that there are two partitions: Y and Z. Create this such that A belongs to Y, B belongs to Z, and Y and Z are disjointed and together contain all the vertices. Let X be the cut that would divide G into two subgraphs with vertices in Y and Z. Since A belongs to Y and B belongs to Z, the edge E between A and B belongs to X. Since X is a cut and S is a spanning tree, there must be exactly one edge in X that is part of S; in this case, it has to be the edge E. Now, since T is also a spanning tree and E is not a member of T, there must be another member of X that is in T; let it be **f**.

If we remove the edge E from S, we will have two different trees, which would be joined again if we insert f. This is because f is an edge between the vertices in Y and Z, and the two parts are already trees. So now we are left with another spanning tree.

All the costs are different; the cost of E is different from the cost of f. If the cost of f is lower than that of E, the total cost of the new spanning tree is lower than that of S. Although, this is not possible because S is a minimum spanning tree. So, the cost of f is higher than that of E.

We can do this for every edge in S that is not in T; S will transform into T when no more edges are available. In every step of this process, the total cost of edges will increase. This means the total cost of edges in T must be higher than that in S. However, this is impossible because S and T are both minimum spanning trees. So our original assumption that there can be two different minimum spanning trees is wrong. Therefore, each minimum spanning tree is unique in a graph where all the costs of the edges are different.

Finding the minimum spanning tree

With the properties we just discussed, we can now define an algorithm for finding the minimum spanning tree of a graph. Suppose a set of edges F is already given and they are members of the minimum spanning tree G. Now we are trying to find another edge that is also a member of the minimum spanning tree. First, we choose an edge e whose cost is minimum when compared to the rest of the edges, E and F in this case. Since some of the edges are already given, some of the vertices are already connected. If the chosen edge e is between two vertices that are already connected, we simply reject this edge and find the next edge with minimum cost. We do this until we find an edge f between two vertices that are not already connected. Our claim is that f is a new member of the minimum spanning tree. To confirm this, let's assume that f is between the vertices A and B. From the description of our procedure, A and B are not connected. Let's make two partitions of the vertices: H and J. Let's have all the vertices that are connected to A, including A in H, and all the vertices connected to B, including B in J. The rest of the vertices are assigned to the set H. Since H and J are partitions of the vertices in the original graph G, we have a cut X in the original graph G that splits the graph G in a way that all the vertices in H are placed in one of the subgraphs and all the vertices in J in the other. We know that the member of X that has the minimum cost is a member of the minimum spanning tree G. Now, of course, f is a member of X as it connects A to B. It is also the edge with the minimum cost among all the edges in X. This is because all the edges in X are in the remaining edges (otherwise some vertices in H and some in J would be connected, which cannot be true because of the way we have created the two sets), and f is the minimum cost in all the remaining edges. This means f is a new member of the spanning tree. Therefore, we use the following steps to build the minimum spanning tree:

1. Start with an empty set of edges as the spanning tree.

2. If more edges are remaining and all the vertices are not connected, choose the one with the minimum cost.

3. If the edge is between two connected vertices, discard it and go back to step 2.

4. Otherwise, add the edge to the set of edges of the minimum spanning tree.

5. Repeat from step 1.

The problem now is how to efficiently know whether the two vertices are connected. The solution is a data structure called a union set forest.

Union find

The purpose of union find is to be able to tell whether the two given objects are members of the same set. This data structure allows you to first specify all the members of a universal set and then specify which ones are members of the same partition, thus joining the two partitions to make a single partition. It represents a collection of partitions of the universal set, and it lets us query whether the two members of the universal set are members of the same partition.

A tree is kept in an opposite pointer form, that is, the child knows its parent; however, the parent does not have any pointers to the children. The idea is to have connected values in the same tree. Each tree in a forest has a representative node that is its root. If two nodes have the same representative roots, they are in the same partition; otherwise, they are not.

This data structure has three important operations:

- Add a new object to the universal set.
- **Union two objects**: This will result in the partitions those objects belong to joining together to make a single partition.
- **Find**: This will return the representative object of the partition that the object passed belongs to. If the result of the find operations of two different objects is the same, the object would belong to the same partition.

The following is an implementation of a Union find that can hold comparable objects:

```
public class UnionFind<E extends Comparable<E>> {
```

Each node holds a reference to its parent. If there is no parent, that is, if the node is the root of its tree, the parent is null. All nodes also store its rank, which is the height of the tree rooted by itself:

```
private class Node implements Comparable<Node>{
    Node parent;
    E object;
    int rank;

    public Node(E  object) {
        this.object = object;
        rank = 0;
    }


    @Override
```

```
        public int compareTo(Node o) {
            return object.compareTo(o.object);
        }
    }
```

All the nodes are stored in a red black tree so they have a logarithmic search:

```
    BinarySearchTree<Node> allNodes = new RedBlackTree<>();
```

Additionally, we want to keep a count of the number of partitions available:

```
    int partitionCount;
```

The add operation adds a new object to the universal set, which is implemented using a red black tree:

```
    public void add(E object){
        Node n = new Node(object);
        allNodes.insertValue(n);
        partitionCount++;
    }
```

This is an internal method that traverses the parents one by one until it finds the root of the tree that the object passed belongs to:

```
    Node findRoot(Node n){
        if(n.parent==null){
            return n;
        }else{
            return findRoot(n.parent);
        }
    }
```

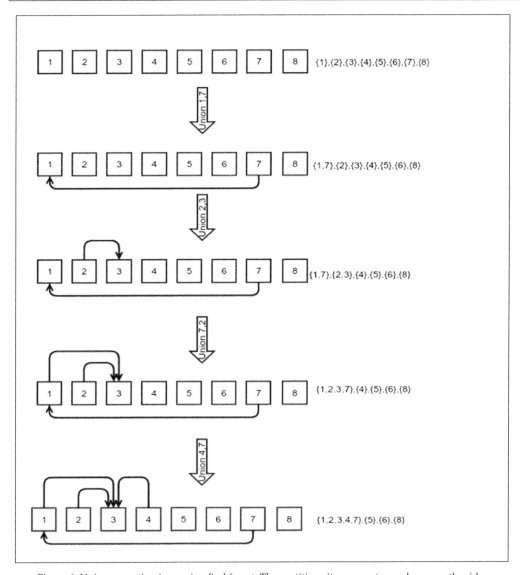

Figure 6. Union operation in a union find forest. The partitions it represents are shown on the side.

The union operation merges two trees. This is achieved by setting one of the roots of the two trees as the parent of the root of the other tree. When merging two trees of unequal height, the root of the taller tree is set as the parent of the root of the shorter tree; otherwise, any one of the two is chosen as the root. The rank of the root increases only when two equal trees are merged. When unequal trees are merged, the height of the merged tree is the same as the height of the taller tree. *Figure 6* shows the union operation:

```
public void union(E o1, E o2){
    BinaryTree.Node<Node> node1 = allNodes.searchValue(
        new Node(o1));
    BinaryTree.Node<Node> node2 = allNodes.searchValue(
        new Node(o2));
    if(node1==null || node2==null){
        throw new IllegalArgumentException("Objects not found");
    }
    Node n1 = node1.getValue();
    Node n2 = node2.getValue();
    Node p1 = findRoot(n1);
    Node p2 = findRoot(n2);
    if(p1==p2){
        return;
    }
    int r1 = n1.rank;
    int r2 = n2.rank;
    if(r1>r2){
        p2.parent = p1;
    }else if(r2>r1){
        p1.parent = p2;
    }else{
        p2.parent = p1;
        p1.rank++;
    }
    partitionCount--;
}
```

The `find` operation involves looking up the node related to the object first and then finding the root node. The object contained in the root node is returned:

```
public E find(E object){
    BinaryTree.Node<Node> node1 = allNodes.searchValue(
        new Node(object));
    if(node1==null){
        throw new IllegalArgumentException("Objects not found");
    }
    Node n = node1.getValue();
    return findRoot(n).object;
}
```

Complexity of operations in UnionFind

First, let's consider the complexity of finding the root node of any node; this is an internal operation. The complexity of this operation is $\theta(h)$, where h is the height of the tree. Now what is the upper bound of the height of the tree? Let $f(h)$ be the minimum number of nodes in a tree of height h. Trees are always created by merging two smaller trees. If the trees being merged have unequal heights, the height of the merged tree is the same as the taller of the two initial trees, and now it has more nodes than the original taller tree. This is not the way to create the worst tree, which is the tree with minimum nodes with the same height. The worst tree must be created by merging two equal trees, both of which are worst trees themselves. After you merge them, the height of the merged tree is one more than the height of either of the trees being merged. So, for creating a worst tree of height $h+1$, we must merge two worst trees of height h. The operation to do this is $f(h+1) = 2 f(h)$. So, if $f(0) = C$, where C is some constant, $f(1) = 2C, f(2)=4C, \ldots, f(h) = 2^h C$. Therefore, if the number of nodes is n, then $n \geq f(h) = 2^h C \Rightarrow lg\ n \geq lg\ (2^h\ C) = h + lg\ C \Rightarrow h \leq lg\ n - lg\ C \Rightarrow h = O(lg\ n)$. This means the complexity of finding the root of a given node is also $O(lg\ n)$.

- Adding a new object involves inserting a new node in the red black tree, so the complexity is $\theta(lg\ n)$.

- **Find**: This operation involves looking up the node that corresponds to the object first. This is a search operation in the red black tree; hence it is $\theta(lg\ n)$. After this, it involves looking up the root of this node, which is $O(lg\ n)$. And at the end, we return the object in the node, which is constant time. Hence, the complexity of the entire find operation is $\theta(lg\ n)$.

- Union involves three operations. The first is to search the nodes for the objects, which is $\theta(lg\ n)$. The second is to find the roots of each of the trees associated with the nodes, which is also $O(lg\ n)$. And finally, it involves the merging of the trees, which is a constant time operation. So the complexity of the entire operation is $\theta(lg\ n)$.

Implementation of the minimum spanning tree algorithm

Now we can implement our minimum spanning tree algorithm. First, we create a class that we will use for the implantation. The `CostEdge` class represents an edge along with its cost. The `compareTo` method is overridden to compare the costs instead of IDs:

```
class CostEdge extends Edge{
        Integer cost;

        public CostEdge(int source, int target, int cost) {
```

```
                super(source, target);
                this.cost = cost;
        }


        @Override
        public int compareTo(Edge o) {
                return cost - ((CostEdge)o).cost;
        }
    }
```

The argument costFinder is a lambda that returns the cost of an edge from the value that is stored in it. edgeQueue is a priority queue that lets us consider the edges in the order of their costs. We can dequeue the edge with the minimum cost every time, as our algorithm requires. The purpose of unionFind is to keep track of which vertices are connected after some edges are already chosen. First, we traverse through all the edges and enqueue them to the priority queue, then we traverse through all the vertices to add them to unionFind. After this, as described in our algorithm, we pick the edges in the order of their costs and add them only when they are not between the vertices that are already connected. The unionFind keeps track of which vertices are connected. The edges of the spanning tree are returned in a linked list:

```
default LinkedList<Edge> minimumSpanningTree(OneArgumentExpression<E,I
nteger> costFinder){
        if(!isUndirected()){
            throw new IllegalStateException(
              "Spanning tree only applicable to undirected trees");
        }
        LinkedList<Edge> subGraph = new LinkedList<>();

        PriorityQueue<CostEdge> edgeQueue = new
          LinkedHeap<>((x, y)->x.compareTo(y));

        UnionFind<Integer> unionFind = new UnionFind<>();

        this.visitAllConnectedEdges(getAllVertices()
          .getRoot().getValue(), (s,t,v)-> edgeQueue.enqueue(
            new CostEdge(s,t,costFinder.compute(v))),
                    TraversalType.DFT);

        this.getAllVertices().traverseDepthFirstNonRecursive(
          (x)->unionFind.add(x),
              BinaryTree.DepthFirstTraversalType.PREORDER);
```

```
while((unionFind.getPartitionCount()>1
                    && edgeQueue.checkMinimum()!=null){
    Edge e = edgeQueue.dequeueMinimum();
    int sGroup = unionFind.find(e.source);
    int tGroup = unionFind.find(e.target);
    if(sGroup!=tGroup){
        subGraph.appendLast(e);
        unionFind.union(e.source, e.target);
    }
}
return subGraph;
}
```

Complexity of the minimum spanning tree algorithm

Visiting all the edges and adding them to the priority queue can be as low as $\Theta(|V| + |E| + |E|\ lg\ |E|)$ because traversing through the edges is $\Theta(|V| + |E|)$ and adding all of them to the priority queue is $\Theta(|E|\ lg\ |E|)$. Since a connected graph has $|E| \geq |V| -1$, $\Theta(|V| + |E| + |E|\ lg\ |E|) = \Theta(|E|\ lg\ |E|)$. Inserting all the vertices to the union find is done through $\Theta(|V|\ lg\ |V|)$ because adding each vertex has the complexity $\Theta(lg\ |V|)$.

Now let's consider the core of the algorithm. For each edge, dequeueing the minimum edge is $\Theta(lg\ |E|)$, finding each of the source and the target in `unionFind` is $\Theta(lg\ |V|)$, adding to the linked list is constant time, and doing a union on `union find` is $\Theta(lg\ |V|)$. So, for each edge, the complexity is $\Theta(lg\ |V| + lg\ |E|)$. This is $\Theta(lg\ |E|)$ for each edge, as $|E| \geq |V| -1$. Therefore, the complexity of the core part is $\Theta(|V|\ lg\ |E|)$ because we stop after $|V| - 1$ number of edges are added and all the vertices are already connected.

Adding the complexity of all the preceding steps, we get the total complexity of the minimum spanning tree algorithm as $\Theta(|E|\ lg\ |E|) + \Theta(lg\ |V|) + \Theta(|V|\ lg\ |E|) = \Theta(|E|\ lg\ |E| + |V|\ lg\ |V|) = \Theta(|E|\ lg\ |E|)$ as $|E| \geq |V| -1$.

This algorithm is called Kruskal's algorithm, invented by Joseph Kruskal. Kruskal's algorithm works with the complexity $\Theta(|V|\ lg\ |E|)$ if a sorted list of edges is already available. Since we have checked until all the edges are processed, if a graph is passed that is not connected, it will give a set of minimum spanning trees, one for each connected subgraph.

Summary

In this chapter, we saw what a graph is and some real-world scenarios where they can be applicable. We saw a few ways of implementing a graph data structure in memory. We then studied ways to traverse a graph, in both BFT and DFT. We used traversals to detect cycles in a graph. Finally, we saw what spanning trees are, what minimum spanning trees are, and how to find them in a graph.

In the next chapter, we will drift a bit to explore a simple and elegant way of implementing some concurrent programming, called reactive programming.

11
Reactive Programming

This chapter is a little detour to reactive programming. It lets us handle the concurrency requirements of an application in some cases. It provides an abstraction to handle concurrency. Even though the concepts are old, it has gained interest in recent years due to the beginning of large inflow of data. In modern times, billions of devices generate data every day. Tapping into this data is essential for the growth of business; in some cases, processing the data to statistically analyze it or feeding it to some machine learning algorithm may be the entire business in itself. This makes it essential to support the processing of this large in-flow of data, provide a quick response, and be resilient to failures. Of course, one can do these things even using a traditional or imperative programming paradigm, just as one can, in theory, build any application using an assembly language. However, this makes the application extremely complex to maintain and impossible to modify according to business needs. In this chapter, we will discuss the following topics:

- Basic idea of reactive programming
- Building an example reactive framework
- Building example programs using our framework

What is reactive programming?

Suppose we have a web server that lets us query some data or save it. This web server serves multiple requests at the same time, and each request is a short task that involves some computation. What is the usual way of achieving this? Well, the naive way would be to spawn a new thread for each request. But one can easily realize that this leads to an explosion in the number of threads in the application. Plus, the creation and deletion of threads are heavyweight activities; they slow down the entire application.

Next, you can use a thread pool so the same threads can be used over and over to avoid the overhead of creation and deletion of threads. However, if you want to serve thousands of requests at the same time, this will require a thread pool with thousands of threads. Thread scheduling in an operating system is complex and involves a lot of logic, including priority and so on. Operating systems do not expect threads to just run short bursts of computation; they are not optimized that way. Therefore, the solution is to use the same thread for multiple simultaneous requests. This can, in general, be done if we stop blocking for IO and use the same thread for another task when one task is waiting for I/O. Managing these things, however, is extremely complicated. Hence, we would need a framework to carry out these activities for us. Such a framework can be called a reactive framework.

Reactive programming takes care of the following:

- **Scalability**: This property is the capability of the application to cater to proportional number of requests as the number of available resources increases. If one processor serves 500 requests per second, two processors should do 1,000.

- **Responsiveness**: We want the application to be responsive; for example, it should show a status when it is computing some result or fetching it from some other place.

- **Resilience**: Since we use the same thread for multiple tasks, handling errors is more complicated than usual. How do we let the user know of an error? So instead of propagating the exceptions back down the call stack, we move forward and explicitly tackle the error situations.

There are different techniques for using reactive programming; it depends on the actual problem we are trying to solve. We will not discuss all of them but will focus on the commonly used ones.

Producer-consumer model

A producer-consumer model is a design that divides processing into small components that send messages to other components. One produces a message and the other consumes and acts on it. It provides an abstraction to easily implement an application optimized to utilize all the resources. A producer-consumer model starts with a queue of messages. Producers publish messages in this queue and consumers receive them. This queue is different from the queues we have studied so far in a few ways. We want this queue to be thread-safe, which is required for the queue to work correctly in a multithreaded environment. We do not need to worry about the exact order of the messages being dequeued. After all, the order of messages does not matter when they are being received by different threads. In these conditions, we optimize the delivery of the messages. Before implementing this queue, let's discuss a few thread synchronization techniques beyond what we have learned so far using the synchronized keyword. These techniques are required for more optimal usage of resources while maintaining the correctness of the program.

Semaphore

A semaphore is a special variable that lets us limit the number of threads that can use a particular resource. The following code shows an example of a semaphore that gives us a thread-safe counter:

```
public class SemaphoreExample {
    volatile int threadSafeInt = 0;
    Semaphore semaphore = new Semaphore(1);
    public int incrementAndGet() throws InterruptedException{
        semaphore.acquire();
        int previousValue = threadSafeInt++;
        semaphore.release();
        return previousValue;
    }
}
```

Here, the semaphore has been initialized to 1, which means it will allow only one thread to acquire it. No other thread can acquire it until it is released. Unlike synchronization, there is no requirement here that the same thread has to call the release method that had acquired it, which makes it particularly flexible.

A call to the `acquire` method of a semaphore will be blocked until it successfully acquires it. This means that the calling thread will be taken off the thread scheduler and put aside in such a way that the operating system's thread scheduler will not be able to see it. Once the semaphore is ready to be acquired, this thread will be put back in place for the thread scheduler to see it.

Compare and set

Compare and set is an atomic operation that lets you update the value of a variable if and only if the existing value matches a specific value. This enables us to update a variable based on its previous value. The CAS operation returns a Boolean. If the comparison is a match, which means the set operation is successful, it returns `true`; otherwise, it returns `false`. The idea is to keep trying until this set operation is successful. The following diagram shows the basic strategy:

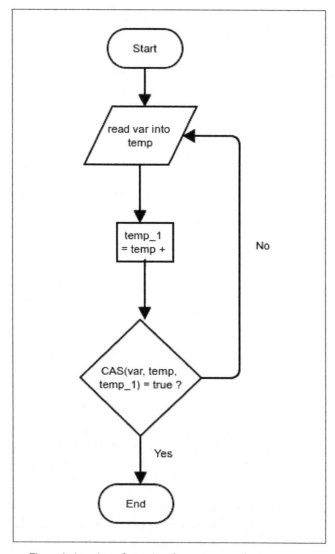

Figure 1: Atomic update using the compare and set operation

In *Figure 1*, we are trying to increment the value of the shared variable **var**. The operation requires us to read the value in a thread-specific temporary location, then increment the temporary value and reassign it to the shared variable. However, this operation can cause problems if there are multiple threads trying to perform the update simultaneously. It can happen that both the threads read the value simultaneously in order to get the same temp value. Both these threads can update the shared variable with the incremented value. This will increment the value only once, but it should have actually caused two increments. To avoid this, we check whether the value of **var** is still the same and update only when it is so; otherwise, we read the value of **var** again and repeat the process. Since this compare and set operation is atomic, it guarantees that no increments will be lost. The following is the Java code that does the exact same thing:

```
public class ThreadSafeCounter {
    AtomicInteger counter;
    public int incrementAndGet(){
        while (true){
            int value = counter.get();
            if(counter.compareAndSet(value, value+1)){
                return value;
            }
        }
    }
}
```

To use any atomic operation, we need to use classes from the `java.util.concurrent.atomic` package. `AtomicInteger` is a class that encapsulates an integer and enables the `compareAndSet` operation on it. There are other utility methods as well. In particular, it has methods to perform atomic increments and decrements, just like the one we have implemented here.

Volatile field

Suppose we have a field that is being written to and read from multiple threads. If all the threads run on the same single CPU, the writes can simply happen on the CPU cache; they need not be synced to the main memory often. This would not be a problem as the value could also be read from the same cache. However, multiple CPUs can have their own caches, and in such a case, a write to a cache from one CPU will not be visible from another thread running on a different CPU. Most programs accept this and work accordingly. Java, for example, maintains a separate copy of a shared variable for each thread, which is occasionally synced. If we, however, want to mandate that the writes from one thread should be visible from another thread, we need to declare the field volatile. All fields involved in atomic operations are declared volatile.

Thread-safe blocking queue

Now we are ready to implement our thread-safe blocking queue. Thread-safe means that multiple threads can share the same queue; blocking means that if a thread tries to dequeue an element and the queue is currently empty, the call to dequeue will be blocked until some other thread enqueues an element. Similarly, if a thread tries to enqueue a new element and the queue is full, the call to the queue will be blocked until another thread dequeues an element and frees some space.

Our queue will store elements in a fixed length array and maintain two counters that would store the next index for queuing and dequeuing. Two semaphores block threads when the queue is either empty or full. Along with this, each array position is provided with two semaphores that ensure that enqueuing and dequeuing operations do not overwrite or repeat any elements. It does this by ensuring that once a new element is enqueued in a particular position, it is not overwritten before it is dequeued. Similarly, once a particular array index is dequeued, it is never dequeued again before another enqueue stores another element in it:

```
public class ThreadSafeFixedLengthBlockingQueue<E> {
```

The `underflowSemaphore` ensures that dequeues are blocked when the queue is empty, and `overflowSemaphore` ensures that enqueues are blocked when the queue is full:

```
    Semaphore underflowSemaphore;
    Semaphore overflowSemaphore;

    AtomicInteger nextEnqueueIndex;
    AtomicInteger nextDequeueIndex;
```

The array store is the space that holds the elements:

```
    E[] store;
```

Both `enqueueLocks` and `dequeueLocks` are individual position-based locks that allow only a dequeue after an enqueue and vice versa:

```
    Semaphore [] enqueueLocks;
    Semaphore [] dequeueLocks;

    int length;
```

The `alive` flag can be used by the dequeuing threads to know when they can stop running, and no more elements would be expected. This flag needs to be set by the enqueuing threads:

```
    boolean alive = true;
```

All initializations are pretty much self-evident:

```
public ThreadSafeFixedLengthBlockingQueue(int length){
    this.length = length;
    store = (E[]) new Object[length];
    nextEnqueueIndex = new AtomicInteger();
    nextDequeueIndex = new AtomicInteger();
    underflowSemaphore = new Semaphore(length);
    overflowSemaphore = new Semaphore(length);
    underflowSemaphore.acquireUninterruptibly(length);
    enqueueLocks = new Semaphore[length];
    dequeueLocks = new Semaphore[length];
    for(int i=0;i<length;i++){
        enqueueLocks[i] = new Semaphore(1);
        dequeueLocks[i] = new Semaphore(1);
        dequeueLocks[i].acquireUninterruptibly();
    }
}
```

The enqueue operation first makes sure that the queue is not full by acquiring `overflowSemaphore`:

```
public void enqueue(E value) throws InterruptedException {
    overflowSemaphore.acquire();
```

The `nextEnqueueIndex` is then incremented and the previous value is returned, which is then used to compute the index in the array where the element would be stored. The seemingly complicated expression ensures that the index rolls over properly even after the `nextEnqueueIndex` integer rolls over, provided the length of the queue is an integer power of 2:

```
int index = (length + nextEnqueueIndex.getAndIncrement()
    % length)
    % length;
```

Once the index is selected, we must acquire an enqueue lock on the position, store the value, and then release the dequeue lock to mark this position as ready for dequeuing. At the end, we release one count on `underflowSemaphore` to mark the fact that there is one more element in the queue to be dequeued:

```
enqueueLocks[index].acquire();
store[index] = value;
dequeueLocks[index].release();
underflowSemaphore.release();
}
```

The dequeue operation is very similar to the enqueue operation, just the role of the semaphores are reversed. There is slightly more complicated code before the actual operation starts. This is to enable the dequeuing threads to quit when no more elements are available:

```
public E dequeue() throws InterruptedException {
```

Instead of directly acquiring `underflowSemaphore`, we use `tryAcquire`, which will wake up the thread after 1 second if there are no elements are available to be dequeued. This gives us a chance to check the value of the `alive` Boolean flag and quit the dequeue operation in case it is no longer alive. If the queue is no longer alive, we interrupt the current thread and exit. Otherwise, we compute the index and dequeue the element to the enqueue operation in a similar manner:

```
while (alive && !underflowSemaphore.tryAcquire(1,
        TimeUnit.SECONDS));
if(!alive){
    Thread.currentThread().interrupt();
}
int index = (length + nextDequeueIndex.getAndIncrement()
        % length)
        % length;
dequeueLocks[index].acquire();
E value = store[index];
enqueueLocks[index].release();
overflowSemaphore.release();
return value;
}
```

This is a utility method to return the current number of elements in the queue. This is useful for knowing when to kill the queue (set the `alive` flag to `false`) in a producer-consumer setup:

```
public int currentElementCount(){
    return underflowSemaphore.availablePermits();
}

public void killDequeuers(){
    alive = false;
}

}
```

Producer-consumer implementation

We can now implement a producer-consumer setup using the queue we have created. In simple words, the producer-consumer queue is a queue of events that the producers produce and the consumers consume. There are three kinds of events. The INVOCATION type refers to the regular events that propagate processing. The ERROR type event is raised when an exception needs to be propagated. The COMPLETION event is produced when it is required that the dequeue threads need to be terminated and the queue needs to be closed. The ProcerConsumer queue takes Consumer as input:

```
public interface Consumer<E> {
    void onMessage(E message);
    default void onError(Exception error){
        error.printStackTrace();
    }
    default void onComplete(){


    }
}


public class ProducerConsumerQueue<E> {
    enum EventType{
        INVOCATION, ERROR, COMPLETION
    }
```

The Event class represents single events. Depending on the type, it can have a value or exception:

```
class Event{
    E value;
    Exception error;
    EventType eventType;
}
ThreadSafeFixedLengthBlockingQueue<Event> queue;
boolean alive = true;
Thread [] threads;
```

The constructor of ProducerConsuerQueue creates consumer threads. It also takes consumer code as input. The consumer must implement the Consumer interface:

```
public ProducerConsumerQueue(int bufferSize, int threadCount,
            Consumer<E> consumer){
    queue = new ThreadSafeFixedLengthBlockingQueue<>(bufferSize);
    threads = new Thread[threadCount];
```

The consumer thread runs code that dequeues events and calls the methods on
`consumerCode` as per the event type in the loop. The loop ends when the termination
event is received and no more events are there in the queue to be processed:

```
Runnable consumerCode = ()->{
    try{
        while(alive || queue.currentElementCount()>0){
            Event e = queue.dequeue();
            switch (e.eventType) {
                case INVOCATION:
                    consumer.onMessage(e.value);
                    break;
                case ERROR:
                    consumer.onError(e.error);
                    break;
                case COMPLETION:
                    alive = false;
                    consumer.onComplete();
            }
        }

    } catch (InterruptedException e) {

    } finally{

    }
};
```

Consumer threads are spawned:

```
for(int i=0;i<threadCount;i++) {
    threads[i] = new Thread(consumerCode);
    threads[i].start();
}
}
```

The `produce` method is invoked from a producer thread. Notice that the queue does
not manage producer threads; they need to be managed separately:

```
public void produce(E value) throws InterruptedException {
    Event event = new Event();
    event.value = value;
    event.eventType = EventType.INVOCATION;
    queue.enqueue(event);
}
```

Once a producer thread marks the stream of events to be completed, no more new events could be generated and the dequeuing threads will be terminated after they process all the events:

```
public void markCompleted() throws InterruptedException {
    Event event = new Event();
    event.eventType = EventType.COMPLETION;
    queue.enqueue(event);
}
```

This is to propagate an exception:

```
public void sendError(Exception ex) throws InterruptedException {
    Event event = new Event();
    event.error = ex;
    event.eventType = EventType.ERROR;
    queue.enqueue(event);
}
```

If we need to wait for all the dequeuing threads to terminate, we use this:

```
public void joinThreads() throws InterruptedException {
    for(Thread t: threads){
        t.join();
    }
}
}
```

To see how to use this producer-consumer queue to actually solve a problem, we will consider a dummy problem. We will work on a file — com-orkut.ungraph.txt — that is open to public and contains all the friendships between users in **Orkut**, which was a social networking site in the past. The file can be downloaded from https://snap.stanford.edu/data/bigdata/communities/com-orkut.ungraph.txt.gz. To protect privacy, all the users are simply referenced by some arbitrary ID and the mapping with the actual users is not shared. We will also use another file called ulist that would contain the list of user IDs we are interested in. Our task is to find the number of friends that each user in the second file has. The following commands show how the two files look:

```
$ head com-orkut.ungraph.txt
1   2
1   3
1   4
1   5
1   6
```

```
1    7
1    8
1    9
1    10
1    11
$ head ulist
2508972
1081826
2022585
141678
709419
877187
1592426
1013109
1490560
623595
```

Each line in com-orkut.ungraph.txt has two IDs that are separated by a whitespace. The meaning is that there is friendship between these two users. It is given that each friendship is mentioned only once in the file and is undirected. Note that this means each line should increase the friend count for both the IDs. Each line in ulist has a single ID. All IDs are unique, and we must find the friend count of each of these IDs. Note that some of these have no friends and thus are not mentioned in com-orkut.ungraph.txt.

We will first create a utility class that will let us read integer IDs from the files. The purpose of this class is to read integer values from any text file so that not too many objects are created in the process. This is just to reduce garbage collection to some extent. In this case, we used file-channel-based logic that uses ByteBuffer as a buffer:

```java
public class FileReader {
    ByteBuffer buf= ByteBuffer.allocate(65536);
    FileChannel channel;
```

The readCount variable keeps track of how many characters are left in the buffer:

```java
    int readCount = 0;

    public FileReader(String filename) throws FileNotFoundException {
        channel = new FileInputStream(filename).getChannel();
        buf.clear();
    }
```

To read an `int`, keep reading the bytes in a loop until you hit a byte that is not a digit. In the meantime, keep computing the integer that the string of characters represents:

```
public int readIntFromText() throws IOException {
    int value = 0;
    while(true){
```

First check whether the buffer is empty; if yes, refill it by reading from the file:

```
if(readCount<=0){
    buf.clear();
    readCount = channel.read(buf);
```

If no more bytes are available in the file, don't care to flip the buffer:

```
if(readCount<0){
    break;
}
buf.flip();
}
```

We read a byte and decrement `readCount` because now the buffer has one less byte:

```
byte nextChar = buf.get();
readCount--;
```

If the character is a digit, keep computing the integer; otherwise, break the loop and return the calculated integer value:

```
if(nextChar>='0' && nextChar<='9') {
    value = value * 10 + (nextChar - '0');
}else{
    break;
}

}
    return value;
    }
}
```

With the help of this, we will create a program to create a file output, which will contain the user IDs provided in `ulist` along with the corresponding friend count. The idea is that reading the file is made asynchronous by computing the friend count. Since the counting involves a binary search, we want two threads doing it instead of one:

```
public class FriendCountProblem {
    private static final String USER_LIST_FILE = "ulist";
```

```
private static final String EDGES_PATH = "com-orkut.ungraph.txt";
private static final String OUTPUT_FILE_PATH = "output";

public static void main(String [] args)
  throws Exception {
    FileReader userListReader = new FileReader(USER_LIST_FILE);
```

First, we simply count the number of lines present in `ulist`. This will let us create the correct size array:

```
int count = 0;

while(true){

    int lineValue = userListReader.readIntFromText();
    if(lineValue==0){
        break;
    }
    count++;
}
```

We create two arrays: one containing the keys and the other containing the friend count of each of the keys. The counts are stored in `AtomicInteger` objects so that they can be incremented from multiple threads:

```
Integer [] keys = new Integer[count];
AtomicInteger [] values = new AtomicInteger[count];
```

We read `userIDs` from `ulist` in an array:

```
userListReader = new FileReader(USER_LIST_FILE);


int index = 0;

while(true){

    int uid = userListReader.readIntFromText();
    if(uid==0){
        break;
    }
    keys[index] = uid;
    values[index] =  new AtomicInteger(0);
    index++;

}
```

Now we sort the array of `userID` so that we can perform binary search on it:

```
ArraySorter.quicksort(keys,(a,b)->a-b);
```

The job of our consumers is to search for each user encountered in `com-orkut.ungraph.txt` and increment the corresponding count in the array values. Note that creating `ProducerConsumerQueue` does not start any processing; only consumer threads are created through this. Processing will start only when we produce events, which we will do after reading from `com-orkut.ungraph.txt`:

```
ProducerConsumerQueue<Integer> queue
        = new ProducerConsumerQueue<>(4092, 2, (v)->{
    int pos  = ArraySearcher.binarySearch(keys,v);
    if(pos<0){
        return;
    }
    values[pos].incrementAndGet();
});
```

We use the main thread for producing the events. We use the same `FileReader` class for reading each user ID separately. This is because both the users in a line in `com-orkut.ungraph.txt` have a friend (which is the other one in the same line) for each line in the file. So we simply read the users and post them as events so that the consumers can process them:

```
FileReader edgeListFileReader = new FileReader(EDGES_PATH);
while(true){
    int val = edgeListFileReader.readIntFromText();
    if(val == 0){
        break;
    }
    queue.produce(val);
}
```

Once we are done processing the entire `com-orkut.ungraph.txt` file, we simply mark the queue as completed and wait for the consumer threads to be terminated:

```
queue.markCompleted();
queue.joinThreads();
```

Now all the counts must be updated in the values array. So we simply read them one by one and output them in the file output:

```
PrintStream out = new PrintStream(OUTPUT_FILE_PATH);
for(int i=0;i<count;i++){
    out.println(keys[i] +" : "+values[i].get());
}
out.flush();
    }
}
```

The preceding example demonstrates how an actual problem can be solved using the reactive technique of **producer-consumer**. Now we will discuss another way of implementing our event queue; it does not involve blocking on semaphores.

Spinlock and busy wait

A semaphore normally blocks a thread before the thread acquires it. This blocking is achieved by the operating system by removing the thread from the list of threads that are ready to be scheduled for processing time on the CPU. The list of threads ready to be scheduled are called running threads. Every semaphore has a list of threads waiting on it, and these threads are removed from the list of running threads. Once the semaphore is released, threads from the list attached to the semaphore are removed and put back on the list of the running threads. This operation is somewhat heavyweight and requires processing time. Another way to stop a thread from accessing a shared resource is to use a spinlock. A spinlock is generally implemented using an atomic variable and compare and set operation. A thread in a spinlock simply tries to perform compare and set on a variable in a loop; it does so until it succeeds. To the operating system, this thread is as good as a running thread and is scheduled just like any other thread. The thread itself, however, keeps trying a compare and set operation and consumes processor time. This is why it is called a busy wait. The thread can proceed to do something meaningful once the compare and set operation is successful. Spinlocks are useful when the resource would not be available only for a short period of time. It simply does not make sense to do all the heavy lifting of removing the thread from the list of running thread and blocking on a semaphore if the resource is unavailable for a brief period of time.

We can implement our thread-safe queue with spinlocks instead of semaphores as shown in the following code. Each array location for storing the queue elements is protected by two `AtomicBoolean` variables, stored in the `enqueueLocks` and `dequeueLocks` arrays. The only thing we want to make sure is that after each dequeue, there should only be a single enqueue, and after each enqueue, there should only be a single dequeue for a particular array location. Different array locations should be independent of one another:

```
public class ThreadSafeFixedLengthSpinlockQueue<E> {
    int nextEnqueueIndex;
    int nextDequeueIndex;
    E[] store;
    AtomicBoolean[] enqueueLocks;
    AtomicBoolean[] dequeueLocks;
    AtomicInteger currentElementCount = new AtomicInteger(0);
    int length;
    volatile boolean alive = true;
    public ThreadSafeFixedLengthSpinlockQueue(int length){
        this.length = length;
        store = (E[]) new Object[length];
        enqueueLocks = new AtomicBoolean[length];
        dequeueLocks = new AtomicBoolean[length];
```

When `enqueueLocks[i]` is `false`, it means there is no element being stored at the position i. When `dequeueLock[i]` is `true`, it means the same thing. The reason we need both is for protection when an element is in the process of being enqueued or dequeued:

```
        for(int i=0;i<length;i++){
            enqueueLocks[i] = new AtomicBoolean(false);
            dequeueLocks[i] = new AtomicBoolean(true);
        }
    }
```

Here is the core of the lock. We simply take the next index to enqueue and try to get `enqueueLock`. If it is `false`, which means nothing is already enqueued, it is atomically set to `true` and it starts the enqueue process; otherwise, we keep doing the same thing in a busy loop until the compare and set operation is successful. Once the process is complete, we release `dequeueLock` by simply setting it to `false`. A compare and set operation is not necessary here because it is guaranteed to be `true`. The number of elements are maintained using another atomic variable:

```
public void enqueue(E value) throws InterruptedException {

    while (true) {
        int index = nextEnqueueIndex;
        nextEnqueueIndex = (nextEnqueueIndex+1) % length;
        if(enqueueLocks[index].compareAndSet(false,true)){
            currentElementCount.incrementAndGet();
            store[index] = value;
            dequeueLocks[index].set(false);
            return;
        }
    }
}
```

The dequeue operation is very similar, just that the enqueue and dequeue locks have switched places:

```
public E dequeue() throws InterruptedException {
    while(alive) {
        int index = nextDequeueIndex;
        nextDequeueIndex = (nextDequeueIndex+1) % length;
        if(dequeueLocks[index].compareAndSet(false,true)){
            currentElementCount.decrementAndGet();
            E value = store[index];
            enqueueLocks[index].set(false);
            return value;
        }
    }
    throw new InterruptedException("");
}
```

The rest of the code is self-evident:

```
    public int currentElementCount(){
        return currentElementCount.get();
    }

    public void killDequeuers(){
        alive = false;
    }

}
```

We can simply replace the queue in the `ProducerConsumerQueue` class to use this spinlock-based queue. In the case of our example problem, the spinlock version of the queue performs better.

Let's solve another problem using `ProducerConsumerQueue`. Our problem is to find all the perfect numbers between 2 and 500,000. What is a perfect number? A perfect number is a number that is the sum of all its divisors, excluding itself. The first perfect number is 6. 6 has three divisors excluding itself, namely 1, 2, and 3 and 6=1+2+3. This is what makes 6 a perfect number. To find all the perfect numbers between 2 and 500,000, we will check whether each number in the range is a perfect number. We can write the following code to figure out whether a given number is a perfect number. For every number *div*, we check whether the number *x* is divisible by *div*; if so, we add it to the sum. In such a case, if we divide *x* by *div*, we will of course get another divisor of *x* as a result stored in the variable quotient. This must also be added to the sum, unless it is equal to *div*. We stop this process when we pass through the square root of *x*, that is, when *div* is bigger than the quotient we get when *x* is divided by *div*. Since we, originally, exclude *1* as a divisor to avoid adding the number itself, we add *1* to the sum at the end and check whether it is equal to *x*; if so, *x* is a perfect number:

```
public static boolean isPerfect(long x){
        long div = 2;
        long sum=0;
        while(true){
            long quotient = x/div;
            if(quotient<div){
                break;
            }
            if(x%div==0){
                sum+=div;
                if(quotient!=div){
```

```
                    sum+=quotient;
            }
        }
        div++;
    }
    return 1+sum==x;
}
```

As you can see, checking whether a given number is a perfect number is a computationally expensive operation, which makes it desirable to use all the CPUs to compute it. We will use our producer-consumer framework to do this. The code is self-explanatory. Our consumer code simply checks whether a given number is a perfect number and then prints the number if it is so. The producer simply generates and queues all the numbers. Since the consumer is run in multiple threads and it is the part that is computationally intensive, it should work faster than the single-threaded version:

```java
public static void findPerfectNumberWithProducerConsumer() throws
InterruptedException{
        long start = System.currentTimeMillis();
        ProducerConsumerQueue<Long> queue
                = new ProducerConsumerQueue<>(4096, 4, (x)->{
            if(isPerfect(x)){
                System.out.println(x);
            }
        });

        for(long i=2;i<5_00_000;i++){
            queue.produce(i);
        }
        queue.markCompleted();
        queue.joinThreads();
        System.out.println("Time in ms: "+(
          System.currentTimeMillis()-start));
    }
```

Since my computer has four CPU cores, I used four threads to do the heavy lifting. On my computer, this program takes 1,596 milliseconds as compared to 4,002 milliseconds for the single-threaded program, as shown in the following code:

```java
public static void findPerfectNumberWithSingleThread(){
        long start = System.currentTimeMillis();
        for(long i=2;i<5_00_000;i++){
            if(isPerfect(i)){
```

```
                    System.out.println(i);
            }
        }
        System.out.println("Time in ms: "+(
          System.currentTimeMillis()-start));
    }
```

Functional way of reactive programming

Most reactive programming frameworks provide functional APIs for reactive programming, which makes it even easier to work with. In this section, we will build a functional reactive API and solve a problem with it. The idea is to use the concept of a stream. A stream is a data generator or source that can provide input when requested. Functional APIs provide map, filter, and consume operations on the stream. The map and the filter operations create a new stream, and the consume operation gives a EventConsumer instance. The idea is that when EventConsumer is asked to start processing, it would spawn its own producer threads and consumer threads and treat each map, filter, or consume operations as a separately scheduled operation in a producer-consumer queue. This is just to highlight what we are really trying to achieve.

For example, I will put the code to use the functional API to solve the same perfect number problem. We will replace the pseudo-method someWayCreateAStream with the actual code to create a stream later. The point is to show how an event stream can be manipulated using the map, filter, and consume method. The processing really starts when the process method is called, and in each step of map, filter, and consume are decoupled processing steps and are potentially run in different threads:

```
    public static void findPerfectNumbersWithFunctionalAPI(){
        EventStream<Long> stream = someWayCreateAStream();
        stream.filter((x)->x>1)
                .filter(EventStream::isPerfect)
                .consume((x)->{System.out.println(x);})
                .onError((x)->System.out.println(x))
                .process(4096,1,4);

    }
```

When we create an instance of EventStream or EventConsumer, no processing happens; only metadata is created. It is when the method process is invoked that the processing starts. This is done by the process method spawning the producer and consumer threads. The producer threads create and enqueue events that contain the initial value and the processing code (like map, filter, or consume operations). A dequeuer runs the first piece of processing and enqueues another event for the next level of processing; it does this for map and filter operations. A consume operation is the end of the processing chain, and it does not return any value. This is when no more events are scheduled.

This requires that a dequeuer thread must also do some enqueue operations. What can be a problem with this? There are two kinds of threads that enqueue. One of these threads is responsible for dequeueing too. These threads may get blocked while trying to perform enqueue operations when the queue is full. But this would mean that they would not be able to do any dequeue operation either; this is because if they do this, the queue would never have more space again. This situation is a deadlock; all the threads are blocked and are expecting other threads to do something to unblock them.

To see why this deadlock happens, let's imagine a queue with length 4. Suppose there are two dequeuing threads that also perform an enqueue operation once in some cases. Let's have another enqueuer thread too. Since the threads can run in any order, it is possible that the enqueuer runs first and enqueues four new elements to make the queue full. Now say two dequeuers run, each dequeuing one element. Before these threads get a chance to enqueue once more, the enqueuer thread is run again, and this time it enqueues two new elements to fill the queue. Now the dequeuer threads are run, but they are blocked because the queue is full. They cannot even dequeue any element because they are themselves blocked from enqueuing more elements. This is a deadlock situation. *Figure 2* shows this situation:

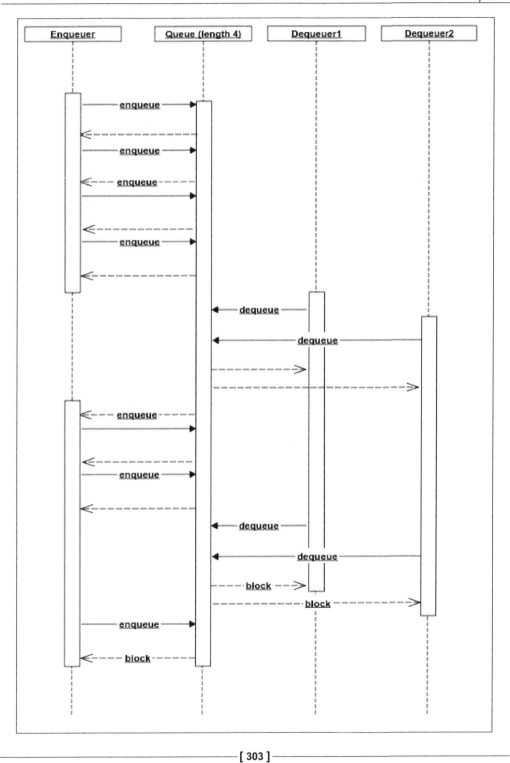

What we really want is threads that will not only perform the enqueue operation, but also block the queue before it is completely full. This is so that the dequeueing threads can use some space to keep dequeuing and enqueuing until they reach a point where they will not have to enqueue anymore (because they have reached the last step of the processing chain). Eventually, the queue gets empty and the enqueuer threads can be unblocked again. To do this, we need to have two different kinds of enqueue operations. One that does not block until the queue is full, and another that blocks once the queue is half or more full. We can implement the second type using the following code in the ThreadSafeFixedLengthSpinlockQueue class. The enqueueProducerOnly method is just like the enqueue method, except it performs an atomic check of the currentElementCount variable instead of just incrementing it. If, while enqueueing, it is seen that the queue is already full, we release the enqueue lock and restart. The thread that does only enqueue operations and no dequeue operation must use this method instead of the regular enqueue method:

```
public void enqueueProducerOnly(E value ) throws InterruptedException{
        int halfLength = length/2;
        while (true) {

            int index = nextEnqueueIndex;
            nextEnqueueIndex = (nextEnqueueIndex+1) % length;
            if(enqueueLocks[index].compareAndSet(false,true)){
                int numberOfElements = currentElementCount.get();
                if(numberOfElements>=halfLength
                    || (!currentElementCount.compareAndSet(
                    numberOfElements, numberOfElements+1))){
                    enqueueLocks[index].set(false);
                    continue;
                }
                store[index] = value;
                dequeueLocks[index].set(false);
                return;

            }
        }
}
```

We can now use this method to implement a corresponding method in the
`ProducerConsumerQueue` class. This method is exactly the same as the produce
method, except that here, the call to enqueue has been replaced by a call to the
`enqueueProducerOnly` method:

```
public void produceExternal(E value) throws InterruptedException {
        Event event = new Event();
        event.value = value;
        event.eventType = EventType.INVOCATION;
        queue.enqueueProducerOnly(event);
}
```

Now let's see the `EventStream` class. The whole point of the `EventStream` class is
to create metadata in a functional way. It is an abstract class with only one abstract
method called `read()`. A call to the `read` method should return the next object that
needs to be processed. The class maintains a pointer to the previous `EventStream`
on which this `EventStream` will work. This means that the operation represented
by `EventStream` will work on the data obtained after all the previous `EventStream`
have been processed. It is really a linked list of `EventStream`. Depending on the kind
of operation the current `EventStream` represents, it either has a mapper, a filter, or
nothing. The `read` method is applicable only to the first `EventStream` that generates
the data. Both the map filter methods return another `EventStream` that represents
the corresponding processing. After all the map and filter calls, the list linked by
`EventStream` will store all the operations from the last to the first:

```
public abstract class EventStream<E> {
    EventStream previous;
    OneArgumentExpressionWithException mapper;
    OneArgumentExpressionWithException filter;
    public <R> EventStream<R> map(
      OneArgumentExpressionWithException<E,R> mapper){
        EventStream<R> mapped = new EventStream<R>() {

            @Override
            public R read() {
                return null;
            }
        };
        mapped.mapper = mapper;
        mapped.previous = this;
        return mapped;
    }
    public EventStream<E> filter(OneArgumentExpressionWithException<E,
      Boolean> filter){
```

```
EventStream<E> mapped = new EventStream<E>() {

    @Override
    public E read() {
        return null;
    }
};
mapped.filter = filter;
mapped.previous = this;
return mapped;

}
```

The consume method, however, returns an instance of EventConsumer. This is the terminal processing in any chain that does not compute a new value. The EventConsumer class, as would be shown a little later, contains all of the logic to actually start the processing:

```
public EventConsumer<E> consume(
    OneArgumentStatementWithException<E> consumer) {
        EventConsumer eventConsumer = new EventConsumer(
            consumer, this) {
    };
    return eventConsumer;
}
public abstract E read();

}
```

Since we need to store the details of the processing inside an EventConsumer instance, we will first make a few classes to store this information. The first one is a Task interface that represents any of the map, filter, or consume operation:

```
public interface Task {
}
```

This interface is implemented by three classes that represent each kind of operation. To store the code, we need two additional functional interfaces that represent an expression and a statement that would allow you to throw exceptions:

```
@FunctionalInterface
public interface OneArgumentExpressionWithException<A,R> {
    R compute(A a) throws Exception;
}
@FunctionalInterface
public interface OneArgumentStatementWithException<E> {
    void doSomething(E input) throws Exception;
}
```

The following classes implement the `Task` interface:

```
public class MapperTask implements Task {
    OneArgumentExpressionWithException mapper;
    Task nextTask;

    public MapperTask(
            OneArgumentExpressionWithException mapper,
            Task nextTask) {
        this.mapper = mapper;
        this.nextTask = nextTask;
    }

}

public class FilterTask implements Task{
    OneArgumentExpressionWithException filter;
    Task nextTask;

    public FilterTask(
            OneArgumentExpressionWithException filter,
            Task nextTask) {
        this.filter = filter;
        this.nextTask = nextTask;
    }
}
```

Both `MapperTask` and `FilterTask` have a pointer to the next task because they are intermediate operations. They also store the piece of code associated with the processing. The `ProcessorTask` represents the terminal operation, so it does not have a pointer to the next task:

```
public class ProcessorTask<E> implements Task{
    OneArgumentStatementWithException<E> processor;

    public ProcessorTask(
            OneArgumentStatementWithException<E> processor) {
        this.processor = processor;
    }
}
```

We will now create the `EventConsumer` class that will create a task chain and run it:

```
public abstract class EventConsumer<E> {
    OneArgumentStatementWithException consumptionCode;
    EventStream<E> eventStream;
    Task taskList = null;
    private ProducerConsumerQueue<StreamEvent> queue;
    private OneArgumentStatement<Exception> errorHandler =
      (ex)->ex.printStackTrace();
```

A `StreamEvent` is a processing request that is an element of the producer-consumer queue. It stores `value` as `Object` and `task`. The `task` can have more tasks pointed to by its next reference:

```
class StreamEvent{
    Object value;
    Task task;
}
```

An `EventStream` stores its previous operation—that is to say that if we read the head of the list, which would be the last operation. Of course, we need to arrange the operations in the order of execution and not in reverse order. This is what the `eventStreamToTask` method does. A `MapperTask` or `FilterTask` stores the next operation, so the head of the list is the first operation to be carried out:

```
private Task eventStreamToTask(EventStream stream){
    Task t = new ProcessorTask(consumptionCode);
    EventStream s = stream;
    while(s.previous !=null){
        if(s.mapper!=null)
            t = new MapperTask(s.mapper, t);
        else if(s.filter!=null){
            t = new FilterTask(s.filter, t);
        }
        s = s.previous;
    }
    return t;
}
```

The constructor is package-accessible; it is intended to be initialized only from inside the `consume` method of an `EventStream`:

```
EventConsumer(
        OneArgumentStatementWithException consumptionCode,
        EventStream<E> eventStream) {
    this.consumptionCode = consumptionCode;
    this.eventStream = eventStream;
```

```
            taskList = eventStreamToTask(eventStream);
    }
```

The following is the piece of code responsible for actually carrying out the operations. The `ConsumerCodeContainer` class implements `Consumer` and acts as the consumer of the producer-consumer queue for processing events:

```
class ConsumerCodeContainer implements Consumer<StreamEvent>{
    @Override
    public void onError(Exception error) {
        errorHandler.doSomething(error);
    }
```

The `onMessage` method is invoked for every event in the producer-consumer queue. Based on the actual task, it takes the corresponding action. Notice that for `MapperTask` and `FilterTask`, a new event is enqueued with the next operation:

```
    @Override
    public void onMessage(StreamEvent evt) {
```

The `ProcessorTask` is always the end of a processing chain. The operation is simply invoked on the value and no new event is queued:

```
        if(evt.task instanceof ProcessorTask){
            try {
                ((ProcessorTask) evt.task).processor
                        .doSomething(evt.value);
            } catch (Exception e) {
                queue.sendError(e);
            }
        }
```

For a `FilterTask`, the event with the next task is enqueued only if the condition is satisfied:

```
        else if(evt.task instanceof FilterTask){
            StreamEvent nextEvent = new StreamEvent();
            try {
                if((Boolean)((FilterTask) evt.task)
                    .filter.compute(evt.value)) {
                    nextEvent.task =
                            ((FilterTask) evt.task).nextTask;
                    nextEvent.value = evt.value;
                    queue.produce(nextEvent);
```

```
            }
        } catch (Exception e) {
            queue.sendError(e);
        }
    }
```

For a `MapperTask`, the next task is enqueued with the value computed by the current map operation:

```
else if(evt.task instanceof MapperTask){
    StreamEvent nextEvent = new StreamEvent();
    try {
        nextEvent.value = ((MapperTask) evt.task).mapper
                            .compute(evt.value);
        nextEvent.task = ((MapperTask) evt.task).nextTask;
        queue.produce(nextEvent);
    } catch (Exception e) {
        queue.sendError(e);
    }
}
        }
    }
```

The process method is responsible for kicking the actual processing of the tasks. It uses a `ProducerConsumerQueue` to schedule events that are processed by the consumer previously discussed:

```
public void process(int bufferSize, int numberOfProducerThreads,
int numberOfConsumerThreads) {
    queue = new ProducerConsumerQueue<>(bufferSize,
    numberOfConsumerThreads, new ConsumerCodeContainer());
```

Only the original `EventStream` on which map and filter were called has the `read` method implemented. So we simply get a reference to the original `EventStream`:

```
EventStream s = eventStream;
while(s.previous !=null){
    s = s.previous;
}
```

The `startingStream` variable points to the original `EventStream`:

```
EventStream startingStream = s;
```

The producer code also runs in separate threads. The Runnable producerRunnable contains the producer code. It simply keeps calling the read method of the EventStream until null is returned (which marks the end of the stream) and enqueues a StreamEvent with the value and the task chain we have created with the help of the eventStreamToTask method:

```
Runnable producerRunnable = ()->{
    while(true){
        Object value = startingStream.read();
        if(value==null){
            break;
        }
        StreamEvent nextEvent = new StreamEvent();
        try {
            nextEvent.value = value;
            nextEvent.task = taskList;
            queue.produceExternal(nextEvent);
        } catch (Exception e) {
            queue.sendError(e);
        }
    }
    try {
        queue.markCompleted();
    } catch (InterruptedException e) {
        e.printStackTrace();
    }
};
```

Now we spawn the producer threads and wait for them to finish with the join calls:

```
Thread [] producerThreads = new Thread[
  numberOfProducerThreads];
for(int i=0;i<numberOfProducerThreads;i++){
    producerThreads[i] = new Thread(producerRunnable);
    producerThreads[i].start();
}
for(int i=0;i<numberOfProducerThreads;i++){
    try {
        producerThreads[i].join();
    } catch (InterruptedException e) {
        e.printStackTrace();
    }
}

}
```

This is a method to register a custom error handler and return a new
EventConsumer:

```
public EventConsumer<E> onError(
        OneArgumentStatement<Exception> errorHandler){
    EventConsumer<E> consumer
     = new EventConsumer<E>(consumptionCode, eventStream) {};
    consumer.taskList = taskList;
    consumer.errorHandler = errorHandler;
    return consumer;
    }
}
```

Going back to our original problem of perfect numbers, all we have to do now is
to define an EventStream with a read method that generates all the numbers and
then does maps and filters on them as follows. Notice that the EventStream.read()
method may be invoked by multiple threads simultaneously if we use more than one
producer thread, so it is better for it to be thread-safe.

The read method simply increments an AtomicLong and returns the previous value,
unless the previous value is greater than 5_00_000L; in this case, it returns null,
marking the end of the stream. We have already seen the rest of the code:

```
public static void findPerfectNumbersWithFunctionalAPI(){
    long start = System.currentTimeMillis();
    EventStream<Long> stream = new EventStream<Long>() {
        AtomicLong next = new AtomicLong(0L);
        @Override
        public Long read() {
            Long ret = next.incrementAndGet();
            if(ret<=5_00_000L){
                return ret;
            }
            return null;
        }
    };
    stream.filter((x)->x>1)
            .filter(EventStream::isPerfect)
            .consume((x)->{System.out.println(x);})
            .onError((x)->System.out.println(x))
            .process(4096,1,4);

    System.out.println("Time in ms: "+(
        System.currentTimeMillis()-start));
}
```

This code runs for almost the same time as the previous reactive version without a functional API. I will leave it up to you to use the functional API to implement the friend count solution, as it is fairly simple as one gets the hang of it. All you need to think about is how to implement the read method to return the integers from the file.

Summary

In this chapter, we learned how to do advanced thread synchronization using volatile fields, atomic operations, and semaphores. We used these to create our own reactive programming framework and also created a functional API for reactive programming. We used our frameworks to solve sample problems and saw how multithreaded scalable apps can be written easily with a reactive framework.

There are many reactive programming frameworks available, such as RxJava, Akka, and many more. They are slightly different in their implementation and features. They all provide a lot more features than the one we used. This chapter is just an introduction to the topic; interested readers can learn more about reactive programming from the books dedicated to this subject.

In this book, I tried to give you a head start in the world of algorithms, with implementations in Java. Algorithms are a vast field of study. Every computation problem needs to be solved by an algorithm. A further study would include complexity classes of algorithms, equivalence of algorithms, and approximate algorithms for highly complex problems. A complex problem is a problem that guarantees that any algorithm that solves it must have a certain amount of complexity. This gives rise to the concept of the complexity classes of problems. There are also formal/mathematical ways of proving the correctness of algorithms. All these areas can be pursued by you.

The book also covers functional and reactive programming a little bit. This should work as a head start in those areas; you can learn more about them in the books dedicated to these topics.

Index

Made in the USA
Middletown, DE
01 July 2020